D1541246

Communion Ecclesiology

Communion Ecclesiology

Vision and Versions

Dennis M. Doyle

ORBIS BOOKS
Maryknoll, New York 10545

The Catholic Foreign Mission Society of America (Maryknoll) recruits and trains people for overseas missionary service. Through Orbis Books, Maryknoll aims to foster the international dialogue that is essential to mission. The books published, however, reflect the opinions of their authors and are not meant to represent the official position of the society. To obtain more information about Maryknoll and Orbis Books, please visit our website at www.maryknoll.org.

Copyright © 2000 by Dennis M. Doyle

Published by Orbis Books, Maryknoll, New York, U.S.A.

Some materials in this book have appeared in earlier versions elsewhere. Chapters 2, 3, and 4 are revisions of articles that appeared in *Theological Studies* 57 (September 1996) 467-80; 58 (September 1997) 461-79; and 60 (June 1999) 209-27. Chapters 7 and 9 are revisions of articles that appeared in annual volumes of the College Theology Society: *Religion, Ethics, and the Common Good*, 185-205, eds. James Donahue and M. Theresa Moser (Mystic, CT: Twenty-Third Publications, 1996) and *Theology: Expanding the Borders*, 200-18, eds. Maria Pilar Aquino and Roberto S. Goizueta (Mystic, CT: Twenty-Third Publications, 1998). Some passages from chapter 5 appeared in an article in *Living Light* 32 (Spring 1996, copyright © United States Catholic conference, Inc.) 6-11; passages from chapter 6 appeared in an article in *Church* 13 (Summer 1997) 48-51; passages in chapter 5 are adapted from an article in *America* 167 (September 12, 1992) 139-43; and passages from chapter 11 appeared in an article in *Pro Ecclesia* VI (Winter 1997) 7-12. I give my thanks to the editors and publishers who gave me permission to make further use of these materials in this book.

All rights reserved. No part of this publication may be reproduced or transmitted in any form or by any means, electronic or mechanical, including photocopying, recording, or any information storage or retrieval system, without prior permission in writing from Orbis Books, P.O. Box 308, Maryknoll NY 10545-0308, U.S.A.

Manufactured in the United States of America.

Library of Congress Cataloging-in-Publication Data

Doyle, Dennis M.
    Communion ecclesiology : vision and versions / Dennis M. Doyle.
       p. cm.
    Includes bibliographical references and index.
    ISBN 1-57075-327-X
    1. Church—Catholicity. 2. Church—Unity. I. Title.

BV601.3 .D68 2000
262'.7—dc21   00-061183

Contents

Acknowledgments

There are many more people to thank than I can reasonably name here. Several graduate assistants from the Religious Studies Department at the University of Dayton gave me much help, especially Christine Vandenbosch, Prudence Hopkins, and Richard Drabik. Those who helped me with various chapters at various stages include Brad Hinze, Susan Wood, Joseph Komonchak, Elizabeth Johnson, Roberto Goizueta, and Miroslav Volf. A discussion group at the University of Dayton, consisting in Michael Barnes, Terrence Tilley, Maureen Tilley, Sandra Yocum Mize, M. Therese Lysaught, Una Cadegan, Jim Heft, and Jack McGrath, gave me invaluable guidance through several versions of my vision. Dean Paul Morman and Provost John Geiger provided monetary support for course reductions and a sabbatical. The University of Augsburg and Chaminade University in Hawaii allowed me the use of their facilities and materials. My wife, Patricia, and our children, Thomas, Michael, Patrick, and Christopher, kept me grounded in the real world, and provided me with plenty of practice in mediating among various compelling yet competing views. My deep thanks to them all.

Introduction

Vision and Versions

The vision of the Church as a communion enlightens and inspires. The process of dialogue in a spirit of communion fosters hope and encouragement. This vision of the Church and this process of dialogue, however, exist in various versions in the theological world. The purpose of this book is twofold: first, to promote a Catholic vision of communion ecclesiology as an approach for understanding the Church; second, to mediate among the various, sometimes competing, versions to explore a vision which is broadly and inclusively Catholic.

Communion ecclesiology can be found today in Catholic, Orthodox, and Protestant versions. I write as a Roman Catholic who focuses mainly on Roman Catholic versions. Differences among Protestant and Orthodox and Roman Catholic approaches at times enter into this study, but the main focus will be on the Roman Catholic versions of the vision of communion ecclesiology. It is my hope that the inclusive Catholic vision of communion ecclesiology toward which I am working will have ecumenical benefits insofar as it will provide points of connection with various Christian denominations.

When releasing the document, "Some Aspects of the Church Understood as a Communion," Joseph Cardinal Ratzinger said of communion ecclesiology that

> ultimately there is only one *basic ecclesiology*, which certainly can be approached and worked out in different ways, depending on which of the various aspects are stressed or highlighted. Nevertheless, every exposition must always take into account the harmony of the various essential elements of an ecclesiology which intends to be Catholic.[1]

_____

[1]*L'Osservatore Romano* [English Edition], 17 June 1992, 1.

Four points important to this book can be derived from Ratzinger's brief statement. First, communion ecclesiology is the one basic ecclesiology. Second, communion ecclesiology can exist legitimately in different versions. Third, Catholic versions of communion ecclesiology need to take into account the full range of certain essential elements of the Church. Fourth, the meaning of "communion ecclesiology" is bound up with the meaning of "Catholic."

For Catholics, the meaning of communion ecclesiology is connected with Vatican II. Twenty years after the Council, the Extraordinary Synod of 1985 met to discuss progress in implementation. In the Final Report of that synod, the bishops presented communion ecclesiology as the key to a proper understanding of the Vatican II documents, one that would go beyond the overly selective readings of the right and the left. They called communion "the central and fundamental idea of the Council's documents."[2] But this claim also implies its reverse, that the documents of Vatican II provide the key to a Catholic understanding of communion ecclesiology. Catholic theologians cannot interpret either Vatican II or communion ecclesiology apart from each other.

The bishops at the Synod of 1985 invited all parties in the Church to a fuller reading of the entire texts. The bishops included even themselves in this call toward a higher vision:

> We are probably not immune from all responsibility for the fact that especially the young critically consider the church a pure institution. Have we not perhaps favored this opinion in them by speaking too much of the renewal of the church's external structures and too little of God and of Christ? From time to time there has also been a lack of the discernment of spirits, with the failure to correctly distinguish between a legitimate openness of the Council to the world and the acceptance of a secularized world's mentality and order of values. (I, 1, 4)

Such humble willingness to admit to limitations constitutes a key element in any authentic version of communion ecclesiology. As Johann Adam Möhler held in *Unity in the Church*, love and humility lead to a broad and inclusive orthodoxy; egoism and pride lead to the narrow confines of heresy.[3] A communion ecclesiology that reflects the bishops' approach is an understanding of the Church that will emerge from a full engagement with the documents of Vatican II. Communion

---

[2]Extraordinary Synod of 1985, "The Final Report," *Origins* 15 (19 December 1985) 448.

[3]Johann Adam Möhler, *Unity in the Church*, trans. Peter C. Erb (Washington, DC: The Catholic University of America Press, 1996 [German original: Mainz, 1825]) 122-65.

ecclesiology can serve as a path beyond left-right dichotomies because it calls Catholics on all points of the spectrum beyond a selective reading of the Council documents.

John Paul II has also been emphasizing the importance of Vatican II for our times. In *Tertio Millennio Adveniente* (1994), he says, "The best preparation for the new millennium, therefore, can only be expressed in a renewed commitment *to apply*, as faithfully as possible, *the teachings of Vatican II to the life of every individual and of the whole Church*.[4] Of course the documents of Vatican II need to be read against the background of the Christ event, the scriptures, the patristic witness, and the entire tradition.

Common Ground, Contrasting Approaches

My own approach constructs "communion ecclesiology" as necessarily a broad and inclusive category that makes room for a range of legitimate approaches. If communion ecclesiology is to be touted as the one basic ecclesiology and as the only method that is truly Catholic, then it must be broad enough to include a variety of approaches that legitimately trace their heritage to Vatican II and to other currents within the Catholic tradition.

In one sense I am presenting another perspective among the many. What makes this perspective different is that it seeks to harvest the best from a range of perspectives and to show how each perspective contributes to a fuller vision.

My initial interest in communion ecclesiology grew out of my reading of the final statement of the Extraordinary Synod of 1985. My concern for mediating among a variety of versions of communion ecclesiology has come mainly from my experience of teaching from a variety of texts in graduate courses. As I have completed this study, I have found that my approach overlaps with and lends theological support to the Catholic Common Ground Initiative that is associated with the late Cardinal Bernardin.[5]

My approach to communion ecclesiology contrasts with that of David L. Schindler, long-term editor of *Communio* and author of *Heart of the World, Center of the Church*.[6] Schindler criticizes the initial docu-

---

[4]Pope John Paul II, *Tertio Millennio Adveniente* (As the Third Millennium Draws Near), *Origins* 24 (24 November 1994) 407.

[5]The initial statement of the project, issued by the National Pastoral Life Center in conjunction with Joseph Cardinal Bernardin, is "Called to Be Catholic: Church in a Time of Peril," *Origins* 26 (29 August 1996) 165-70.

[6]David L. Schindler, *Heart of the World, Center of the Church: Communio Ecclesiology, Liberalism, and Liberation* (Grand Rapids, MI: Eerdman's / Edinburgh: T&T Clark, 1996).

ment of the Common Ground Initiative for implicitly promoting notions of dialogue that carry modern baggage concerning the priority of process over content and the need to place one's most cherished convictions in brackets as a condition of participation.[7] I tend to agree more with Robert Imbelli, who argues that the Common Ground Initiative statement already contains many safeguards that Schindler does not adequately acknowledge.[8]

I think also, though, that Schindler underemphasizes the real potential of moderately open-ended dialogue as well as the good dimensions of what is often labeled "modernity." Modernity is, admittedly, at best a mixed bag for Catholics. But Catholicism and modernity cannot be so easily and simply separated and set against each other as Schindler seems to think. I presuppose throughout this book that Roman Catholic communion ecclesiology represents a coming to grips with modernity that is much more complex than a simple rejection of it. My arguments rest not on modern assumptions about the glories of authentic dialogue but on the nature of catholicity and on a critical consideration of the particular voices that are trying to contribute to the current theological conversation. The communion ecclesiology of Vatican II lends support both to those who stress *ressourcement* (return to the sources) and to those who stress *aggiornamento* (updating). Admittedly, dialogue does not create truth *ex nihilo*. But in a situation in which various parties are stressing dimensions of the truth that others are not, fuller and more satisfying portions of truth can be enjoyed by all who are willing to partake in the discussion.

Schindler works with his particular version of communion ecclesiology as if it were the only correct version, and then uses it to criticize other versions such as neo-conservatism and liberation theology, and to ignore the more pneumatological approach of Karl Rahner.[9] I find a distinct, though related, problem in the approach to communion ecclesiology taken by Michael Lawler and Thomas Shanahan in *Church: A Spirited Communion*.[10] Although their work is on a more pastoral level, like Schindler they make a very important contribution to communion ecclesiology. These authors, however, stand on a very different point on the theological spectrum than Schindler. They are more directly influenced by Yves Congar and by Karl Rahner. Their notion of sacramentality is broader than that of Schindler.

---

[7]David L. Schindler, "On the Catholic Common Ground Project: The Christological Foundations of Dialogue," *Communio* 23 (Winter 1996) 823-51.

[8]Robert Imbelli, "The Unknown Beyond the Word: The Pneumatological Foundations of Dialogue," *Communio* 24 (Summer 1997) 326-35.

[9]Joseph A. Komonchak, "Missing Person," *Commonweal* 124 (12 September 1997) 34-5.

[10]Michael G. Lawler and Thomas J. Shanahan, *Church: A Spirited Communion* (Collegeville, MN: Liturgical Press, 1995).

Lawler and Shanahan take very progressive and potentially controversial stands on issues such as the lay-clergy distinction, the meaning of "ministry," the preference for the broadly catholic over the "narrowly Roman Catholic," and the option for spirituality as engagement with the world in contrast to what they depict as an outmoded monastic ideal. In spite of the partisan nature of these positions, however, they do little to acknowledge viewpoints other than their own that also regard the Church as a communion. They tend to present their positions as the truth, without contextualizing them within the larger theological conversation and without highlighting that theirs is one theological perspective among others. Readers not deeply familiar with a wide range of theological literature, such as some of my students, at times have difficulty recognizing from their text the particularity of their positions and where they stand among the alternatives.

Dangers and Limitations

This book can be read as an attempt to undertake a task called for by well-known ecclesiologist Joseph Komonchak, which is to:

> elaborate a truly critical notion of communion that will avoid two temptations visible today. One would evaporate communion into a nebulous fellow-feeling, a content-less "agreement to disagree," or into a purely spiritual or eschatological ideal with no historical form or force, while the other would exploit it ideologically, covering with its spiritual and mystical connotations an ecclesiological theory and an ecclesiological practice that do not differ substantially from the old *societas perfecta* notion.[11]

The second of the "temptations" to which Komonchak refers, that of using *communio* as a conservative ideology, is the one to which Schindler is potentially most susceptible. The first "temptation," that of casting communion ecclesiology as so inclusive that it has nothing substantial to say, is a danger in my own approach, one which I hope to have avoided by specifically naming dimensions that need to be included and by rejecting relativism in favor of a particular range of theological diversity understood within certain frameworks of inclusion.

Nicholas Healy makes a similar criticism of communion ecclesiology. He finds the meaning of the term to be so flexible from one author to another that, "To say that 'communion' is a necessary model of the church is to say remarkably little, since the model can be used in

---

[11]Joseph A. Komonchak, "Conceptions of Communion, Past and Present," *Cristianesimo nella storia* 16 (1995) 339.

conflicting ways and have conflicting theological meanings, depending upon its context."[12] It is precisely this difficulty that I hope to have overcome by naming the various dimensions of communion and by presenting communion ecclesiology, as did the bishops at the Synod of 1985, as an overall vision, linked to Vatican II, which legitimately exists in different versions. Communion ecclesiology thus understood manifests within itself an analogical richness that can help to mediate among its various particular renderings.

Healy also characterizes communion ecclesiology as too world-affirming. I do not think, however, that this latter critique applies to the versions offered by Schindler or by Leonardo Boff. In contrast to communion ecclesiology, Healy opts for a narrative approach that focuses on the practical and concrete rather than on the ideal and abstract. My own construction of what communion ecclesiology is differs from Healy. I strongly prefer a "both/and" concerning the interplay of ideal images and concrete, practical concerns.

In line with Healy, John Ford cautions against too much optimism concerning communion ecclesiology, especially insofar as it may function as a cover for latent tensions.[13] My own construction of communion ecclesiology acknowledges existing tensions, yet still looks toward communion as a tool for unity.

Any rendering of the vision of communion ecclesiology will be a particular version. One of the strongest thrusts in theology today is to emphasize the importance of the inculturated faith expressions of various communities of believers. Theological approaches emphasizing social location, ethnicity, and gender offer fruitful standpoints from which to describe, reappropriate, construct, and articulate diverse and distinctive versions of the Christian vision.

As Roberto Goizueta emphasizes, theologies that stress social location do reach toward the universal, but always in and through particular expressions in relation to other particular expressions. In fact, Goizueta goes so far as to argue that only in and through particulars can the universal be known.[14] In a similar vein, Joseph Komonchak calls for a "recognition that an ecclesiology remains merely formal and abstract as long as it remains at the level of the merely theological and the universal, ignoring the human subjects and local communities in and out of which the Church exists and realizes itself in mission."[15]

---

[12]Nicholas Healy, "Communion Ecclesiology: A Cautionary Note," *Pro Ecclesia* 4 (1995) 450.

[13]John Ford, "*Koinonia* and Roman Catholic Theology," *Ecumenical Trends* 26 (March 1997) 42-4.

[14]Roberto S. Goizueta, *Caminemos con Jesús: Toward a Hispanic/Latino Theology of Accompaniment* (Maryknoll, NY: Orbis Books, 1995) 11; 97; 151-62.

[15]Joseph A. Komonchak, "Conceptions of Communion," 337-8.

Such particularity is a current thrust in theology, and it is much more than a passing trend. Yet attempts to articulate the Christian vision in ways that intend a high degree of universality with less conscious attention to social location will also continue to have currency. One of the great human paradoxes is how we can all be so different and yet so similar. The Vatican II documents *Gaudium et Spes* and *Ad Gentes*, for example, celebrate cultural diversity and the need to evangelize in ways that honor this diversity; these documents also, however, recognize that certain concerns remain relevant to human beings as human beings no matter what their particular culture. Not only do all human beings need to eat, sleep, and breathe, but they also all need to reason, feel, imagine, decide, and make commitments. They all need meaning in their lives. They all need to love and to be loved. They have all been created in the image and likeness of God. They all know the reality of sin, both individual and social. And, according to the documents of Vatican II, ultimately they all need the light of Christ.

All theologies stem from a particular social location whether they stress that fact or not. The Catholic tradition, however, places a strong emphasis on belonging not just to a local church but also at the same time to a Church universal. In line with this need to stress simultaneously the particular and the universal, systematic approaches to Christian theology that do not stress particular social location, while less grand and universal than in the past, will continue in the future as a necessary complement to approaches that do stress particular social location. A legitimate Catholic theological diversity will require an inclusive policy on this point of tension.

Whether I have successfully avoided the dangers associated with universalizing or not, however, a consideration of the perspectives of Komonchak, Healy, and Goizueta impresses upon me certain limitations of my study. I have offered here a somewhat aerial view of historical and current Catholic discussion concerning the nature of the Church. I have paid more attention to mountaintops and to the types of villages that theoretically might lay beneath the mountaintops than I have actually investigated the life in those villages. And I have been necessarily selective even in the particular mountain ranges that I have addressed. A great deal more remains to be done toward constructing a concept of communion ecclesiology that is well-grounded historically, critically, socially, and theologically; I hope that I have contributed to a good start.

Carving Out a Historical Trajectory

Some Protestants might want to point to Luther and Calvin as the originators of an ecclesiology that focuses on communion or fellowship rather than juridical understandings of the Church. Free Church Christians might wish to find in groups such as the Anabaptists and the Quakers the combination of witness, community, and action from which communion stems. Some Orthodox theologians like to argue that communion ecclesiology is what the East has preserved all along as the West underwent the battles of the Reformation and the Enlightenment. Yet other theologians might see in communion ecclesiology an articulation of the faith of the people, a popular and relational and devotional experience of the real nature of the Church prior to abstract theologies. Each of these approaches has some credibility; each of them, however, would construct a communion ecclesiology that is to some extent pre-modern, or at least that does not emphasize engagement with issues characteristic of the modern world.

In this text, I treat communion ecclesiology as a form of theology expressly in dialogue with modernity.[16] In carving out a historical trajectory I take Friedrich Schleiermacher to be an originating voice expressing a modern Protestant version of communion ecclesiology. I find important his historically dynamic view of religion as well as his acknowledgment of the need for a Catholic pole in a Protestant-Catholic dialectic. I take Johann Adam Möhler to be the originator of a modern Catholic version of communion ecclesiology. In the contrast between the "early" Möhler and the "later" Möhler, I find the roots of tensions that continue in Catholic thought before, during, and after Vatican II. These tensions exist between a version that is historical-pneumatological-organic and another that is mystical-christological-aesthetic. Similar tensions are manifested in the contrast between Charles Journet and Yves Congar in their work leading up to the Council. They surface again in the contemporary tensions between the approaches of Rahner and Hans Urs von Balthasar, as well as in those between a Balthasarian such as Joseph Ratzinger and Rahnerians such as the Brothers Himes.

I find in Henri de Lubac a theologian of remarkable balance whose work not only spans the Balthasar-Rahner tension but also anticipates some of the thrust of liberation theology. Liberation theology stands as a corrective to both Balthasar and Rahner. Theologies that stress ethnicity and social location, such as those offered by Elizabeth A. Johnson and Roberto Goizueta, do overlap with liberation theology and its focus on political and social transformation, but they also stress other dimensions of Christianity such as relationality and popular devotion. Catholic theologies that stress reform, such as that of Hans Küng, provide

---

[16]I will not enter here into the current discussion about the relationship between modernity and post-modernity. By "modernity" I intend to include our contemporary world. I leave debates about nomenclature, identity, and difference, etc. to others.

important voices that serve to keep alive certain key elements of the reforming thrust of Vatican II. Yet each of these views has its limitations, which, if made rigid, can lead to theological exclusivity and marginalization.

If communion ecclesiology is to be the "one basic ecclesiology," then it must be able to engage seriously this range of theological approaches in order to be fully Catholic. It would be absurd to think that the call beyond left-right dichotomies is simply a call for one side to surrender to the other. Communion ecclesiology is a content and a process, a vision and a summons to higher ground.

ONE

What Is Communion Ecclesiology?

Images and Dimensions

A few years ago, I spoke to a group of catechumens in a Catholic parish about the topic of "Church." I wrote on the board two sets of three phrases describing the Church.

Mystical Body of Christ	People of God
Bride of Christ	Pilgrim Church
Communion of Saints	Servant Church

After brief explanations of each phrase, I asked those present to write down which of the two sets they were either more interested in or felt more drawn to, the ones on the left or the ones on the right. As we went around the room and shared responses, each of the five catechumens and the majority of sponsors and other team members expressed a preference for the images on the left. They said that these were what inspired them, these were what the Church is most about at its heart.

The Director of Religious Education, however, who was leading the catechumenate and who went last, expressed his strong preference for the phrases on the right. He told the group he associated the phrases on the left with the old Church, and that, to him, the phrases on the right represented the heart of Vatican II. He implied, I felt, that most of those present were of a pre-Vatican II mentality, but that was okay with him, because as the sessions progressed they would learn the more current views. He appeared bewildered when I, a supposedly up-to-date theologian, tried gently to suggest that there were other ways of reading what happened at the Council, and that those who preferred either set of phrases could find plenty of support in the Council documents. The conversation overall was positive and upbeat, but I left with the impression that many of those present were quite relieved to hear that there exist alternatives to the "progressive" view favored by the group leader.

The group leader, in my opinion, could use a better understanding of

11

the communion ecclesiology associated with Vatican II. His worthy commitments to social justice and religious freedom and ecclesial reform stand juxtaposed to images that represent the glorious mystery of the Church rather than in interconnected harmony with them. This is a man who is bright and well educated, with a Master's Degree in Theology. And there is a history behind the development of such views among his teachers that can itself be read very sympathetically. The fear stemming from the way in which mystical images of the Church have been used to mystify rather than enlighten and to maintain power structures that mitigated against what became the progressive forms of Vatican II is a strong and understandable one. Holy Mother Church evokes concrete memories for some people that are less than pleasant. Some people do not like to be told that now all of a sudden such images can serve to promote rather than prohibit the progressive reforms of the Council. Yet I think that those who take such positions, no matter how understandable, are seriously out of touch with Vatican II when they characterize the Mystical Body of Christ and the Communion of Saints as the old views that Catholics have grown beyond.

The Director of Religious Education favored a view of the Church that emphasizes historical development, practical change, and the service of the Church to the world. Others present favored a mystical, relational, and aesthetic view. A consideration of communion ecclesiology, historically and in contemporary discussion, can shed light on these views.

A Web of Interwoven Relationships

Communion ecclesiology is an approach to understanding the Church. It represents an attempt to move beyond the merely juridical and institutional understandings by emphasizing the mystical, sacramental, and historical dimensions of the Church. It focuses on relationships, whether among the persons of the Trinity, among human beings and God, among the members of the Communion of Saints, among members of a parish, or among the bishops dispersed throughout the world. It emphasizes the dynamic interplay between the Church universal and the local churches. Communion ecclesiology stresses that the Church is not simply the receiver of revelation, but as the Mystical Body of Christ is bound up with revelation itself.

Communion ecclesiology is popular in Roman Catholic, Eastern Orthodox, and Protestant circles.[1] Its promoters claim it holds great

---

[1]See papers and addresses from the World Council of Churches 1993 meeting in Santiago de Compostela, *On the Way to Fuller Koinonia: Official Report of the Fifth World Conference on Faith and Order*, Faith and Order Paper no. 166, ed. Thomas F. Best and Günther Gassmann (Geneva: WCC, 1994).

potential for inner-Church renewal and for ecumenical progress. There exists, however, a tension in communion ecclesiology. It is simultaneously a call to a higher vision of Christian unity and something that exists in particular, sometimes contrasting, versions.

Amid the various versions of communion ecclesiology, four elements remain fairly constant. First, communion ecclesiology involves a retrieval of a vision of the Church presupposed by Christians of the first millennium, prior to the divisions among Eastern Orthodox and Roman Catholic and Protestant manifestations of Christianity. Second, communion ecclesiology emphasizes the element of spiritual fellowship or communion between human beings and God in contrast to juridical approaches that over-emphasize the institutional and legal aspects of the Church. Third, communion ecclesiology places a high value on the need for visible unity as symbolically realized through shared participation in the Eucharist. Fourth, communion ecclesiology promotes a dynamic and healthy interplay between unity and diversity in the Church, between the Church universal and the local churches.

Those who promote communion ecclesiology emphasize that the Church has its origin in the love shared among Jesus and the disciples. By thus locating the origin of the Church, theologians avoid descriptions of the Church as consisting most basically in institutional arrangements. They stress that the love which is the core of Christian revelation is generated through the intimate connection of Jesus with the Father and is sustained through the sending of the Holy Spirit; the growth of the Church is the spread of this divine love within Christian communities. To live in Christian community is to share in the life and love of the three persons in one God.

Communion ecclesiology emphasizes that the Church is basically a "communion" or fellowship among human beings and God. In contrast with overly institutional approaches, communion ecclesiology places its primary emphasis on relationship. Personal being and interconnectedness lie at the heart of what the Church is. Love, acceptance, forgiveness, commitment, and intimacy constitute the Church's very fabric.

The Church is a web of interwoven relationships. It cannot be understood simply as a modern institution or corporation. While it has important institutional aspects, the Church is also the Mystical Body of Christ, in which all the members make up one body with Christ as their head. The Church is the Communion of Saints, a community that spans past and present, earth and heaven, in its sharing in the grace of God. The Church offers a share in the life of the Trinity, as well as passage to a journey along with a Pilgrim people called to act as leaven in the world.

I do not intend this point, that the mystical elements of the Church's make-up are more basic to grasping its nature than the institutional elements, to downplay the value of applying various social and organizational theories and techniques to the Church for improving both understanding and functioning. I agree with ethicist James Gustafson in *Treasures in Earthen Vessels* that it is important to engage neither in a social reductionism that sees the Church merely as a human community nor in a doctrinal reductionism that ignores the human elements of the Church.[2] I agree also with the point of the well-known ecclesiologist Joseph Komonchak that social theory can be applied fruitfully to the Church without being reductionist.[3]

Reductive Distortions, Corrective Images, and Dimensions

A narrowly institutional view of the Church results in a type of reductive distortion. By "reductive distortion" I mean an approach that excludes or seriously de-emphasizes important dimensions of a phenomenon being studied. This is not to say the institutional aspects of the Church are themselves to be neglected or disparaged. Communion ecclesiology, while not making these elements primary, must identify and value them. Versions of communion ecclesiology with anti-institutional tendencies quickly become muddled in self-contradictions. Those who de-value institutions and structures often end up operating with institutions and structures that they do not acknowledge as such.

Institutionalism is not the only form of reductive distortion that communion ecclesiology addresses. The following discussion addresses five types of reductive distortions concerning the nature of the Church, as well as five corrective images that can be drawn from the communion ecclesiology associated with Vatican II. I label the reductive distortions as *individualism, the merely human, juridicism, mystification, and exclusivism.* The corrective images are *the Trinity, the Body of Christ, Communion of Communions, People of God,* and *Leaven in the World.*

Individualism is the insistence that the individual is the basic unit of human reality and that all types of community are secondary and accidental. Communion ecclesiology's attention to *the Trinity* places community at the center of things. God is the deepest reality, infinitely deeper than the created universe. Within the reality of God there exists not only oneness but also community. There is one God, but within that one God is a relation among three persons. God's relationality and God's oneness are mutually interdependent; neither has priority over the other. Individuality remains crucial and basic, but not more basic than community. The first chapter of the Vatican II document *Lumen*

---

[2]James M. Gustafson, *Treasure in Earthen Vessels: The Church as a Human Community* (New York: Harper, 1961) 105-7.
[3]Joseph A. Komonchak, "Ecclesiology and Social Theory: A Methodological Essay," *The Thomist* 45 (April 1981) 262-83.

Gentium puts the origin and sustenance of the Church in the ongoing work of the Father, Son, and Spirit. Another Vatican II document, *Gaudium et Spes*, expresses the intrinsically social nature of human persons. Like the Trinity, the Church exists at the same time as a community and as a group of distinct persons.

Treating the Church as *merely human*, as simply the fallible receiver of divine revelation, is common not only among many Protestants but also among some first-world Catholics. Communion ecclesiology, at least its Catholic versions, rejects this approach as a reductive distortion. Focusing on the Church as the *Body of Christ* and as the *Communion of Saints* brings in the mystical and transcendent elements needed to counter this view. The Church is not simply the human receiver of revelation but is also itself a dimension of that which is revealed. *Lumen Gentium*, in the second half of chapter one, draws upon images and symbols from the scriptures in order to articulate dimensions of the mystery of the Church, the Body of Christ foremost among them.

Juridicism is another label for institutionalism or legalism. It is for Catholics the most familiar form of reductive distortion. Communion ecclesiology highlights the *sacramental* nature of the Church. As expressed in *Lumen Gentium*, the Church must be considered "as forming one complex reality comprising a human and a divine element" (LG 8). Understood as sacrament, the Church is a human and visible reality that makes present and effective the divine and the invisible. Each local church, or diocese, is a community of love linking human beings with God. The Eucharist expresses the unity of love. The bishop, whose office is linked with the Eucharist, also expresses symbolically this unity. The communion among all the Catholic bishops of the world, with the pope as their head, symbolizes this unity of love on the level of the Church universal. The Church is thus, in the phrase associated with Jean-Marie Tillard, *a Church of Churches, a Communion of Communions.*[4]

At the other extreme, *mystification* labels a form of reductive distortion that downplays or ignores the human elements and processes in the Church. What is practical, human, and sometimes arbitrary has unfortunately sometimes been justified by a vague appeal to "mystery." In contrast, communion ecclesiology draws upon *Lumen Gentium*, especially chapters two and seven, to present a Church that is the *People of God* making its way through history, as well as a *Pilgrim Church* that is on a journey and not yet finished. Within the historical Church there have been many developments, changes, and downright errors. Any approach to understanding the Church that minimizes the dark side of its historical track record is severely lacking.

---

[4]Jean-Marie Tillard, *Church of Churches: An Ecclesiology of Communion*, trans. R.C. De Peaux (Collegeville, MN: Liturgical Press, 1992 [French orig. 1987]).

Finally, *exclusivism* is that form of reductive distortion by which the presence of grace and goodness outside of the visible confines of the Church is ignored, minimized, or denied. Communion ecclesiology draws upon both *Lumen Gentium* and *Gaudium et Spes* for the image of the Church as a *leaven in the world*. This image expresses a vision of the world, with all of its ambiguities and negativities, as the essentially good arena in which the lives of those who belong to the Church are lived out. This image of the Church as a leaven in the world can be extended to include questions not just about the relationship between Catholics and other human beings, but also ecological questions about the relationship between human beings and other elements of the cosmos. The Church that is as a leaven in the world of human events can also be construed as a leaven in the larger cosmos.

The Church-world relation is legitimately a subject for debate these days. There are many Catholic voices that react with good reason against naive evaluations of the world's goodness and against modern assumptions about automatic and unlimited human progress. But to ignore the basic goodness of creation, of human beings, and of many traditions apart from the Church is reductionist and un-Catholic (not to say that we Catholics haven't done our share of it).

The following chart maps out the five corrective images along with the five reductive distortions as indicating five dimensions of the Church understood as a communion. These five dimensions are not simply ideal types, but they represent various meanings of "communion" as that term is actually used by contemporary theologians in current discussion.[5]

REDUCTIVE DISTORTION	CORRECTIVE IMAGE	DIMENSION
individualism	Trinity	divine
the merely human	Body of Christ/ Communion of Saints	mystical
juridicism	Communion of communions	sacramental
mystification	People of God/ Pilgrim Church	historical
exclusivism	Leaven in the World	social

[5]Komonchak explores how the word "communio" has functioned in quite different ways in earlier Roman Catholic contexts, at times itself being used to express juridical concepts. See Joseph A. Komonchak, "Conceptions of Communion, Past and Present," *Cristianesimo nella storia* 16 (1995) 321-40.

The connections made in this chart are not intended to be exact. The dimensions of communion overlap and interpenetrate. Each in its own way can be understood as containing all the others. Which dimension addresses which type of reductive distortion could easily be re-organized. Moreover, an image such as the Body of Christ, which I use here as a counter to views that focus on the merely human to the neglect of the transcendent dimensions of the Church, has in some historical instances been used in support of juridicist views. The particular way in which I have lined up these dimensions and images reflects, then, not a systematic necessity but something of the way they often function in current theological discussion.

Another use for the chart is to help sort out different theological approaches that label themselves as communion ecclesiology. One way of getting at differences is by examining how particular theologians emphasize some dimensions more than other dimensions.

The chart that identifies these five reductive distortions, corrective images, and dimensions can help in understanding the Church in a dif-ferentiated fashion. As noted in the 1992 Sacred Congregation for the Doctrine of the Faith (CDF) document, "Some Aspects of the Church Understood as a Communion," the term "communion" needs to be employed in an analogical fashion.[6] One cannot give communion ecclesiology a flattened-out, univocal reading, as if everything that applies to one dimension also applies to the others. For example, one does not have to attribute sinfulness to the Church understood as the Mystical Body of Christ. On the other hand, one should be at least as careful not to attribute perfection to the Church understood as on a pil-grim journey. One should not, furthermore, confuse the communion that exists among the persons of the Trinity with that which exists among the bishops. Yet it would be even worse to give communion ecclesiology an equivocal reading that would not recognize the connec-tions among the various dimensions of communion. In addition, it is important to see the interconnections among the communion that exists among all Catholics and among all Christians and among all human beings. Ultimately there is but one Church, one complex reality that comes together from all of these elements. One needs to operate with what Catholic theologian David Tracy calls the "analogical imagi-nation" to even begin to apprehend what it means to say that the Church is a communion.[7]

---

[6]CDF, "Some Aspects of the Church Understood as a Communion," *Origins* 22 (25 June 1992) 108-112.

[7]David Tracy, *The Analogical Imagination: Christian Theology and the Cul-ture of Pluralism* (New York: Crossroad, 1981), esp. chapter 10.

Dimensions and Models

The Jesuit ecclesiologist Avery Dulles' 1974 *Models of the Church* is a classic text of post-Vatican II Catholic ecclesiology.[8] His models of institution, mystical communion, sacrament, herald, and servant helped Catholics to sort out some of the various themes that stemmed from the Council. In the expanded edition of 1987, Dulles expressed concern that the five models alone might be misinterpreted or misused as promoting disconnected views in support of a polarized pluralism rather than as starting points leading toward unity. He offered a sixth model, that of the Church as a Community of Disciples. This was not one model among others, but a synthesis of points important in the other models. The Community of Disciples model contains elements of community, institution, sacrament, herald, and servant at the same time. Dulles still recognized the validity of various starting points and final configurations, but he emphasized that not everything is optional, and that models can be measured according to the extent that they finally incorporate the best of the original five.

There are some similarities between Dulles' five models and the five dimensions of the Church discussed above. Indeed I am indebted to Dulles. What I am calling the social dimension lines up roughly with Dulles' servant model, and the sacramental dimension is close to the sacrament model. What I divide into the mystical and historical dimensions, however, are subsumed by Dulles into the single mystical communion model. This difference is significant, because I find the contrast between the mystical and the historical to express one of the greatest points of tension in Catholic ecclesiology today. This tension is reflected in the struggles between those who see the historically oriented People of God image as the main thematic thrust of Vatican II, and those who insist that the reforming themes associated with the People of God need to remain subordinate to those associated with the more mystical and traditional Body of Christ. Those who have explicitly stated that the Mystical Body of Christ image should have priority over what they call the more "sociological" People of God include Henri de Lubac, Hans Urs von Balthasar, Joseph Ratzinger, and John Paul II. Although I argue in the end for the ultimate complementary of these images and their associated themes, I think it helpful to distinguish these dimensions when analyzing current tensions.

I designate the divine as a distinct dimension; this reflects the practice in many contemporary theological circles of making connections between the relation of persons in the Trinity and the relations of persons in the Church. The Church considered as a communion includes

---

[8]Avery Dulles, *Models of the Church* (Garden City, NY: Image Books, 1974, expanded edition 1987).

relation with the Triune God. Emphasizing this connection does not lead to a simplistic divinization of the Church as long as other dimensions of the Church are also given emphasis, especially the historical and the social.

Dulles' later Community of Disciples model begins with the Church as a communion, and then incorporates elements of the other models from that standpoint. What I view here as Dulles' version of communion ecclesiology manifests its own particularity. For example, Dulles argues the debatable position that it is better to have small churches of the truly committed rather than large churches that include many who are only nominally or communally Catholic. All versions, though, will be particular to some degree. Dulles' Community of Disciples model serves as one example of what a multi-dimensional communion ecclesiology can be.

Various Versions

In doing the comparative studies that comprise the body of this book, I have found at least six contemporary Catholic versions of communion ecclesiology.

1. A CDF version, notable for its emphasis on the priority of the Church universal and the importance of certain visible church structures.

2. A Rahnerian version, notable for its emphasis on the sacramentality of the world and on the communion with God that exists within all of humankind.

3. A Balthasarian version, notable for its emphasis on the uniqueness of Christian revelation and its aesthetic character.

4. A liberation version, notable for its emphasis on the option for the poor and on the political implications of communion.

5. A contextual version, notable for its emphasis on gender, ethnicity, and social location as the context for appreciating relationality.

6. A reforming version, notable for its emphasis on the need for Roman Catholics to challenge radically their own ecclesiological presuppositions in the interest of ecumenical progress.

All six of these theological approaches properly contribute to a Catholic vision of communion ecclesiology. Any ecclesiological approach that would systematically exclude one of these versions would be less than "Catholic." Yet none of these versions is in itself complete. Like the

Church that it studies, communion ecclesiology manifests its own dialectic of the universal and the particular, of the one and the many, of the vision and the versions.

These versions of communion ecclesiology need not be exclusive of each other. They overlap on many issues. At the same time, however, I do not intend to endorse a relativism or simply a spineless pluralism, but rather a limited and particular range of diversity. Random theological diversity is not being promoted for its own sake; however, a particular range of the diversity that in fact exists within Catholic theology is legitimate and basically healthy. Every one of the above six schools of thought contributes something important to a Catholic vision.

This is not to say that these six versions of communion ecclesiology have a strictly "equal" voice in this Catholic dialogue about the meaning of communion ecclesiology and the meaning of catholicity. Scripture and tradition provide normative sources. The magisterium has a privileged voice. Balthasar and Rahner can each be recognized as being more grounded in the specifically Roman Catholic tradition than is, for example, Hans Küng.

An authentic communion ecclesiology should put more energy into embracing legitimate diversity than into excluding marginal positions. Ecclesial and theological diversity in and of itself is not the problem. If communion ecclesiology simply becomes associated with one selective reading of the Vatican II documents, it will not be able to function as the one basic ecclesiology or as the path beyond left-right dichotomies. If, however, in addition to having important content, communion ecclesiology also generates a process, an ideal vision, and a call beyond narrowness, then it can offer a Catholic vision of unity for the start of the third millennium.

The particular range of theological diversity here being described rests upon a host of deeply shared presuppositions. There is a method to this madness. The seemingly large differences among Catholic ecclesiological approaches are all being played out within the same ballpark.

Communion ecclesiology is like a playing field within which various theological approaches co-exist. Vatican II is subject to a wide range of interpretation even among Catholics who are striving to think beyond narrow camps and theological cliques. Various credible schools of thought operate within Catholic theology today. These schools of thought constitute the existing theological contexts in which Catholic versions of communion ecclesiology are taking shape.

Frameworks of Inclusion

A guiding principle that I employ in arguing for the inclusion of the six versions listed above in the construction of a Catholic communion ecclesiology is that each of them carries forward something of the ecclesial vision of Vatican II. Not to include one or more of them would constitute a selective reading of the Council documents and would be less than Catholic. To repeat, this is not to say that all are equal or that some approaches are not already more inclusively Catholic than others; at this time, however, no one version of communion ecclesiology has the corner on the market.

Two additional frameworks of inclusion have emerged during the writing of this book that buttress my argument for including these various versions. First is the idea that to be "Catholic" is to be "inclusive." Both Johann Adam Möhler and Henri de Lubac find such an understanding of catholicity in the patristic authors. They argue that the errors of the early heretics were not simply falsehoods, but partial truths. The heretics were often condemned not for what they affirmed but for what they denied.

To be "inclusive" here does not mean that no one can ever be excluded; rather, it means, paradoxically, that the only reason to exclude someone would ultimately be for their own lack of inclusivity. The intent is not to marginalize people or views, but simply to acknowledge that certain positions themselves marginalize what should be central. The Catholic impulse is to favor the "both/and" over the "either/or." It is to be open to truth wherever it may be found. It is to opt for unity, sometimes at the cost of other goods.

My third framework of inclusion concerns sacramentality. Drawing upon several twentieth-century thinkers such as Henri de Lubac, Karl Rahner, Edward Schillebeeckx, and Bernard Cooke,[9] I use "sacramentality" to refer to an awareness of the presence and activity of God simultaneously both in the sacraments and in the context of everyday life. I find this principle expressed in a distinction that Thomas Aquinas made in his *Summa Theologiae*.[10] There are two kinds of sacraments: those whose grace represents something incommensurable with what human beings can achieve in their own lives, and those whose grace is more in proportion with what human beings are naturally inclined to achieve on their own. As examples of the first type, Aquinas mentions baptism, confirmation, and the anointing of the sick. For the second type, he mentions matrimony and reconciliation. The first type have as

---

[9]Henri de Lubac, *Catholicism*, trans. Lancelot C. Sheppard (London: Burns and Oates, 1950; Universe Books edition, 1961 [French orig. 1938]); Edward Schillebeeckx, *Christ the Sacrament of Encounter with God*, trans. Paul Barrett; English text rev. Mark Schoof and Laurence Bright (New York: Sheed and Ward, 1963 [Dutch orig. 1960]); Karl Rahner, *The Church and the Sacraments*, trans. W.J. O'Hara (Freiburg: Herder, 1963); Bernard Cooke, *Sacraments and Sacramentality* (Mystic, CT: Twenty-Third Publications, 1983).

[10]*Summa Theologiae* (1273), part III, q. 84, a. 1.

their matter (material cause) external bodily substances such as water and oil. The second type have as their matter perceptible human actions, such as expression of commitment or of repentance.

This distinction brings out a crucial point: there is a sense in which there is a sacramentality that offers to the world that which the world lacks; and there is a sense in which there is a sacramentality that blesses and enhances what the world, through God's grace, already has. Both of these meanings of sacramentality are grounded in the Catholic tradition. Balthasar tends to emphasize sacramentality in the first sense. Rahner tends to emphasize the second sense. In this difference lies one of the great theological fissures among Catholics of the late twentieth century. A truly Catholic vision of communion ecclesiology must find a way to emphasize simultaneously both of these senses of sacramentality. Such a balance, I argue, is critical for understanding what it means to say that the Church itself is a "sacrament."

Both Balthasar and Rahner were theologians of great breadth and vision. But either of their emphases can be taken to an exclusionary extreme. A neglect of sacramentality in the first sense can lead to an underemphasis on the need for an explicit Christianity and an explicit Church. A neglect of sacramentality in the second sense can lead to a mystified understanding of the Church and to a de-valuing of the Spirit's presence in the world. The result in either case is a self-marginalizing narrowness.

The chart that maps out various dimensions is intended as a tool to mediate among the various versions of communion ecclesiology operative in Catholic circles today. At this point the chart is only systematic and abstract. Yet the ideas for it grew out of a series of comparative studies, both historical and contemporary. These studies constitute the chapters that follow. One advantage of comparative studies is that they can sometimes open up an opportunity to build bridges between contrasting viewpoints.

T W O

Communion and Modernity

Johann Adam Möhler and
Friedrich Schleiermacher

Johann Adam Möhler (1796-1838) is recognized as a seminal figure in the development of communion ecclesiology. It would be anachronistic to suggest that he would have explicitly applied the term "communion ecclesiology" to his own work, but his approach to the Church has had an important, formative impact upon theologians associated with the twentieth-century development of communion ecclesiology, such as Yves Congar, Henri de Lubac, Karl Rahner, Joseph Ratzinger, and Walter Kasper. Ratzinger has christened Möhler "the great reviver of Catholic theology after the ravages of the Enlightenment."[1]

In this chapter I explore the nineteenth-century roots of three important versions of communion ecclesiology. Friedrich Schleiermacher (1768-1834), in his 1821-22 *The Christian Faith*,[2] provides a classic and originating Protestant version. Möhler's 1825 work, *Unity in the Church*,[3] provides a dynamic and organic Catholic version. Although Möhler later distanced himself from *Unity*, his first book, many of its concerns remained important in his work throughout his short life. (He

---

[1]Joseph Cardinal Ratzinger, *Church, Ecumenism, and Politics* (New York: Crossroad, 1988 [German orig. 1987]) 4.

[2]Friedrich Schleiermacher, *The Christian Faith*, 2 vols., ed. H.R. Mackintosh and J.S. Stewart (New York: Harper and Row Torchbook edition, 1963 [orig. English trans. one vol., Edinburgh: T&T Clark, 1928; German orig. 1821-22; revised edition 1830]). Hereafter in text as *CF*.

[3]Johann Adam Möhler, *Unity in the Church, or The Principle of Catholicism Presented in the Spirit of the Church Fathers of the First Three Centuries*, trans. Peter C. Erb (Washington, DC: The Catholic University of America Press, 1996 [German original: Mainz, 1825]). Hereafter in text as *Unity*.

died at 42.) Möhler's subsequent works, especially the 1827 *Athanasius der Grosse*[4] and various editions of *Symbolik*,[5] altered the positions he took in his first book. The communion ecclesiology of the "early" Möhler differs from the communion ecclesiology of the "later" Möhler. In this difference lies the root of a basic tension in Catholic theology that still exists today.

Both Schleiermacher and the early Möhler constructed their ecclesiologies over against what they took to be a medieval, juridical view of the Church that focused too much or even exclusively on the Church's institutional aspects to the neglect of its communal and personal aspects. Both approached the Church as being most basically a fellowship or communion carrying forth in history the relationship between Jesus and his disciples. In comparison with what they cast as the juridical view, their own views were personal, historical, and grounded in human experience.

At the same time both Schleiermacher and Möhler, though more directly the former than the latter, were reacting against an individualistic Pietism whose theology tended to belie the strong role of community that often actually existed among Pietists. Schleiermacher, in ways for which Möhler had sympathy, drew deeply upon the piety, the personalism, and the strong sense of community among the Pietists while emphasizing simultaneously the theological importance of community.

Schleiermacher and Möhler also found a shared dialogue partner in the modern scientific and often reductionistic views associated with the Enlightenment. Both constructed ecclesiologies that were modern insofar as they relied upon an historical reconstruction of the origin and spread of Christianity. That is, they countered supernaturalistic, static views of revelation by re-imagining the emergence of Christianity as it was grounded in historical human experience. At the same time, though, they both fought against the anti-supernaturalism of the modern, retaining a strong, inviolable place for Christian revelation.

The intellectual currents from which both figures borrowed and against which both reacted ran broad and deep; also deep are the similarities in their respective ecclesiologies. I will present four basic points where the ecclesiologies of *The Christian Faith* and *Unity in the Church* converge, points very important for communion ecclesiology today. Yet there are also important junctures at which their ecclesiologies diverge.

---

[4]Johann Adam Möhler, *Athanasius der Grosse und die Kirche seiner Zeit* (Mainz: Florian Kupferberg, 1827).

[5]Johann Adam Möhler, *Symbolism: Exposition of the Doctrinal Differences between Catholics and Protestants as Evidenced by Their Symbolical Writings*, trans. James Burton Robinson (New York: Crossroad Herder, 1997 [German orig. 4 editions between 1832 and 1835]).

These points, too, are crucial to the discussion of communion ecclesiology today. To illustrate this I will then present four further points, ones where the early Möhler will agree with Schleiermacher to some extent, but then qualify with a strongly contrasting position. Finally, I will discuss contrasts between Möhler's early work and his later work.

I want to clarify that I am not claiming that Möhler wrote *Unity in the Church* directly in response to Schleiermacher, though on a few points he possibly did. It is well documented that Möhler was quite familiar with Schleiermacher,[6] and he does refer to him twice in *Unity in the Church*.[7] Schleiermacher is but one of many figures to whom Möhler is responding, though a very important one at that. I have recognized in Schleiermacher's *On Religion* points seminal to Tillich's "new being," Otto's "idea of the holy," Maslow's "peak-experiences," Ricoeur's "second naivete," Rahner's *Vorgriff* and "anonymous theist," Boff's "ecclesiogenesis," and many other well-known concepts associated with later theologians.

What I am claiming is that a comparison and contrast of the ecclesiologies of *The Christian Faith*, *Unity in the Church*, and Möhler's later works will prove fruitful for weighing the elements that in various combinations comprise communion ecclesiology in its twentieth-century manifestations. For all of Möhler's similarities to Schleiermacher, there is a chasm that separates the two. Moreover, for all of the important continuities between the early Möhler and the later Möhler, yet another chasm emerges. Both in those similarities and in those chasms are to be found the roots of contemporary Western versions of communion ecclesiology.

Four Points of Basic Agreement

In this section I will draw mainly upon *The Christian Faith* to highlight those dimensions of Schleiermacher's approach to the Church that overlap with Möhler's *Unity* to provide a basis for what is today called communion ecclesiology.

The paste that holds Schleiermacher's ecclesiology together is his

---

[6]Möhler's simultaneous regard for and distance from the thought of Schleiermacher is discussed in Michael J. Himes, "'A Great Theologian of Our Time': Möhler on Schleiermacher," *Heythrop Journal* 37 (January 1996) 24-46; Hervé Savon, *Johann Adam Möhler: The Father of Modern Theology* (Mahwah, NJ: Paulist Press, 1966) 13-7; 21-2; and Peter C. Erb's Introduction to Möhler's *Unity in the Church*, 49-59. Erb discusses the influence of *Unity* on later theology in his Introduction, 61-6.

[7]Himes, "A Great Theologian of Our Time," 24-5.

consistent concern for unity in the Church. I would even suggest that the title of Möhler's book, *Unity in the Church*, might not unreasonably have been given to *The Christian Faith*. In fact, ecclesiology provides the starting point and the framework for the whole of Schleiermacher's theology, with the Church's unity providing one of its most pervasive themes. Schleiermacher finds in the Church a concrete historical alternative to beginning his theology with abstract *a priori* principles. In his discussions of Church unity, he highlights many themes that overlap with concerns that are today associated with communion ecclesiology. The following four points are important to both Schleiermacher and Möhler:

1. The Church is basically a fellowship or communion with God through Jesus and the Spirit that is shared among Christians.

As mentioned above, if getting beyond an overly institutional view of the Church to a focus on spiritual fellowship while still valuing institutional structures were the sole defining factor in what constitutes a communion ecclesiology, then Schleiermacher could be seen as offering a communion ecclesiology *par excellence* (*CF* 26; 358-69).

Möhler begins *Unity in the Church* with this point (*Unity* 81). He emphasizes that *"the Church exists through a life directly and continually moved by the divine Spirit, and is maintained and continued by the loving mutual exchange of believers"* (*Unity* 91; italics in text).

2. The Church is the corporate life brought about by Jesus. Its origins must be grasped historically and dynamically. It has its foundation in a religious intimacy between Jesus and his followers that grows organically through the spread of like relationships.

Schleiermacher identifies religious self-consciousness, which is also a consciousness of God, as the basis of religion. This consciousness or piety leads naturally to fellowship or communion, which in the case of Christianity is the Church. In *On Religion*, Schleiermacher lingers on the topic of intimacy, discussing how religious consciousness dissolves the artificial boundaries of our personalities and immerses our selves within the feeling of comradeship.[8] It is in *The Christian Faith*, though, that he discusses Christian redemption arising through fellowship with Jesus and the emergence of the Church as a necessary extension of such fellowship (*CF* 26-9; 62-70; 358-73).

The early Möhler emphasized the Spirit more than Christ when he

---

[8]Friedrich Schleiermacher, *On Religion: Addresses in Response to Its Cultured Critics*, trans. Terrence N. Tice (Richmond: John Knox Press, 1969) 127-9.

discusses the origin of the Church, but he explains in his preface that he does so not to ignore Christ but to stress more what is not already so well known (*Unity* 77). He explains the spread of the Church as the communication of a new life principle through the Spirit, shared outwardly by those who received it, so that new lives are engendered. Those who receive new life in this way can then engender it in others (*Unity* 85). This new life is a love given by the divine Spirit (*Unity* 210). The Church grows as a living organism (*Unity* 166 and *passim*).

3. The Church is an intrinsic dimension of revelation, not an added extra.

Schleiermacher argues that whether in the modern era or in the time of Christ, Christian redemption takes place always and necessarily within the context of a fellowship. It is not simply the case that individuals have their own personal transforming experiences and then come together to form a fellowship (though for Schleiermacher it is also this). Christ's ministry took place within a context in which a collective need for redemption and the expectation of it already existed. Moreover, each personal Christian experience takes place within and is conditioned by a fellowship that took form with Christ's first public appearance. The resulting organization finds its roots in this initial self-organizing principle (*CF* 526-7).

Möhler argues that without the Church there is no access to Christ (*Unity* 94). The Church is not simply "a construction or an association, founded for the preservation of the Christian faith. Rather, she is much more an offspring of this faith, an action of love living in believers through the Holy Spirit." The Church develops as an outgrowth of an inner need to express divine love (*Unity* 209).

4. The Lord's Supper is the highest representation of Church unity, bringing together fellowship with Christ and fellowship among believers. The image that most aptly describes the Church is that of the Body of Christ.

Although he explicitly rejects the Roman view that insists upon transubstantiation, Schleiermacher also rejects views that characterize the Lord's Supper as merely figurative. He sees the Lord's Supper as the primary way of maintaining the living fellowship with Christ, such that all other forms of "enjoyment" of Christ are either an approximation to it or a prolongation of it (*CF* 589; 638-60). Schleiermacher is not given to the use of images in his systematic discussion of the Church. He finds the body of Christ, however, to express the irreplaceable importance of each individual member in union with Christ, their head. The concept of a mystical union of Christ with all the members captures well the heart of Schleiermacher's organic understanding of the Church (*CF* 580).

At the beginning of *Unity*, Möhler links the Eucharist with the Spirit, the begetting of a community, and Unity of all. In this connection he quotes Clement drawing upon Paul's image of the Body of Christ (*Unity* 82). This image recurs at various points in *Unity* to describe Möhler's organic view of the Church.

Four Points with Some Overlap Yet Strong Differences

Möhler's *Unity* was published just four years after the third and fullest edition of Schleiermacher's *On Religion* appeared, and just three years after the second volume of the first edition of *The Christian Faith*. Although *Unity* can be read simply as a study of patristic writers, much of Möhler's correspondence and other supporting documents, not to mention the slightest degree of reading between the lines, make clear that Möhler's main concerns involved the theology of his present day.[9] That is, although modern theological arguments are often present in the work only implicitly, they constitute a main thrust of the entire book.

Möhler was a baker for several years in his youth. The communion ecclesiology that he concocted might thus appropriately be imaged as a cake with many layers. From Möhler's perspective, Schleiermacher's approach to the Church gives one all of the internal layers, but it lacks the topmost and the bottommost. The topmost layer is the inner life of the Trinity, the communal life that exists among the three persons in God and which is shared with believers. The bottommost layer is the visible Church as it developed organically in an interconnected way through history, with its unity expressed in episcopal communion and in the papacy. Yet the lack of the topmost and the bottommost layers lends a certain flavor to all of the remaining layers, a flavor that Möhler found less than pleasing.

As Michael Himes has brought out, Möhler paid relatively little attention to what I am calling the topmost layer of communion ecclesiology, the inner life of the Trinity, in *Unity*.[10] In his work of two years later, *Athanasius der Grosse*, Möhler takes these issues on more fully and engages in an explicit and extensive critique of Schleiermacher's affection for Sabellianism. *Athanasius* can thus be seen as representing the second stage of a two-stage construction of communion ecclesiology. The first stage, *Unity*, focuses more on communion

---

[9]Erb, Introduction to *Unity in the Church*, passim.
[10]Himes, "A Great Theologian of Our Time," 24-46.

ecclesiology's bottommost layer, that of the visible, unified Church, although the Trinity does receive some mention.

To draw on what was said earlier, if getting beyond a narrow focus on institutional structures to concentrate on the Church as a spiritual fellowship were the sole factor in determining what constitutes a communion ecclesiology, then Schleiermacher and Möhler could be linked arm in arm as co-founders of a movement. Yet the points at which Möhler departs from Schleiermacher are not small ones, and they pervade the whole of *Unity*.

Schleiermacher held that the Church developed organically, but that due to human finitude and corruption it was necessary at various points for groups to break off. There remain real, organic connections among all Christians, and it is important to work to resolve differences on the visible level, but it is simply an unfortunate fact that legitimate divisions do exist. Möhler, in contrast, held that the Church in the early centuries developed in an organic unity that found a necessary and permanent expression in the worldwide episcopacy. Like Schleiermacher, he finds the deepest and most essential unity in the bondedness of all Christians through the Holy Spirit, and he recognizes diversity and various forms of disagreement as healthy signs of vitality and progress in Christian life. But Möhler does not brook complete institutional break-offs and new beginnings as ever being legitimate. According to Möhler, the Catholic Church remains always the legitimate, if oftentimes poorly implemented, visible expression of the deeper underlying unity that comes from the bondedness of all Christians in the Spirit. This anti-Protestant Catholic apology provides a main theme of *Unity*. Virtually the entire book can be read as an argument that Schleiermacher's concern for unity of the Church, while starting on the right track, simply does not go far enough because it does not include as necessary the type of visible unity that developed organically in the first three centuries.

The communion ecclesiology that arises from Möhler takes on a contour quite different from Schleiermacher's ecclesiology. I use the following four points to try to capture the balance of his concerns. The point to which Schleiermacher and Möhler agree is given in regular type; the point at which Möhler departs with a strong qualification is given in italics.

1. Unity present in Christian fellowship requires certain essential elements. *However, these essential elements include the episcopacy as it developed in the first three centuries, as well as the papacy.*

Schleiermacher held that since Christian fellowship must exist alongside the world it will have organizational elements, such as laws, structures of authority, etc. Most of these elements are historically variable, but there must be certain essential elements that account for continuity in self-identity. Schleiermacher identifies these elements as Holy Scripture; Ministry of the Word of God; Baptism; the Lord's Supper; the Power of the Keys; and Prayer in the Name of Jesus. He links these six elements with the threefold ministry of Christ as prophet, priest, and king, and as such he considers them to be the continuation of the activities of Christ himself (*CF* 586-91).

Möhler devotes the second of two parts of *Unity* to the organic development of structures of authority in the Church. He argues that the love present in Christian congregations found its visible expression and center in the bishop (*Unity* 209; 218); the dynamic unity already present among all believers in the Spirit found further expression in the metropolitan and then in a worldwide episcopacy; finally, it found a necessary expression in the papacy (*Unity* 230-62). Möhler draws frequently upon the testimony of the patristic writers to demonstrate the apostolic origin, importance, inevitability, and necessity of these structures. He does not claim that Jesus or the apostles directly instituted the forms of the structures, but that they developed organically from an inner need (*Unity* 209; 258).

2. Historical manifestations of the Church will legitimately be diverse. Church unity is not a narrow uniformity but something that exists amid the dynamic interplay of many diverse elements; unity and diversity are complementary rather than contradictory. The main purpose of Church authority is to counter those who insist on making their own mode of thinking obligatory, as the only expression of the common spirit. *However, the church contains within itself all legitimate antitheses. Moving beyond the boundaries of the church that developed organically is heretical and contradictory by its very nature.*

Schleiermacher held that, because it exists within the world, the visible Church has many mutable and corruptible elements. It is subject to error and division. Only the invisible Church is infallible and unified. Each part of the visible Church should be aware of its own incompleteness, and open to fellowship with other parts (*CF* 676-92). Even Protestantism and Roman Catholicism can be viewed as incomplete mediations of Christianity, each needing the other.[11]

Möhler supports strongly the concept that the Church, as a living organism, has many diverse elements (*Unity* 166). He speaks in favor of individuality properly understood (*Unity* 186), and he rejects any narrow concept of authority that would impose a rigid uniformity (*Unity* 194-6). But Möhler also argues insistently that the Church

---

[11]Schleiermacher, *On Religion*, 336-44.

founded by Christ is a visible one (*Unity* 211); that separation is of the very nature of heresy (*Unity* 124-5); that moving beyond the visible Church dissolves its organic unity (*Unity* 143); and that what exists as legitimate diversity when held in tension with its contrary within the bounds of church unity becomes an egoistical contradiction when carried outside the visible Church (*Unity* 178; 196). All true apostolic communities are generated directly by prior apostolic communities. No authentic community is generated through a complete breaking off with the communities that preceded it. Möhler explicitly rejects the argument that the Church should form a higher unity with those heresies that had separated themselves from it (*Unity* 197).

3. Church unity requires some normativity in the basic expressions of revelation. *However, scripture needs the living tradition and the church to function properly. A true understanding of the church demands a retrieval of the patristic witness as a key to the normative tradition.*

According to Schleiermacher, scripture is the most basic norm of revelation; Protestants are bound also by Evangelical confessional documents (*CF* 112-7); dogmas are necessary but provisional (*CF* 689-92). Sources of dogma such as the witness of the patristic writers and the decrees of Church Councils can be valuable but are not binding (*CF* 117-8).

Möhler finds scripture alone to be insufficient. The theological method of *Unity* manifests Möhler's position that to grasp the vision of the patristic authors is to grasp essential elements of what the Church is. Scripture is itself a necessary witness, but it must be complemented by the living tradition that preceded it and that carries it on (*Unity* 112-21). Church doctrine is not simply a human work, but a work of the Spirit (*Unity* 103). At the core of many heresies is the belief that Christianity was delivered complete at the beginning, and that any developments that took place were corruptions rather than the guidance of the Holy Spirit who continually preserves the Church; in other words, many heresies are at root denials of the principle of organic development (*Unity* 125-7).

4. The Church is trinitarian. *However, the Trinity is much more than simply a symbolic way of speaking about the Church; the Christian way of encountering God reveals something of the reality of God.*

For Schleiermacher, the Holy Spirit is the vital unity of the Christian fellowship as a moral personality; it is the Being of God as it is present in the Church and it continues the communication of the perfection and blessedness of Christ. The doctrine of the Trinity is first and foremost a way of talking about Christ and the Church; it is a way of firmly asserting that the Divine Essence considered as united to human nature is the same as the Divine Essence in itself. Any assertions about the Trinity beyond this ecclesial framework should not be considered binding (*CF* 535-6; 738-51). In particular, Schleiermacher thought that the Sabellian view has many attractive elements when compared with the Athanasian view that prevailed at Nicaea.[12]

The opening paragraph of the preface of *Unity* shows Möhler's grasp of the doctrine of the Trinity to be as dynamic and historical as that of Schleiermacher. The Trinity is the understanding of God that grows from the Christian experience of the economy of salvation (*Unity* 77). In contrast to Schleiermacher, however, Möhler explicitly rejects Sabellianism as a heresy (*Unity* 111), and he speaks throughout in a way that highlights that the Holy Spirit is more than just the moral personality of the Church. The Trinity as it is encountered in the economy of salvation is the same as the Trinity in its own immanent existence. That a dogma lies beyond our understanding does not preclude its being grasped as a truth.

Möhler's ecclesiology in *Unity* shares much with that of Schleiermacher. As opposed to the medieval juridical view, it emphasizes a spiritual communion among human beings with God. As opposed to scientific rationalism, it is mystical and transcendent and sacramental. In line with Romanticism, it finds a grounding in religious experience. It is organic, dynamic, and historically conscious. It values unity as the broker of a legitimate diversity, not as its oppressor. But against the prevailing Romanticism of the time, it values not only religiousness but a particular historical revelation as sacrosanct. It recognizes the Trinitarian nature of Christianity. It identifies amid changing times and circumstances certain essential elements that constitute the Church. It finds in the Eucharist the highest expression of Christian community, and it recognizes the need for certain sources of revelation and structures of authority. Möhler and Schleiermacher both address the challenges of modernity by being modern themselves to a great degree, while retaining a strong faith in Christ and the Church as expressing, in a privileged way, God's revelation.

Yet the early Möhler's communion ecclesiology needs to be understood in contrast to Schleiermacher's approach as identifying the Church that developed organically in the first few centuries as the visi-

---

[12]Friedrich Schleiermacher, "On the Discrepancy between the Sabellian and Athanasian Method of Representing the Doctrine of the Trinity in the Godhead," trans. M. Stuart, in *Schleiermacher and Stuart on the Doctrine of the Trinity* (reprinted in book form [no publication data] from the *Biblical Repository and Quarterly Observer*, April and July 1835).

ble Catholic Church, and in seeing the structures of authority that emerged as secondary but essential expressions of unity in love. At the heart of Möhler's communion ecclesiology is a link between mystical communion and the episcopacy. The faith as witnessed by the patristic writers and as formulated in the early councils is normative and binding, not as abstract propositions, but as expressing the heart of the Christian life as it is actually lived.

Apologetic Yet Ecumenical

Before examining ways in which Möhler later modified his views, it will be good to reflect on the ecumenical dimensions of the interplay between the positions of Möhler and Schleiermacher. Although Schleiermacher remained always a strong apologist for the Protestant churches, his ecumenical contribution was considerable. In *The Christian Faith*, Schleiermacher took the position that Protestantism and Catholicism were both incomplete mediations of Christianity, each needing the other for its fulfillment. Schleiermacher continued to reject the papacy, and he held that Catholicism would do better to return to an older, "aristocratic" form of episcopacy rather than a monarchical one. Still, his recognition of Protestantism's incompleteness and its dialectical link with Catholicism provides a strong thrust in an ecumenical direction.

Schleiermacher's viewpoint on this issue is of course not identical with the official Catholic one. The Sacred Congregation for the Doctrine of the Faith, when criticizing Leonardo Boff's "ecclesiological relativism," expressly rejects the position that Catholicism and Protestantism exist in the kind of dialectical relationship described by Schleiermacher.[13] There are, however, many Protestants who to this day hold simply that Catholicism constitutes a corrupt and infantile form of Christianity and that Protestantism represents the mature form. There are many other Protestants who still hold that church and fellowship are so purely secondary to an individual's relationship with Christ that current congregations are as complete as they need to be; denominational matters are really not important. In comparison with these viewpoints, the ecumenical outreach of Schleiermacher can be appreciated. Also, although the CDF's technical qualifications about the essential completeness of the means of salvation to be found in Catholicism need to be taken seriously, there is also some legitimacy to the claim that, considered historically, Catholicism and Protestantism

---

[13]CDF, "Doctrinal Congregation Criticizes Brazilian Theologian's Book," *Origins* 14 (4 April 1985) 683-7.

have functioned dialectically. This is a complex matter that will resist easy attempts to be sorted out.

Möhler's own approach represents a strong Catholic apologetic. Why is it, then, that communion ecclesiology is often hailed as being a tool for ecumenical progress? On one level, with its focus on the patristic authors, the Trinity, sacramentality, and the episcopacy, it has functioned preeminently as a tool for Roman Catholic dialogue with the Eastern Orthodox. But it has also played a role in Catholic-Protestant relations. How is it that something which in its roots is so blatantly apologetic could play such a role?

Möhler was ecumenical in several ways. He thought of it as his duty to love Protestants and to engage in serious ongoing dialogue with them. But his ecumenism was also substantive. Like Schleiermacher, he contrasted his own understanding of the Church with the Roman Catholic view of the Middle Ages. Whether his grasp of medieval Catholicism was accurate is highly debatable, but nevertheless he saw that view, which he called in an earlier work "the papal system,"[14] as static, institutional, monarchical, and overly centralized. Although he judged the great Reformers to have been illegitimate in their moving beyond a Catholic framework, he strongly sympathized with them concerning the need for reform and the frustrations of trying to accomplish such reform in union with a hierarchy that misconceived the nature of its own authority. In constructing his ecclesiology over against the medieval juridical view, Möhler offered a view of Church that is dynamic, organic, collegial, and pluraform.

Möhler held in *Unity* that the main job of the episcopacy and the papacy is not to impose a narrow uniformity but rather to affirm and hold in tension the diverse and often contrary forms of expression that the Christian life will generate. The papacy is the completion of the ways in which unity of the Church manifests itself, but Möhler has as much to say about the need for papal reform and limits as he has to say about its necessity. As Möhler conceived of himself, he affirmed strongly the heart of what Protestant reformers legitimately wanted, to understand the Church as primarily a fellowship of believers united in the Spirit, while retaining a reformed notion of the Catholic episcopacy and the papacy.

Realizing how Möhler's differences from Schleiermacher contribute to a Roman Catholic apologetic, therefore, should not lessen one's appreciation of how his similarities with Schleiermacher contribute to an ecumenical vision. For once communion, that is, fellowship among believers with God, becomes the primary reference point for identifying

---

[14]Savon, *Johann Adam Möhler*, 24-6.

what constitutes the Church, many ecumenical avenues open up. Institutional issues remain important, even essential, but they are still secondary to the spiritual dimension of communion. Communion with each other and with God is the deepest thing that Christians share. It is this basic conceptual scheme that allowed Vatican II's *Unitatis Redintegratio* and *Lumen Gentium* to replace the language of heresies and sects with talk of our "separated brothers and sisters" who remain in imperfect but real communion with Catholics (UR 3) and in whom the Holy Spirit is active in a salvific manner (LG 15).

The Later Möhler

Not long after the publication of *Unity*, Möhler began to develop further his ecclesiology in qualification of his earlier positions and even in reaction against some of the implications of those positions.[15] Möhler found that his pneumatological approach ran the dual danger both of collapsing the transcendence of God into the spirit of the community and of allowing the real freedom of humans to be lost within the transcendence of God. This is because, on the one hand, the Holy Spirit could become too closely identified simply with the community spirit. The revelation of God in this regard becomes not something that comes as it were from outside to speak a word to Christians, but is limited to what emerges from within the workings of the community. What begins as a healthy stress on history and human subjectivity can end up in a subjectivism and a denial of the ultimate transcendence of revelation.

On the other hand, if the spirit of the community is too closely identified with the Holy Spirit, the Church can be divinized and its human elements become absorbed and lost. Möhler came to see a need for protecting the integrity of the human person and of human freedom. Only by maintaining a clear distinction between the Holy Spirit and the community spirit that emerges from within human beings can the ability of

---

[15]In this section, I rely significantly upon Michael J. Himes, *Ongoing Incarnation: Johann Adam Möhler and the Beginnings of Modern Ecclesiology* (New York: Crossroad, 1997), which presents a detailed study of the various changes and stages that Möhler's work underwent. Hereafter in text as *Ongoing*. Erb discusses Möhler's repudiation of *Unity in the Church* in his Introduction, 2-3; on 56-61 he reviews Josef Rupert Gieselmann's outlines of Möhler's shifts. Another valuable overview of some of Möhler's shifts is found in Bradford E. Hinze, "The Holy Spirit and Catholic Tradition: The Legacy of Johann Adam Möhler," in *The Legacy of the Tübingen School: The Relevance of Nineteenth-Century Theology for the Twenty-First Century*, ed. Donald J. Dietrich and Michael J. Himes, 75-94 (New York: Crossroad, 1997).

human beings to cooperate freely within divine grace be preserved.

Möhler's solution to these problems was to shift away from a pneumatological emphasis to a distinctively christological emphasis in his ecclesiology. Möhler wrote in *Symbolism*,

> The visible church is the Son of God appearing within mankind in human form in a continuous fashion, constantly renewed, eternally rejuvenated, his ongoing incarnation, just as the faithful are also called in holy scripture the body of Christ. (Himes' translation. *Ongoing* 259)

As Himes puts it, for Möhler:

> The church is the development in time of the incarnation: it is the expansion to all human beings at all times in all places of that divine-human relation established in Christ, a relationship to which they are receptive because of the "image," the "religious capacity" within them, which can now, by the reestablishment of the communication of God to humanity, grow again to "likeness." (*Ongoing* 207)

In the Church, as in Christ, there is a union yet distinction between the divine and the human elements. Because humans remain human, they are able still to be free as they grow to be more like God. Because the divine element in the Church is real and transcendent, what human beings encounter through the Church is really God and not simply a spirit of their own manufacture.

The hypostatic union in Christ, as defined by Chalcedon, becomes for Möhler the model upon which to fashion an understanding of the Church. As Christ is one entity, both truly divine and truly human, so too is the Church. As Himes brings out, Möhler tried to avoid the extremes of an ecclesiological Nestorianism and ecclesiological monophysitism (*Ongoing*, 332-4). The former extreme would so separate the divine elements and the human elements of the church as to make them two completely separate entities. The latter extreme would collapse the divine and the human such that both the divine and the human elements of the Church would be treated simply as if they were all divine. The proper way to understand the Church is as one reality that is both divine and human.

Möhler moved in the direction of this balance throughout the revisions of the five editions of *Symbolik*, but he did not fully achieve it. In reaction to some of the dangers present in *Unity in the Church*, Möhler placed great emphasis on the Church's supernatural character and its external, visible dimensions. A rough contrast of different emphases can be drawn as follows:

Unity in the Church	Symbolik
low, ascending ecclesiology	high, descending ecclesiology
pneumatological origin and nature of the Church	Christological origin and nature of the Church
visible Church structures as strictly secondary	visible Church as a temporal priority
revelation begins within and grows organically in external expression	revelation begins in external human signs in which the divine is present
what has been revealed unfolds historically and organically	what has been revealed calls for aesthetic appreciation
authority represents an inner-unfolding of love	authority represents stability, authenticity, and truth

This contrast is indeed rough, because, as Himes argues, Möhler gradually reintegrated themes associated with *Unity* throughout the various revisions of *Symbolik*. That is, if the first edition of *Symbolik* in many ways stands over against *Unity*, the later editions show much evidence of redressing the balance. Himes demonstrates how, in later editions, Möhler complemented his supernaturalist emphasis on the Church with a further stress on how this Church corresponds to the deepest longings of the human heart. To the external sign of the Church is added the internal inclinations of believers toward such a Church. Himes demonstrates also how Möhler's theological anthropology, which grounds his entire approach in *Symbolik*, shifted away from a supernaturalist stress to a greater appreciation of the freedom of human beings and the integral nature of their contribution to the Church.

Conclusion

Schleiermacher provides an early modern Protestant version of communion ecclesiology. Möhler's early work provides a modern Catholic version with a pneumatological stress. It has affinities with the twentieth-century approaches of Yves Congar and Karl Rahner. Möhler's later work provides another modern Catholic version of communion ecclesiology. It has affinities with the twentieth-century approaches of Journet, Balthasar, and Ratzinger. The tensions between the early Möhler and the later Möhler will re-surface in the chapters that follow.

THREE

Communion, Mystery, and History

Charles Journet and Yves Congar

The contrasting concerns of the authors to be treated in the present chapter present a parallel with the contrasting concerns of the early Möhler and the later Möhler as discussed in the previous chapter. The French Dominican Yves Congar (1904-1996), with his focus on the Holy Spirit and his attention to the dynamic, historically developing Church, shares much in common with the early Möhler. Swiss theologian Charles Journet (1891-1975), with his focus on the Church as an objective, aesthetically engaging given, shares much in common with the later Möhler.

The tension between these approaches is important for two reasons. First, Journet and Congar represent two distinct schools of theological reform leading into Vatican II. Second, the tension between them remains today a major underlying issue in contemporary Catholic theology.

Congar stands as one of the great figures whose work led up to Vatican II. Joseph Komonchak said of Congar that "there is no theologian who did more to prepare for Vatican II or who had a larger role in the orientation and even in the composition of the documents."[1] Richard McBrien has referred to Congar as "the most distinguished ecclesiologist of this century and perhaps of the entire post-Tridentine era."[2]

Congar acknowledged the strong influence of Möhler on his thought: "In him I found a source, the source, which I directly used. What Möhler had done in the 19th century became for me an ideal toward which I

---

[1] Joseph A. Komonchak, "The Return of Yves Congar," *Commonweal* 110 (July 15, 1983) 402.

[2] Richard P. McBrien, "Church and Ministry: The Achievement of Yves Congar," *Theology Digest* 32 (1985) 203.

would aim my own reflections in the 20th century."[3] A French translation of Möhler's *Unity in the Church* became the second volume in the well-known *Unam Sanctam* series that Congar edited. Beginning with ecumenical concerns, Congar became a premier theologian of *ressourcement*. The first volume of that series is his own *Chrétiens désunis*, in which he discusses as one of his "grand lines of a concrete program for a Catholic ecumenism" the need for a "return to the sources," a theme that would occupy him throughout his life.[4] He championed the position that the best way to understand the Church is as the Mystical Body of Christ, a communion, which goes beyond simply visible structures to constitute a relationship between the Trinity and those who are devoted to Christ.

For two decades prior to the Council, though, Congar worked under the shadow of great suspicion from Rome. He was at times refused permission to attend certain ecumenical conferences and to publish some of his works. In the early 1950's he spent several years "in exile" in Jerusalem, away from his home at the Saulchoir. Many of the advances at Vatican II can be read as a vindication of Congar's life work.

Journet, although not nearly so well remembered as Congar, is also a figure whose work was influential in leading up to Vatican II. Journet founded the journal *Nova et vetera* in 1926, and served as its editor until his death. He was known for his humility as well as his gracious wit. At first he refused the cardinal's hat offered to him by Paul VI, only to accept it when he was urged to do so for the sake of his country. He was made a cardinal on January 25, 1965. Journet is also notable for having written the only formal systematic treatise on the Church in the twentieth century, his three volume *L'Eglise du Verbe incarné*.[5] He authored about nineteen books in addition to this treatise, including *The Primacy of Peter*[6] and *The Meaning of Evil*.[7] His reaction to the changes brought about by Vatican II, as evidenced in his post-conciliar writings, was one of disappointment that in some respects the Catholic Church was going too far in adjusting itself to the modern world.

---

[3]From Pablo Sicously's essay in J. Puyo, *Une vie pour la vérité: Jean Puyo interrogé le Père Congar* (Paris: Le Centurion, 1975) 48. Cited in Bradford E. Hinze, "The Holy Spirit and Catholic Tradition: The Legacy of Johann Adam Möhler," in *The Legacy of the Tübingen School: The Relevance of Nineteenth-Century Theology for the Twenty-First Century*, ed. Donald J. Dietrich and Michael J. Himes (New York: Crossroad, 1997) 91.

[4]Yves Congar, *Chrétiens désunis* (Paris: Cerf, 1937) 330-3; Eng. ed. *Divided Christendom*, trans. M. A. Bousefield (London: G. Bles, 1939).

[5]Charles Journet, *L'Eglise du Verbe incarné*, 3 vols. (Paris-Bruges: Desclée De Brouwer, 1941, 1951, 1969).

[6]Charles Journet, *The Primacy of Peter: from the Protestant and from the Catholic Point of View*, trans. John Chapin (Westminster, MD: Newman Press, 1954 [French orig. 1953]).

[7]Charles Journet, *The Meaning of Evil*, trans. Michael Barry (New York: P.J. Kenedy, 1963 [French orig. 1961]).

Journet is today sometimes interpreted as one who never broke out of the neo-Scholastic model that Congar and Vatican II surpassed.[8] I argue here that this interpretation is at most a half-truth. Journet did make use of neo-Scholastic terms and concepts, but he used them to break open the neo-Scholastic model from within. His attempt to move beyond neo-Scholasticism was well understood in his times. In a 1952 article, for example, Joseph Clifford Fenton of the Catholic University of America defended Robert Bellarmine's concept of the Church against Journet's advances. He identified Journet as a writer in league with Yves Congar and Karl Adam, whose teachings are based on no evidence and should not "influence students and teachers of sacred theology to forsake the doctrine of St. Robert Bellarmine on the visibility of the Catholic Church."[9] Many of the ecclesiological developments of Vatican II were right in line with Journet's work.

Journet: Overturning the Neo-Scholastic Model

In his treatise on the Church, Journet reacted against the prevailing neo-Scholasticism of his time. There are at least a few reasons why Journet is misinterpreted today as one who remained mired in the juridical model of the Church reflected in many seminary manuals. His reaction to the Council is one reason. If Vatican II represented the overcoming of juridicism, then those dismayed by the aftermath of the Council are assumed to be defenders of juridicism. A second reason, important in English-speaking countries, is that only the first volume of *L'Eglise du Verbe incarné* has been translated into English. This volume deals with the role of the hierarchy, and, read out of context, appears simply as traditional fare. It is the other two volumes that fulfilled Journet's project. A third reason is that Journet continued to use neo-Scholastic terminology even as he staged a revolution against certain neo-Scholastic concepts. Where Congar was going behind the sometimes mechanical packaging of Aquinas' *Summa* to the patristic authors and to scripture, Journet retained much of the Thomistic terms and concepts even as he transformed their applications. He did this,

---

[8]See, e.g., Thomas F. O'Meara's treatment of Journet. O'Meara acknowledges the ambiguities of Journet's relationship to neo-Scholasticism, and he gives reasons for treating only the first volume of *L'Eglise du Verbe incarné*. ("The Teaching Office of Bishops in the Ecclesiology of Charles Journet," *The Jurist* 49 [1989] 23-47.) However, his summary and criticism of the first volume apart from the rest seems unfortunately to present Journet in a way that de-emphasizes the ways in which Journet anticipated certain developments at Vatican II.

[9]Joseph Clifford Fenton, "Father Journet's Concept of the Church," *American Ecclesiastical Review* 127 (November 1952) 370-80.

though, by reading Thomas' ecclesiology against the background of the patristic tradition. As Journet wrote in 1939:

> In these great Doctors [Augustine and Aquinas] I have found a theology of the Church more living, more far-reaching and more liberating than that which our manuals commonly contain. In them we feel the active presence of a vision of the Mystery of the Church understood as an extension of the Incarnation. That vision we find in the Fathers, Latin as well as Greek; it is supported by the whole tenor of the New Testament.[10]

This vision is of the Church as the Mystical Body of Christ. By drawing upon the patristic authors, Journet self-consciously presented himself as a theologian of *ressourcement* and declared himself open to the possibility of doctrinal development, citing John Henry Newman and Johann Adam Möhler as pioneers in that area.[11]

Journet used a Thomistic version of the four causes of Aristotle to outline the trajectory of his four-part (three-volume) project. Seminary manuals of the nineteenth and twentieth centuries frequently used these categories to analyze a wide range of theological issues. Human beings were described in these terms; so were the virtues; so were the sacraments. Although not all manuals used these categories to speak of the Church, some did so explicitly, and all taught along similar lines.

Daniel A. Triulzi, S.M. has written a brief survey of five seminary manuals.[12] These manuals concentrated on apologetics. They defended the Catholic Church as the one true Church founded by Christ, the only one that is one, holy, catholic, and apostolic. They used Aristotelian categories of causality (some explicitly, some implicitly) to describe the Church. The formal cause is the hierarchy; the material cause is the laity; the efficient cause is the Trinity (remote) and Christ (immediate}; the final cause is the beatific vision. When it came to defining what the Church is, therefore, it was depicted as formally a hierarchical organization. The formal cause included also the sacraments and rightly defined dogmas. This hierarchical organization included lay people, was founded by God, and was oriented toward eternal life. The understanding of "Church" among Catholics before Vatican II was complex and multi-valent. In certain respects, though, the Church was considered to be identical with the hierarchy, and

---

[10]Charles Journet, *Church of the Word Incarnate*, vol. 1 [French orig. 1941], trans. A. H. C. Downs (New York: Sheed and Ward, 1955) xxx. This passage is from the introduction, dated 1939.

[11]Ibid.

[12]Daniel A. Triulzi, S.M., "The Tract, *De Ecclesia Christi*, in the Seminary Manuals Predating the Second Vatican Council," unpublished (1986).

what the hierarchy taught was what "The Church" taught.

The main achievement of Journet was to cast the hierarchy out of the formal cause of the Church. For Journet, the formal cause of the Church, that which definitively makes it what it is, that which determines its essence, is the Holy Spirit. The hierarchy is given the role of immediate efficient cause.

This change is substantial, if subtle. The first volume of *L'Eglise du Verbe incarné*, dealing with the hierarchy, seems very traditional in its presentation of an "ideal vision" of the Church. The various powers of the hierarchy are outlined and affirmed. There is no stress on historical shifts in structure, on various corruptions, or on the possibility of or need for reform. The hierarchy is presented as having as important and dominant a function as it ever had.

Yet one can read Journet as dealing first with the hierarchy in order to do his duty to this obligatory matter so that he could get on to what he considered more interesting and important. For Journet explicitly says in his preface that he wants to get beyond those treatises that dwell exclusively and apologetically on the hierarchy in order to concentrate on the "deeper study of the intimate constitution and essential mystery of the Church."[13] In Journet's approach, to recognize the Holy Spirit as the formal cause of the Church is to move behind the seminary manuals to the real St. Thomas.

Journet was careful to clarify that he does not want to bifurcate the Church as a hierarchical organization from the organization of charity. He quoted Pius XII favorably:

> It would be erroneous to distinguish between the juridical church and the Church of charity. That is not how things are, rather this juridically established Church, having the Supreme Pontiff for [its] head, is also the Church of Christ, the Church of charity, and of the universal family of Christians.[14]

Journet followed Pius XII's wishes to the letter, but in a quite interesting manner. Using Aristotelian causality, Journet is able to describe analytically a Church whose organization of charity is most basically what it is, while its juridical organization is an essential factor that helps to bring it about. In other words, for Journet, the Church of charity and the juridically organized Church are indeed one and the same; however, the Church conceived of as most basically an organization of charity and the Church conceived of as most basically a juridical organization are not only distinct, but the latter does not even exist, except

---

[13]Journet, *Church of the Word Incarnate*, xxvi.

[14]Ibid. The quote is from *Documentation Catholique*, August 20, 1939, col 1000. Journet also refers the reader to the encyclical *Mystici corporis*, 1943.

as an abstraction. It is an aberration to make the hierarchy the formal cause of the Church. Journet thus overturns any juridically based notion of the Church while maintaining an essential role for the hierarchy within the Church of charity.

From within the tradition of the manuals, this move is revolutionary. However, it was a revolution not concerning Church structures or the need for development, but a revolution in conceptualization and, ultimately, vision and feeling. Journet, for all of his limitations from a contemporary perspective, evokes a sense of awe and mystery and love concerning the Church as the Mystical Body of Christ and as the presence of the Spirit among Christians. Journet loves Mary and the saints and the Church, the Church understood not as a hierarchy but as a mystical communion. This sense of humble devotion permeates his work. Journet loved to repeat a saying from the Russian Vassili Rozanov: "Ma vie, c'est L'Eglise."[15] The hierarchy, for Journet, is most fundamentally a service to help bring about the mystical communion. If Journet was not very interested in reforming hierarchical structures, still he was quite interested in not letting his ecclesiology construe them alone as essential and sufficient. He makes this point most vividly in the introduction to *Church of the Word Incarnate*, where he says that with a proper understanding of the four causes of the Church, "The apostolic hierarchy will then represent no more than the immediate efficient cause of the Church, of the Mystical Body."[16] It is indeed a sad irony that the English translation of only the first book of his treatise made it appear to some that he did so construe them.

Much of the theology that Journet championed found a significant place in *Lumen Gentium*. Journet was a member of the preparatory Theological Commission that produced the first version of the text *De Ecclesia* (drafted in large measure by Sebastian Tromp), which was voted down and thoroughly revised before ultimately becoming *Lumen Gentium*.[17] It would be a mistake, though, to associate Journet's ideas closely with those cast aside at the Council, and this for two reasons.

First, Journet's works show that he fought against juridicism even as he operated within neo-Scholastic categories. As Robert Kress attests:

Cardinal Journet will be remembered for his contributions to the theological model of the Church as the Mystical Body of Christ. His

---

[15]Pierre-Marie Emonet, *Le Cardinal Journet: Portrait Intérieur* (Chambray-les-Tours: C.L.D., 1983) 1.

[16]Journet, *Church of the Word Incarnate*, xxvi.

[17]See Komonchak's discussion of *De Ecclesia* in *History of Vatican II*, vol. 1, ed. Giuseppe Alberigo and Joseph A. Komonchak (Maryknoll, NY: Orbis Books; Leuven: Peeters, 1995) 285-300; 311-3.

Thomistic background enabled him to maintain the balance between the Church's visible and invisible dimensions, which had been so severely sundered in previous theology. Likewise his Thomistic sacramental insight enabled him to understand that the ecclesial institution and structure form the *sacramentum* of the more mystical inner life of grace of the Church. His ecclesiology was a significant contribution to the spirit and theology of Vatican II.[18]

Second, there was much in *Lumen Gentium* to which Journet could lay claim as compatible with his own advances. Foremost among these is having the mystery of the Church be the topic for the opening chapter with the Mystical Body of Christ as its primary image. This focus was the main point of Journet's life work. Also reflective of Journet is the first chapter's use of a broad range of scriptural images to speak of the mystery of the Church. That the chapter on the hierarchy comes third, being contextualized by the Church as mystery, is another point characteristic of Journet.

Chapter five of *Lumen Gentium*, "The Universal Call to Holiness," expresses well Journet's concern that the spiritual life be not something extra, added over and above an institutional Church, but rather that which constitutes the Church's very core. Chapter eight, on Mary, contains something of the outlook of Journet, who could not speak of the Church without including Marian reflection: "*La Vierge est au coeur de l'église.*"[19] Journet's linking of the earthly Church with the heavenly Church, and his weaving together ecclesiology with christology, soteriology, and missiology are also reflected in *Lumen Gentium's* approach. Finally, his inclusion in the Church of non-Christians who have a faith *latent* "*en acte tendancielle*"[20] foreshadows positions taken at the Council toward atheists and those of other faiths.

On the other hand, there were several elements of Vatican II that Journet's work did not anticipate. These elements include a stress on the Church being always in need of reform and renewal; a significantly enhanced role for the laity; and a reconfiguration of the relationship between Church and world. In the end, though, Journet embraced the Council documents, in great contrast with those such as Archbishop Marcel Lefebvre who rejected the Council itself.

Journet's appointment to the cardinalate in 1965 allowed him to give several speeches during the last sessions of Vatican II. He spoke strongly in favor of the Declaration on Religious Liberty (*Dignitatis*

---

[18]*New Catholic Encyclopedia*, vol. 17 (Washington: Catholic University of America, 1979) 310.

[19]Journet, *L'Eglise du Verbe incarné*, II, 382.

[20]Ibid., 1065.

humanae).[21] He defended the indissolubility of marriage during the discussion of the Pastoral Constitution on the Church in the Modern World (*Gaudium et Spes*).[22] And he insisted on the absolute necessity of explicitly Christian evangelization during the consideration of the Decree on the Church's Missionary Activity (*Ad Gentes*).[23] Paul VI's elevation of Journet and Journet's reemergence as an influential voice during the final sessions should be read not as a resurgence of the old guard, but rather as an affirmation of an important strain of the movements for renewal that brought the Council about, the strain that emphasized the Church as the Mystical Body of Christ.

In his work in the decade after Vatican II, Journet supported a stricter reading of the Council documents than was then in vogue. In many articles in *Nova et vetera*, he attacked positions that were too worldly or that applied the teachings of the Council in too liberal a manner. He thought that ecumenical agreements were being reached too facilely without sufficient attention to remaining issues of disagreement, such as the meaning of sacrament, the belief in transubstantiation, and the validity of orders.[24] He emphasized that God does not intend a global religious pluralism and that evangelization is not an option but a command. He critiqued Teilhard de Chardin for leaving out the supernatural from his otherwise powerful synthesis;[25] Rahner for not sufficiently stressing the need for positive revelation;[26] Schillebeeckx for reducing faith to an interior expression and denying there is one true Church beyond the apostolic age;[27] and Schoonenberg for denying the divinity of Christ, the Trinity, and the afterlife.[28] Overall, he argued against those whom he thought were taking an anthropological turn that would rob Christianity of its distinctiveness and dissolve it into a humanism.[29] For Journet, it was a sad reversal for a

---

[21]See Henri Fesquet, *The Drama of Vatican II*, trans. Bernard Murchland (New York: Random House, 1967 [French orig. 1966]) 614-5.

[22]Ibid., 647-52.

[23]*Council Daybook, Vatican II, Session 4*, ed. Floyd Anderson (Washington, DC: National Catholic Welfare Conference, 1966) 111.

[24]Charles Journet, "Intercommunion?" *Nova et vetera* 45 (1970) 1-9. Also "Note sur un accord entre theologians Anglicans et Catholiques touchant la doctrine eucharistique," *Nova et vetera* 46 (1971) 250-1.

[25]Charles Journet, "La synthèse du P. Teilhard de Chardin: Est-elle dissociable?" *Nova et vetera* 41 (1966) 144-51.

[26]Charles Journet, "Cordula ou l'épreuve décisive," *Nova et vetera* 43 (1968) 147-54.

[27]Charles Journet, "Secularisation, hermeneutique, orthopraxis selon E. Schillebeeckx et P. Schoonenberg," *Nova et vetera* 44 (1969) 300-12.

[28]Ibid.

[29]Charles Journet, "De le théologie a l'anthropologie: un périple aujourd'hui centenaire," *Nova et vetera* 41 (1966) 229-34.

Council whose main achievement was a renewed sense of the mystery of the Church to have its initial implementations consist in humanistic reductionisms.

Congar: Mystery and History

Like Journet, Congar acknowledged the existence of disturbing liturgical and doctrinal abuses in the wake of the Council. In contrast with Journet, however, he was even more concerned with the reactions of those whom he thought had "an allergy to any kind of change."[30] Congar rejected such an attitude because he thought that the deeper problems facing the Church after the Council had to do with the real life complexities of the modern world and the genuine questions troubling believers. To focus too much on internal abuses could function as a way of avoiding these real issues.[31]

Congar's work in ecclesiology had long, sustaining roots in his ecumenical concerns. In his 1939 *Chrétiens désunis*, a programmatic work, his ecumenical starting point led to his appreciation of the cultural and historical factors that contributed to disunity and thus surfaced many issues of life-long interest.[32] In that work Congar articulated his understanding of the Church primarily as a communion. He highlighted the connection of the Church with the Trinity. He defined "catholicity" in an inclusive manner. He affirmed that Christianity surpasses the visible reality of the Church. And he found in the ecumenical question a primary motivator for *ressourcement*.

The ecumenical concerns in *Chrétiens désunis* would be influential at Vatican II. One finds there already a recognition of Protestant denominations as "frères séparés," the naming of "éléments d'Eglise" existing within them, the expression of degrees of communion, and acknowledgment of the salvific presence of the Holy Spirit among them.

Congar's early experiences with ecumenical groups in France helped him to think creatively of future possibilities for Roman Catholicism. He undertook a sympathetic study of Luther.[33] He stressed the importance of charism as well as structure, and explored the priest-

---

[30]Yves Congar, *Challenge to the Church: The Case of Archbishop Lefebvre*, trans. Paul Inwood (Huntingdon, IN: Our Sunday Visitor, 1976 [French orig. 1976]) 58 and 56.

[31]Ibid., 58.

[32]An autobiographical essay that traces Congar's intellectual development constitutes the preface of *Dialogue Between Christians*, trans. Philip Loretz (Westminster, MD: Newman Press, 1966 [French orig. 1964]) 1-51.

[33]Yves Congar, *Vraie et fausse reforme dans l'eglise* (Paris: Cerf, 1950. Rev. ed. 1968) 341-85.

hood of all believers and the role of the laity.[34] He championed the superiority of dialogue, respect, and freedom over authoritarianism and dogmatism.[35] Above all, his ecumenical concerns led him to believe that continual internal reform was necessary to any genuine ecumenical progress.[36]

Congar argued against those who thought that tradition meant a lack of change. He thought they confused the tradition with its historical forms of expression. He distinguished between Tradition and the traditions, and demonstrated how a unity of faith has existed through many variations in its concrete renderings.[37] And he argued as well against those who thought all "reform" was bad. Inspired by Möhler, Congar explored the history of the Church with an eye to distinguishing between true and false reform.

Like Journet, Congar was interested in moving beyond the ecclesiology of the manuals to retrieve a sense of the mystery of the Church. In contrast to Journet, however, Congar explicitly included the need for structural reform of the reigning *status quo*. As Archbishop John Quinn put it:

Congar . . . has pointed out the inadequacy of a purely "moral" reform, by which I understand him to mean an attitudinal reform. He believes that any true and effective reform must touch structures. . . . Most of those [in the Middle Ages] who wanted reform, he said, were prisoners of the system, incapable of reforming the structures themselves through the recovery of the original vision, incapable of asking the new questions raised by a new situation. Reform meant to them simply putting the existing structures in order. The further, deeper, long-term questions were never asked.[38]

---

[34]Yves Congar, *Lay People in the Church*, trans. Donald Attwater (Westminster, MD: Newman, 1957 [French orig. 1953]).

[35]This point is found in Congar, *Chrétiens désunis*, 326-30, as well as in other places throughout Congar's work. See, for example, Yves Congar, *After Nine Hundred Years*, trans. faculty and staff at Fordham University (New York: Fordham University, 1959 [French orig. 1954]) 83-90. See also Congar, *Vrai et fausse reforme dans l'eglise*, 227-40.

[36]The need for real reform and renewal on all sides is another pervasive theme in Congar's work. See Congar, *Chrétiens désunis*, 333-41; also Congar, *Vraie et fausse reforme dans l'eglise*, 221-5.

[37]This is a main theme of Yves Congar, *Tradition and the Traditions*, trans. Michael Naseby and Thomas Rainborough (New York: Macmillan, 1966 [French orig. 1960, 1963]).

[38]John Archbishop Quinn, "The Exercise of the Primacy," *Commonweal* 123 (July 12, 1996) 13. See also Jean-Pierre Jossua, *Yves Congar: Theology in the Service of God's People* (Chicago: Priory Press, 1968 [French orig. 1967]) 92.

The issue of how the Church is related to the world is the main point of difference between the work of Congar and that of Journet. Where Journet granted a wholesale exemption to the Church itself in relation to the world with its sin and decay[39] (which makes sense if the Holy Spirit is the formal cause of the Church), Congar established more of a dialectic between the Church as "mystery" and the Church as "historical reality."[40] Congar held that the structures present in the preconciliar Church deserved respect, but that they needed to be understood in the light of their historical development. For example, the present understanding of the "magisterium" considered as the teaching office of the bishops taken together with the pope as their head dates only from the nineteenth century, and might not always remain in that form. Present structural arrangements were not to be taken as absolutes. Congar warned against the problem of "creeping infallibility," by which he meant the growing tendency to regard facilely more and more of the ordinary teaching of the Church as infallible. He argued as well against "hierarchology" which would reduce the study of the Church to the study of the hierarchy. He strongly promoted the structure and practice of collegiality that became central to the Council's approach. He also urged that members of the hierarchy carry out their charge with a sense of humility, service, and poverty.[41]

Like Journet, Congar emphasized the role of the Holy Spirit in the Church. Congar went beyond Journet, however, in exploring how the Holy Spirit has a role in the Church distinct from that of Christ. In other words, Journet taught of a Church that Christ had founded and that was sustained in love by the Holy Spirit. He did not emphasize a distinctive role for the Holy Spirit in shaping the Church in the present age. Congar emphasized that the Spirit, while always in harmony with the christological nature of the Church and never in contradiction to it, still had a distinct role to play.[42] For the Church has an eschatological nature; it isn't finished yet; it is as yet imperfect and on a journey toward its fulfillment. For Congar, the Holy Spirit is available not just for the defense of the *status quo*; the Spirit has a role to play in bringing about structural reform.

Congar, like Journet, used the language of Aristotelian causality to speak about the respective roles of the Holy Spirit and the hierarchy in

---

[39]Journet, *L'Eglise du Verbe incarné*, II, 904.

[40]On this dialectic between mystery and history in Congar, see Richard Beauchesne, "Heeding the Early Congar Today, and Two Recent Roman Catholic Issues: Seeking Hope on the Road Back," *Journal of Ecumenical Studies* 27 (1990) 535-60.

[41]See Yves Congar, *Power and Poverty in the Church*, trans. Jennifer Nicholson (Baltimore: Helicon, 1964 [French orig. 1953]).

[42]See Yves Congar, *The Mystery of the Church*, trans. A.V. Littledale (Baltimore: Helicon, 1969 [French orig., two separate books, 1956]) 160.

the Church.[43] Congar did not, however, follow Journet in removing the hierarchy from the formal cause of the Church. He lists the apostolic body (those who carry on the hierarchical apostolic function) and the Holy Spirit as both being efficient and formal causes of the Church. That is, both the apostolic body and the Holy Spirit play a role in bringing the Church to be;[44] when the Church is considered as established, however, both the apostolic body and the Holy Spirit function as formal causes. The apostolic body is the formal cause that both indwells and composes the Church, while the Holy Spirit is a quasi-formal cause that indwells but does not compose.

In this schema, the Holy Spirit, as quasi-formal cause, is a major factor that determines what the Church is, but the hierarchical structures are also an important dimension of the formal cause. In contrast with Journet, the engagement of the Church with history in the final analysis does touch upon its inner essence. For Congar, it was necessary that the Church own its presence and activity in the world as a major dimension of what it is. Those who would put the temporal structures of the Church beyond reform are engaging not in being open to mystery but in a process of mystification.

Journet gets beyond the manuals by making the Holy Spirit the Church's formal cause and by relegating the hierarchy to the category of immediate efficient cause; in contrast, Congar gets beyond the manuals by allowing both the Holy Spirit and the various structures to be viewed as formal causes of the Church, while distinguishing sharply between structures that are essential and structures that are historically conditioned. He did so in an atmosphere in which the distinction between the essential and the historically conditioned was often blurred, such that a wide range of temporally conditioned manifestations of the Church were mistakenly viewed as timeless and irreformable.

Like Journet, Congar portrays a Church that is not simply a juridical institution,[45] but much more deeply a communion, the Mystical Body of Christ, a fellowship animated by the Holy Spirit.[46] Unlike Journet, how-

---

[43]Congar, *The Mystery of the Church,* 180-81.

[44]Yves Congar, "My Path-Findings in the Theology of Laity and Ministries," *The Jurist* 32 (1972) 176.

[45]Congar insisted, though, that the nature of the Church as an institution must be acknowledged and appreciated. See Congar, *Dialogue Between Christians,* 75-7.

[46]The focus of this chapter has been the preconciliar work of Journet and Congar. Congar's communion ecclesiology, which is already fully present in his early works, can be seen in its postconciliar flowering in Yves Congar, *I Believe in the Holy Spirit,* 3 vols., trans. David Smith (New York: Seabury; London: Geoffrey Chapman, 1983 [French orig. 1979, 1980]) and in Yves Congar, *Diversity and Communion,* trans. John Bowden (Mystic, CT: Twenty-Third Publications, 1985 [French orig. 1982]).

ever, for Congar the Church's engagement with history is a defining characteristic, such that the particular questions encountered by Christians living in the world and the manner in which the Church responds help to shape the Church's very contours.

Yet Congar's insistence on the historical reality of the Church did not prevent him from exploring the deep links between ecclesiology and spirituality that a communion approach forges. In contrast with theologies that become mired in sometimes important but often sterile battles over institutional change, Congar found the core of what makes the Church what it is to be conformity to Christ. He performs his ecclesiology with a range and a reach that one would be hard pressed to find today. Ecclesiologists who can both emphasize the need for structural change and at the same time inspire with a deeply spiritual vision of the Church are a rare breed.

I draw extensively here upon an essay that Congar wrote in the 1950's on the Mystical Body to illustrate something of his range and reach. He writes:

> The Mystical Body is realized once our life belongs to Christ. Then it is that we lead, in this life, a life which is his, his life in us, his life in humanity; then it is that we are truly his members.[47]

His vision of the Mystical Body was not one of the high and the mighty:

> It is only too true that souls are divided according as they are open or closed; the former are ready to receive the life of Christ, the latter are unwilling to risk sacrificing theirs to him. That is why our Lord says that the harlots may well enter the kingdom of heaven before the ostensibly just. For if we are satisfied with ourselves, shut up and placid in our sufficiency, if we think ourselves very well as we are, just and wise in quite an adequate degree, we, in fact, have no need of anything and he who came only for those who were sick will have nothing to give us.[48]

To understand what the Church is as the Mystical Body is above all to understand what love is:

> God's own sovereign love, since it exists prior to the goodness of what it loves and actually creates it, is alone perfectly disinterested and alone merits the name of love. But, when we love with God's own love sent into our hearts by the Holy Spirit, we love from a motive above and beyond our selfish and personal inter-

---

[47]Congar, *The Mystery of the Church*, 118.
[48]Ibid., 121.

ests; we love with a love whose motive and source transcend even the distinction between *another* and *myself*. It is by charity alone that we are able, in absolute truth, to love others as ourselves, without thereby in the least infringing on our own good. This is because, where charity is concerned, there is no longer a neighbour who is really other than me and alien.[49]

This love is a love which is lived out in everyday life:

Those who are truly the friends of Our Lord are the most living members of his Mystical Body. For the same reason, the Mystical Body does not consist in exterior manifestations or ceremonies, however valuable or striking they may be. But it is when a small child, a humble lay-sister, a working mother whose life is taken up with ordinary daily chores, when people like this, unnoticed by the world, love God with all their heart and live a life of ardent charity, then the Mystical Body is realized and increased in stature. Such persons bring about the kingdom of God and grow in holiness to the profit of all, for it is only as Christ's members that we grow in him by charity, so that the whole body benefits from the advance of each.[50]

For Congar, the line between ecclesiology and spirituality dissolves in practice, for spirituality is the living out of what it means to be the Body of Christ in the context of the everyday:

This communion, brought into being by charity, which unites men in the very degree in which they are united to God, is, undoubtedly, what constitutes the Mystical Body of Christ. Charity makes Christ live in us and unites us, one to the other, all together, in God.[51]

There are many authors writing today, both Christian and non-Christian, whose works have deep spiritual insight. So many of these, however, are slanted toward an individualist and exclusive focus on personal life journeys. For Congar, personal spiritual growth and membership in the Body of Christ are deeply intertwined. What stands out here is that Congar's spiritual writing constitutes an ecclesiology, a particular approach to understanding the Church.

---

[49]Ibid., 127.
[50]Ibid., 127.
[51]Ibid., 128.

Different Paths to the Council

The above comparison between Journet and Congar brings out how distinct developments in ecclesiology were present prior to Vatican II. The common view that sees simply an old neo-Scholasticism being challenged and replaced by a new, more historically conscious approach tends to miss or discount the strain of reform represented by Journet's more metaphysical, mystical approach. It is true that a revolution took place at Vatican II which is aptly symbolized by the rejection of the texts of the preparatory commissions and the establishment of new commissions by Pope John XXIII.[52] It is also true, however, that that revolution included not only the historically dynamic vision associated with Congar, but also the emphasis on mystery and grace associated with Journet. Journet's reform was not of institutional structures per se, but of conceptualization concerning the essential nature of the Church. His theology was designed to overcome juridical notions of the Church and thus to awaken Catholics to a deeper sense of what it means to be the Mystical Body of Christ.

This last goal was also of critical importance to Congar. He pursued it, however, in a way that was more historically minded and more attentive to the need for change on the institutional level. Interpreters of Vatican II and of the current range of discussion concerning communion ecclesiology would do well to be mindful of both of these attempts to move beyond neo-Scholasticism in the preconciliar era.

Journet's Continuing Presence

That Congar's influence continues today is without question. That Journet's influence should continue is more in need of explanation. Can an approach to ecclesiology that does not place great emphasis on historical contingency and change still wield influence in theology today? In fact, it does. Journet emphasizes the ideal, essential nature of the Church. His version of communion ecclesiology is still influential in certain Catholic circles. It has much in common with the later work of Möhler and with the aesthetic approach associated with Hans Urs von Balthasar. I do not think that this line of thought can simply be subsumed as representing one side of what already exists in a many-sided way elsewhere. There are a great number of people who would identify themselves as supporting communion ecclesiology and who operate within this line of thought, perhaps as many or more as those who

---

[52]See Komonchak, "The Struggle for the Council during the Preparation of Vatican II (1960-1962)," in Alberigo and Komonchak, eds., *History of Vatican II*, 167-356.

would identify themselves with Congar's line of thought.

To the extent that Journet himself downplayed ways of talking about the Church that allowed for structural change, I find his position highly problematic. But to the extent that he affirmed a way in which the Church can be conceived of as the spotless Bride of the spotless Lamb, I think he makes a contribution to communion ecclesiology that needs to be preserved. Going into the Council, Journet's version of communion ecclesiology, with its connections to *Mystici corporis*, was probably more acceptable to "progressive" bishops than Congar's version. To replace the overly juridical concept of the Church with the mystical Body of Christ was anticipated more than to affirm a vision of a Church that held in tension the Body of Christ with the more historically dynamic People of God.[53]

The influence of Journet's style of theologizing at the Council is most clearly visible by the ambiguous way in which the passage in *Lumen Gentium* 8 on sin and the Church is phrased. In the decade leading up to the Council, Journet was the foremost promoter of the position that the Church, considered theologically with the Holy Spirit as its formal cause, is without sin. In fact, in the discussion of the debate among Catholics concerning sin and the Church in Herbert Vorgrimler's multi-volume commentary, volume two of *L'Eglise du Verbe incarné* is the work cited as representative of the "sinless" side of the debate.[54]

Congar took issue with Journet on the sinlessness of the Church in his 1952 review of volume two of *L'Eglise du Verbe incarné*, which began a series of exchanges between the two authors throughout the fifties.[55] The ambiguous passage in *Lumen Gentium* can be taken as supportive of either Journet or Congar:

While Christ "holy, blameless, unstained" (Heb 7, 26) knew no sin (see 2 Cor 5, 21), and came only to expiate the sins of the people (see Heb 2, 17), the church, containing sinners in its own bosom, is at one and the same time holy and always in need of purification and it pursues unceasingly penance and renewal.[56]

This passage can be read as supporting the position of Congar insofar

---

[53]Raymond Brown, *The Churches the Apostles Left Behind* (New York: Paulist Press, 1984) 60 and 73-4.

[54]Joseph Feiner, "Decree on Ecumenism," in *Commentary on the Documents of Vatican II*, ed. Herbert Vorgrimmler, trans. William Glen-Doepel, et al. (New York: Herder and Herder, 1968 [German orig. 1967]) 2.100.

[55]Congar's side of the discussion is collected in Yves Congar, *Sainte église: études et approches ecclésiologique* (Paris: Cerf, 1964).

[56]Quoted from Norman P. Tanner, *Decrees of the Ecumenical Councils*, 2 vols. (Washington, DC: Georgetown University Press, 1990) v. 2, 855.

as it states directly that the Church is in need of purification.[57]

Yet the passage can also be read as supporting Journet's position. Cardinal Joseph Ratzinger, for example, reads the passage in this way, stressing that it is only the Church considered insofar as it embraces sinners in its bosom that travels the path of penance and renewal, not the Church considered in its inner essence. He explains by looking back to the Latin formula in the Roman liturgy preceding communion: "*Domine Jesu Christe . . . Ne respicias peccata mea, sed fidem Ecclesiae tuae.*" Ratzinger comments:

> *Everybody* in the Church, with no exception, had to confess himself to be a sinner, beseech forgiveness and then set out on the path of his real reform. But this in no way means that the Church as such was also a sinner. The Church—as we have seen—is a reality that surpasses, mysteriously and infinitely, the sum of her members.[58]

Although Ratzinger acknowledges that the Church can be reformed in its human structures, his overall vision of the Church hearkens back to Journet:

> For a Catholic . . . the Church is indeed composed of men who organize her external visage. But behind this, the fundamental structures are willed by God himself, and therefore they are inviolable. Behind the *human* exterior stands the mystery of a *more than human* reality, in which reformers, sociologists, organizers have no authority whatsoever.[59]

Like Journet, Ratzinger stresses the divine element in the Church: "We need, not a more human, but a more divine Church; then she also will become truly human.[60]

Ratzinger's position on the sinlessness of the Church, which could appear to those who hold a different position to promote juridicism and mystification insofar as it identifies a large dimension of the Church as sacrosanct and beyond human criticism, has roots in Journet's attempt to move beyond juridicism to an emphasis on the Church of charity. No

---

[57]Beauchesne describes Congar's position on the sinfulness of the Church in "Heeding the Early Congar Today," 544-8.

[58]Joseph Cardinal Ratzinger, *The Ratzinger Report*, with Vittorio Messori, trans. Salvator Attanasio and Graham Harrison (San Francisco: Ignatius Press, 1985) 52; the full discussion is 45-53.

[59]Ibid., 46.

[60]Joseph Cardinal Ratzinger, *Called to Communion: Understanding the Church Today*, trans. Adrian Walker (San Francisco: Ignatius Press, 1996 [German orig. 1991]) 146.

matter where one finally stands on this issue, this underlying intention needs to be appreciated. It is all too easy to cast those who defend the sinlessness of the Church as narrow institutionalists without acknowledging the many important distinctions made by someone like Journet, especially his concern to avoid any facile identification of the Church, whose formal cause is the Holy Spirit, with the hierarchy, its immediate efficient cause.

Conclusion

When measured against neo-Scholasticism, Journet and Congar worked arm-in-arm to bring about the vision of the Church expressed at Vatican II. They both moved beyond the manuals to a view of the Church as a communion. They often quoted each other favorably in their works, though Congar did explicitly disagree with Journet's idealization on the question of the Church's sinfulness and on the place of the laity.[61] Most importantly, though, for both Journet and Congar, ecclesiology functioned as the key to developing a distinctively Catholic spirituality, rooted in ecclesiology, that would find its expression at Vatican II.

When viewed in terms of their differences, however, Journet and Congar represent two competing visions of reform going into the Council, as well as two competing schools of thought regarding the Council's present interpretation. The split is by no means absolute. Ratzinger can quote favorably from Congar without a problem, though he probably draws the line differently concerning what is human and reformable in the Church and what is divinely ordained.

The differences in the approaches of Journet and Congar reflect many of the differences between the early Möhler and the later Möhler. A historical-pneumatological approach stands in tension with an aesthetic-christological approach. In today's ongoing search to appreciate communion ecclesiology, the theological community can surely profit from the significantly distinctive lines of thought of both Journet and Congar.

---

[61] On Journet as "profound" but "medieval," see Yves Congar, *L'Eglise de Saint Augustin à l'epogue moderne* (Paris: Cerf, 1970) 464; for Journet's understanding of the laity, see *Fifty Years of Catholic Theology: Conversations with Yves Congar*, Bernard Lauret, ed. (Philadelphia: Fortress Press, 1988) 52.

FOUR

Communion, Paradox, and Multi-Dimensionality

Henri de Lubac

Although there are many Catholic theologians of the early to mid-twentieth century whose work had significant influence on the development of the communion ecclesiology that came to fruition at the Second Vatican Council, there is only one figure whose contribution is comparable to that of Yves Congar, that is the French Jesuit Henri de Lubac (1896-1991). De Lubac's ecclesial vision manifested a multi-dimensionality that is unmatched in the twentieth century. Charles Journet offered an ecclesial vision of a pure, undefiled Church open to aesthetic appreciation; Yves Congar offered a vision of the Church that focused on the presence of the ecclesial mystery in the dialectics of history. De Lubac, I argue, more than any other theologian, offered a synthesis or, perhaps better, a many-layeredness. Journet acknowledged the importance of history, but he did not let it touch the Church's essence. Congar, while himself balanced, argued his case within a context that could make him appear to stress the historical dimensions of the mystery a bit more than the unchanging dimensions. De Lubac stressed simultaneously the essential mystery of the Church and the concrete working out of this mystery in the arena of history, and he did so with a deep sense of the Church as a social body.

In a century rife with liberal-conservative theological divisions, de Lubac stands forth as one whose works span the various divides. As Avery Dulles put it:

> Terms such as "liberal" and "conservative" are ill suited to describe theologians such as de Lubac. If such terminology must be used, one would have to say that he embraced both alternatives. He was liberal because he opposed any narrowing of the Catholic tradition,

even at the hands of the disciples of St. Thomas. He sought to reha-
bilitate marginal thinkers. . . . He reached out to the atheist
Proudhon and sought to build bridges to Amida Buddhism. . . . But
in all of these ventures he remained staunchly committed to the
Catholic tradition in its purity and plenitude.[1]

Margaret O'Brien Steinfels attests to de Lubac's contribution:

De Lubac . . . saw his sense of the church come to fruition in the
work of Vatican II. Perhaps more than anyone, he gave a secure
foundation to this idea of communion ecclesiology, one which we
are still trying to achieve.[2]

The purpose of this chapter is to explore how de Lubac's contribution to communion ecclesiology embraces a broad range of concerns
that are unfortunately often pitted against each other in contemporary
discussion. The main tools that enabled him to do this were his sense of
paradox, his vision of catholicity as radical inclusivity, and his ability to
place emphasis simultaneously on various forms of communion and
relationality. De Lubac's multi-dimensionality allows his work to serve
as a resource for building bridges between theological approaches that
might otherwise appear to be incompatible.

Paradox and Mystery

De Lubac was a master of paradox. He envisioned the Church as
both a paradox and a mystery. Of the latter dimension, he said:

The Church is a mystery for all time out of man's grasp because,
qualitatively, it is totally removed from all other objects of man's
knowledge that might be mentioned. And yet, at the same time, it
concerns us, touches us, acts in us, reveals us to ourselves.[3]

De Lubac held, moreover, that the nature of the Church as a mystery is
deeper and more grounding than the nature of the Church as a paradox. But his ability to emphasize simultaneously the mysterious and
paradoxical nature of the Church was one of the skills that gave de

---

[1]Avery Dulles, "Henri de Lubac: In Appreciation," *America* 165 (28 September 1991) 180-2.

[2]Margaret O'Brien Steinfels, "Dissent and Communion," *Commonweal* 121
(18 November 1994) 15.

[3]Henri de Lubac, *The Church: Paradox and Mystery*, trans. James R. Dunne
(New York: Alba House, 1969 [French orig. 1967]) 14.

Lubac his extraordinary range and reach as a theologian.

A mystery, in the theological sense, is something that reveals God to us. The word can often be used interchangeably with "sacrament."[4] We can participate in a mystery, but its ultimate depths go far beyond us. We can experience a mystery intimately, but its final comprehension transcends our powers of understanding. A paradox is something which, while it may incline one toward mystery, is itself more mundane. A paradox results from the co-existence in relational tension of two or more things which appear on the surface to be contradictory or opposite. De Lubac describes paradoxes as

> the simultaneity of the one and the other. . . . They do not sin against logic, whose laws remain inviolable; but they escape its domain. They are the *for* fed by the *against*, the *against* going so far as to identify itself with the *for*; each one of them moving into the other without letting itself be abolished by it and continuing to oppose the other, but so as to give it vigor.[5]

I interpret de Lubac here as meaning that paradoxes do not violate Aristotle's law of non-contradiction, but they operate on such a level of complexity and depth as to transcend any narrow or one-sided application of it.

De Lubac reminded us the gospels are full of paradox, and spiritual truth is in itself of a paradoxical nature. Revelation often presents two assertions which at first seem contradictory, such as the freedom of humans yet their absolute dependency on grace, or such as redemption as a work of pure mercy yet as related to justice.[6] So also is the relationship between unity and diversity a paradox, as well as that between person and society. Another paradox is the relationship between the natural and the supernatural, which, unfortunately, in Scholasticism came to be understood as two separate realms, the one extrinsic to the other. As de Lubac put it, "the work that is called for at the present day . . . demands a comprehensive combination of opposing qualities, each of them brought to a high degree of excellence, one buttressed, so to say, on one another, and braced with the greatest tension" (*Catholicism* 173).

De Lubac found the Church to be full of paradox. As a Patristics

---

[4]Henri de Lubac, *The Splendour of the Church*, trans. Michael Mason (New York: Sheed and Ward, 1956 [French orig. 1953]) 147. Hereafter in text as *Splendour*.

[5]Henri de Lubac, *Paradoxes of Faith*, trans. Paule Simon, Sadie Kreilkamp, and Ernest Beaumont (San Francisco: Ignatius Press, 1987 [French originals 1948, 1955, 1958]) 12.

[6]Henri de Lubac, *Catholicism*, trans. Lancelot C. Sheppard (London: Burns and Oates, 1950 [French orig. 1938]) 177-8. Hereafter in text as *Catholicism*.

scholar and theologian *par excellence* of *ressourcement*, he drew upon the Church Fathers to label the Church a *complexio oppositorum*: a complex of opposites held in tension. The de Lubac who envisioned the Church as the Bride of Christ could also, along with the patristic authors, see the Church as a harlot (*Catholicism* 26). The Church is both a spring and an autumn, an achievement and a hope (*Catholicism* 136). It is the wretched woman saved from prostitution and the bride of the Lamb. De Lubac wrote:

> I am told that she is holy, yet I see her full of sinners. . . . Yes, a paradox is this Church of ours! I have played no cheap rhetorical trick. A paradox of a Church for paradoxical mankind and one that on occasion adapts only too much to the exigencies of the latter! She espouses its characteristics with all the attendant complexities and illogicalities—with the endless contradictions that are in man. We see this in every age, and the critics and the pamphleteers—a proliferating breed, alas—have a joyous time of it, rubbing it all in. Since the early days, indeed while she was taking the first halting steps outside the confines of Jerusalem, the Church was reflecting the traits—the miseries—of mankind.[7]

It is this sense of paradox, along with a sense of mystery, that gave de Lubac the power to articulate a vision of the Church that could travel on several levels at the same time, levels that often seemed in tension with each other.

Catholicity as Radical Inclusivity

Working along with this deep sense of paradox was de Lubac's definition of "catholicity" in terms of a generous and open embrace of all that is good and worthy and true. This inclusive vision informed the whole of de Lubac's life work. De Lubac's programmatic *Catholicism* of 1938 laid out the ecclesial context within which his more philosophical reflections would take place. His most well-known book, *Surnaturel* (1946), focused mainly on metaphysical issues in the history of theology. It is a key text for articulating the shift from neo-Scholasticism to a more historically conscious methodology.[8] The germ of *Surnaturel*, however, is found already in a few passages near the end of *Catholicism* (166-7). This connection is important insofar as communion ecclesiology is not on a first level some abstract metaphysical discovery, the

---

[7]De Lubac, *The Church: Paradox and Mystery*, 2.

[8]Henri de Lubac, *Surnaturel* (Paris: Aubier, 1946; new edition Paris: Desclee de Brouwer, 1985).

implications of which then need to be worked out on a practical, ecclesial plane. On the contrary, communion ecclesiology has its beginnings in trying to understand concretely and practically the Church in both its historical and spiritual dimensions in the face of the challenges of the modern world. Metaphysical reflection on nature and grace and on the relationship between the natural and the supernatural has been essential to this project, but as supporting cast rather than in the leading role.

Joseph Komonchak has demonstrated integral connections among de Lubac's early works within their social context.[9] Komonchak finds the unifying thread in de Lubac's early works to be the freeing of Catholic theology from its narrow confines so that it could engage the problems posed by the modern world. On the one hand, Europe of the 1930's and early 1940's was faced with the rise of repressive totalitarian regimes. On the other hand, much of the then current Catholic theology promoted an extrinsicist view of the supernatural that supported a Catholic sub-culture existing in relative detachment from the outside world.[10] De Lubac's inclusive vision of catholicity as well as his rejection of extrinsicist views of the supernatural were both directed toward bringing the depths of the Catholic tradition into a critical encounter with the pressing issues of the time. He was fighting not only the atheism, neo-paganism, and authoritarianism rampant in Europe, but also the forms of Catholic theology that refused to engage in the fight against these ideologies. De Lubac's risky involvement in the "intellectual resistance" during the war was a concrete expression of the major themes of his theological works.[11]

De Lubac's main principle of engagement with the world lay in his connection between truth and inclusion. According to de Lubac, the Catholic spirit calls for the broadest universality coupled with the strictest unity. As Hans Urs von Balthasar pointed out, in *Catholicism* "it is precisely the power of inclusion that becomes the chief criterion of truth."[12] The true Catholic spirit is the opposite of a sec-

---

[9]Joseph A. Komonchak, "Theology and Culture at Mid-Century: The Example of Henri de Lubac," *Theological Studies* 51 (1990) 579-602. See also Henri de Lubac, *Christian Resistance to Anti-Semitism: Memories from 1940-1944*, trans. Sister Elizabeth Englund, O.C.D. (San Francisco: Ignatius Press, 1990 [French orig. 1988]).

[10]Joseph A. Komonchak, "The Enlightenment and the Construction of Roman Catholicism," *Annual of the Catholic Commission on Intellectual and Cultural Affairs* (1985) 31-59; also Komonchak's "The Cultural and Ecclesial Roles of Theology," *Proceedings of the Catholic Theological Society of America* 40 (1985) 15-32.

[11]Komonchak, "Theology and Culture at Mid-Century," 595-602.

[12]Hans Urs von Balthasar, *The Theology of Henri de Lubac: An Overview*,

tarianism that declares itself right, to the immediate exclusion of all contrary opinions in a knee-jerk manner. The Catholic spirit embraces the mystery that is at times expressed in paradox and refuses to reduce it to anything manageably one-sided and partial. The Church has a "flexible and vigorous structural unity" rather than a "drab uniformity" (*Catholicism* 152).

De Lubac's position on truth and error reflected the influence of Johann Adam Möhler.[13] Heresy is not simply any type of error, but one that arises from one-sidedness and selectivity. Catholic teaching calls for Christians to hold simultaneously the seemingly contrary assertions that Jesus is fully human and that Jesus is fully divine. Those who deny either the humanity or the divinity of Christ usually do so out of a desire to emphasize the contrary quality. They are heretics not for what they affirm but for what they deny. Heresy arises most often from selectively maintaining something that is true to the exclusion of other things that are, however tensively, true at the same time.

Catholicity, then, is a unity that embraces a broad but legitimate diversity. But for de Lubac, catholicity was not to be understood only as spiritual and intellectual, but also as social and historical.[14] De Lubac held the tendency to jettison everything non-Christian in the name of the Gospel as alien to the Catholic spirit as well as unfair. He pointed out that the Fathers spoke of many elements of various human cultures as "preparations for the Gospel" and that Christianity transformed the world by absorbing it (*Catholicism* 144-51). Catholicity is not, however, tolerant of errors that violate its basic principles. De Lubac said of Catholicism, "like its Founder, it is eternal and sure of itself, and the very intransigence in matters of principle which prevents its ever being ensnared by transitory things secures for it a flexibility of infinite comprehensiveness, the very opposite of the harsh exclusivism which characterizes the sectarian spirit" (*Catholicism* 153).

De Lubac's firm stances toward positions that he judged to be errors can be seen in his approaches to atheism and to Buddhism. In *The Drama of Atheistic Humanism*, a masterpiece, de Lubac analyzed the challenges posed by various forms of atheism. He made a fascinating comparison at one point between his own movement of *ressourcement* and Nietzsche's rejection of dry rationalism. Yet he ended with a stunning characterization of Dostoyevsky as one who had already anticipated the difficulties

---

trans. Joseph Fessio, S.J., and Michael M. Waldstein (San Francisco: Ignatius Press, 1983 [German orig. 1976]) 28.

[13]Johann Adam Möhler, *Unity in the Church, or the Principle of Catholicism: Presented in the Spirit of the Church Fathers of the First Three Centuries*, ed. and trans. Peter C. Erb (Washington, DC: Catholic University of America Press, 1996 [German orig. 1825]) 194-8.

[14]Komonchak, "Theology and Culture at Mid-Century," 594.

posed by Nietzsche and who had overcome them with full integrity. De Lubac explored, understood, and even empathized with atheists, but he left no doubt as to the ultimate limitations of their horizons.[15]

In a way that I find somewhat jarring to my contemporary sensibilities concerning inter-religious dialogue, de Lubac treated Buddhism in a manner similar to atheism. For example, in *Aspects of Buddhism*, he gives knowledgeable and penetrating and appreciative accounts of various forms and practices of Buddhism. But in his final analysis, Buddhism is only worthy to the extent that it contains presentiments of Christianity; its lack of foundation in God and in charity make it insufficient and false in and of itself.[16] My point here is not to judge one way or the other whether de Lubac's 1950's critique of Buddhism has continuing merit, but only to illustrate that de Lubac's exigency to embrace truth wherever it can be found co-existed with a deep embrace of Christian revelation as uncontradictable. For de Lubac, catholicity did not mean "anything goes." The Church has a twofold desire to "entertain whatever can be assimilated and to prescribe nothing that is not of faith" (*Catholicism* 148).

Catholicity is more than just statistical or geographical unity. The deepest meaning of catholicity for de Lubac is anthropological. The Church is catholic because it knows what lies in the heart of every human person. If the human being can be compared to a musical instrument, the Church is like a master performer with a masterpiece to play:

> The Church can play on this organ because, like Christ, she "knows what is in man," because there is an intimate relationship between the dogma to which she adheres and human nature, infinitely mysterious in its turn. Now by the very fact that she goes to the very foundation of man the Church attains to all men and can "play her chords" upon them (*Catholicism* 18).

Catholicity, then, for de Lubac, is not only an encompassing of various dimensions of truth held in tension, and not only a socially conscious embrace of all that is good and worthy, but also a radical inclusion of all human beings in all of their depth and mystery.

I find in this anthropological meaning of catholicity a potential bridge between, on the one hand, contemporary theological approaches that stress how Christian revelation expresses most fully what is already in

---

[15]*The Drama of Atheistic Humanism*, trans. Edith M. Riley (New York: Sheed and Ward, 1950 [French orig. 1944]). A good analysis of de Lubac's engagement with atheism can be found in Francesco Bertoldi, "The Religious Sense in Henri de Lubac," *Communio* 16 (Spring 1989) 6-31.

[16]Henri de Lubac, *Aspects of Buddhism*, trans. George Lamb (New York: Sheed and Ward, 1954 [French orig. 1951]) 51-2.

some sense true about human reality and, on the other hand, those that stress how Christian revelation is unique and new in a way that shatters all human expectations. I will develop this point further in the chapter on Rahner and Balthasar. De Lubac develops a "both/and" position on this most paradoxical of issues. There is an intimate relationship between the mystery of Christian revelation and the mystery of human nature; at the same time, however, the Church has its unique chords it can play upon the human instrument. De Lubac's anthropological approach to catholicity constitutes a dynamic holding-in-tension of these often contrasted alternatives that underlie much conflict in contemporary theology.

Multi-Layered Relationships

In chapter one, I identified five basic forms of relationship to which theologians of communion tend to refer: divine, mystical, sacramental, historical, and social. Some contemporary forms of communion ecclesiology can be identified as "conservative" or "progressive" according to their relative emphasis on these various forms. More than any other theologian whom I have studied, de Lubac displayed the ability to emphasize simultaneously all of these forms of relationship. I believe that it was his grasp of the paradoxical nature of religious truth that allowed him to escape the snares of one-sidedness to achieve such a broadly inclusive vision. He was able to take things that others would see only in terms of opposition or of subordination and orchestrate them as a harmonious symphony.

Divine

De Lubac emphasized that the Church is above all an invitation to share in the divine life of the Trinity:

> God did not make us "to remain within the limits of nature," or for the fulfilling of a solitary destiny; on the contrary, He made us to be brought together into the heart of the life of the Trinity. Christ offered himself in sacrifice so that we might be one in the unity of the divine Persons. . . . But there is a place where this gathering-together of all things in the Trinity begins in this world; "a family of God," a mysterious extension of the Trinity in time. . . . "The people united by the unity of the Father and the Son and the Holy Ghost"; that is the Church. She is "full of the Trinity."[17]

---

[17]*Splendour*, 174-5. See also Susan K. Wood's discussion of de Lubac's connection between Church and Trinity in *Spiritual Exegesis and the Church in the Theology of Henri de Lubac* (Grand Rapids, MI: Eerdman's /Edinburgh: T&T Clark, 1998) 132-4, where she cites several passages from *Catholicism*.

For de Lubac, this divine form of relationality permeates the core of what the Church is. It is the *sine qua non* of ecclesial reality. It is the deepest link between the Church and salvation and eternal life. This theme ran throughout his work.[18]

Mystical

De Lubac also grasped well the mystical form of relationality in which images and symbols are used to express glimpses of the Church as mystery. He taught that the Bible is not complete in the literal sense, and that Christians should cultivate along with the Church Fathers a sense of the mystical symbolism of what is revealed (*Catholicism* 83-6). It is quite appropriate, for example, to read the Bride in the Song of Songs as symbolically prefiguring the Church and also as representing the spiritual journey of the individual (*Catholicism* 102-3). A typological reading of scripture is helpful in comprehending it as a book about the relationship between God and human beings and the salvation of human beings in the course of history. The Church is truly the Mystical Body of Christ in that it represents the spiritual and social reunification of the unity of humankind. The Church is truly the Bride of Christ because it is so closely united with him. The Church is our mother because it brings Christians to birth within the Body of Christ (*Catholicism* 19). And the mystery of the Church is bound up inextricably with the mystery of Mary's role in salvation (*Splendour* 240).

De Lubac's use of images drawn from scripture and tradition to express the reality of the Church stands in stark contrast with the ecclesiological approach taken by Hans Küng. In his *Christianity: Essence, History, Future*, Küng excoriates Möhler, Newman, De Lubac, and Balthasar for their Romantic portrayals of the Church. He speaks of their "idealizations, mystifications, and glorifications which, while not uncritical, have virtually no consequences for the Roman system."[19] Küng tells a story of how following a talk he had given in St. Peter's at the time of Vatican II, de Lubac commented, "One doesn't talk like that about the Church. *Elle est quand-meme notre mere*: after all, she's our mother!"[20] He then goes on to speak facetiously of the many clergy who suffer from a "mother-complex." Küng objects to any positing of an ideal essence of the Church that is disconnected from its actual historical manifestations, including its many dark abominations. One of the

---

[18]Gianfranco Coffele points out that a trinitarian anthropology was fundamental for de Lubac as early as his 1929 inaugural lecture; see "De Lubac and the Theological Foundations of the Missions," *Communio* 23 (Winter 1996) 757-75.

[19]Hans Küng, *Christianity: Essence, History, Future*, trans. by John Bowden (New York: Continuum, 1995 [German orig. 1994]) 4.

[20]Ibid.

major strengths of de Lubac, however, is precisely that he is able to operate on the level of ideal, mystical speech about the Church while at the same time acknowledging fully the level of dark abominations. As Susan K. Wood demonstrates, de Lubac is able to avoid the danger, often associated with a Body of Christ ecclesiology, of an uncritical christomonism that can fail to account for human limitation and failure in the Church. He does this by using a range of images, some of which, like the Bride of Christ, highlight the distinction between Christ and the Church.[21] And for de Lubac, the Church is not only a bride; it is also a harlot.

Both Küng and de Lubac are highly aware of how idealized speech about the Church has been used to mystify and to cover-up by clothing all too human decisions and failings in the guise of sacral legitimations. Küng, however, takes this insight to such an extreme that he cuts off all access to this traditional and fruitful avenue toward realizing the depth of what the Church truly is as a dimension of that which has been revealed to Christians by God. I do not wish to take away from Hans Küng's profoundly positive contributions to ecclesiology. On this point, however, as on some others, I think he is wrong. The heritage of de Lubac offers a much-needed corrective in this regard.

Sacramental

A highly developed understanding of the Church as a sacrament is also present already in *Catholicism*: "If Christ is the sacrament of God, the Church is for us the sacrament of Christ; she represents him, in the full and ancient meaning of the term, she really makes him present" (*Catholicism* 29).[22] De Lubac places a great stress upon the simultaneity of the visible and invisible elements of the Church, and the importance of not separating them. For de Lubac, the sacramental form of relationality is the one that ties together the Church as the Mystical Body of Christ with the Church as the historical People of God. It forms "the sensible bond between two worlds" (*Splendour* 147). When in its opening paragraph, *Lumen Gentium* refers to the Church as a sacrament, the voice of de Lubac in *Catholicism* can be heard: "If Christ is the sacrament of God, the Church is for us the sacrament of Christ; she represents him, in the full and ancient meaning of the term, she really makes him present." When *Lumen Gentium* 8 states that the visible Church and the invisible Church coalesce to form one mysterious real-

---

[21]Wood, *Spiritual Exegesis and the Church*, 88-95; Wood also points out that, though it remained largely undeveloped, there exist grounds in de Lubac's work from which the pneumatological dimensions of the Church could be cultivated. See 149-51.

[22]See Wood's discussion of de Lubac on the sacramentality of the Church in *Spiritual Exegesis and the Church*, 109-28.

ity, the reader feels as though a passage from *Catholicism* is being read aloud in the background.

That the Church carries forth the presence of Christ who brings forth the presence of God makes it a mystery and a sacrament. That this visible and flawed Church is at the same time the spotless bride of the spotless lamb makes it a paradox. In de Lubac's view, this Church is Christ present to us (*Splendour* 153-4). This remains true whether one is thinking of the hierarchy or of the eucharistic assembly.

A grounding element of de Lubac's sacramental focus is the link that he makes between the Eucharist and the Church.[23] That the Eucharist is the sacrament of unity, he emphasizes, was at the forefront of the thought of the Church Fathers. For the first thousand years of the Church, the real effect of the Eucharist was held to be Church unity. The Church was experienced most fundamentally as the Mystical Body of Christ. The analogical connections between the elements of bread and wine and the Church as Christ's body were clear and strong (*Catholicism* 35-50; *Splendour* 147-73).

De Lubac also drew important connections between the Eucharist and the episcopacy/priesthood. He lamented the narrow vision of the Church as a constricting hierarchy:

> Instead of signifying, in addition to a watchful orthodoxy, the expansion of Christianity and the fullness of the Christian spirit, [the name of Catholic] came to represent, for some, a sort of preserve, a system of limitations; the profession of Catholicism became linked with a distrustful and factious sectarian spirit. (*Catholicism* 168)

In contrast, de Lubac presents a vision of a Church whose hierarchy has its most basic *raison d'être* in the offering of the Eucharist as the sign of Church unity:

> Though only one cell of the whole body is actually present, the whole body is there virtually. The Church is in many places, yet there are not several Churches; the Church is entire in each one of its parts. . . . Each bishop constitutes the unity of his flock. . . . But each bishop is himself "in peace and in communion" with all his brother bishops who offer the same and unique sacrifice in other places, and make mention of him in their prayers as he makes mention of all of them in his. He and they together form one episcopate only, and are

---

[23]See Paul McPartlan, *The Eucharist Makes the Church: Henri de Lubac and John Zizioulas in Dialogue* (Edinburgh: T&T Clark, 1993). De Lubac's major work on the subject is *Corpus Mysticum: L'Eucharistie et l'église au moyen âge: Etude historique* (Paris: Aubier, 1944).

all alike "at peace and in communion" with the Bishop of Rome, who is Peter's successor and the visible bond of unity; and through them, all the faithful are united. (*Splendour* 105)

For de Lubac, therefore, the sacramentality of the Church links not only the visible and the invisible, but also the local and the universal. The Church, entire in each of its parts, exists as what Tillard calls a "Church of churches, . . . the *communion of communions*, appearing as a communion of local churches."[24]

Historical

As early as *Catholicism*, de Lubac emphasized that the Church that is the Mystical Body of Christ is also at the same time the People of God. He pointed out that for the Church Fathers, a historical, horizontal vision of Christianity is both the condition of and the result of the vertical vision.

De Lubac explored the historical dimension of the Church in at least three ways. First, he emphasized the connections between Christianity and Judaism. What is new and unique in Christianity, he held, represents a transfiguration rather than a creation from nothing. Christ is the fulfillment of the promise made to the seed of Abraham. De Lubac wrote: "Judaism passed on to Christianity its concept of salvation as essentially social. If, having regard to the greater number of the faithful, the Church derives more particularly from the Gentiles—*Ecclesia ex gentibus*—the idea of the Church, none the less, comes from the Jews" (*Catholicism* 23). The Church has a concrete, embodied history that finds its roots in Judaism and continues with the Church as a people of God on a journey. *Lumen Gentium's* use of the image of the People of God to capture the historical dimension of the Church on its journey through history shows the mark of de Lubac.[25]

Second, de Lubac acknowledged clearly that the Church in history has not always lived up to its promises. As noted above, de Lubac referred to the paradox that the Church which is the bride of the lamb is also the harlot in need of redemption. He attests that, on the individual level, among Church members and including the leaders, there are evident human weaknesses; that there exist *milieux* in the Church that

[24]J.-M. R. Tillard, *Church of Churches: An Ecclesiology of Communion*, trans. R.C. Peaux (Collegeville, MN: Liturgical Press, 1992 [French orig. 1987]) 29.

[25]A good source concerning de Lubac's influence on *Lumen Gentium* and other Vatican II documents is Karl Heinz Neufeld, S.J., "In the Service of the Council: Bishops and Theologians at the Second Vatican Council (for Cardinal Henri de Lubac on His Ninetieth Birthday), trans. R. Sway, in *Vatican II: Assessment and Perspectives, Twenty-Five Years After*, 3 vols., ed. René Latourelle, vol. 1, 74-105 (New York: Paulist Press, 1988-89).

foster evil (*Splendour* 58-9); and that the Church has at times reacted narrowly in ways that have betrayed its own catholicity (*Catholicism* 168). John Paul II's willingness to acknowledge the Church's failings as part of the celebration of the new millennium is in line with de Lubac's heritage.

Third, de Lubac stressed that salvation is something that must be worked out in a real way in history: "For if the salvation offered by God is in fact the salvation of the human race, since this human race lives and develops in time, any account of this salvation will naturally take a historical form—it will be the history of the penetration of humanity by Christ" (*Catholicism* 69). De Lubac's insight here goes far beyond the common point that Church doctrine develops historically. He maintained that human history in its varied and concrete forms provides the arena in which the drama of Christian salvation unfolds.

Social

De Lubac saw the Church's historical dimensions as being inextricably linked with the social (*Catholicism* 69). He opened *Catholicism* with an attack on individualistic notions of Christianity. The Church needs to be understood as a society of believers. This is not to say that the individual was unimportant for de Lubac. For him, a distinctive element in Christianity is precisely its ability to assert simultaneously the transcendent destiny of individuals and the transcendent destiny of humankind.

The sacraments have a social dimension because as means of salvation they are instruments of unity. The Eucharist above all is a sacrament of unity. De Lubac demonstrated that the individualistic forms of piety often associated with the Eucharist in the modern age had no precedent in the early Church (*Catholicism* 35-50).

Yet the unity signified by the Eucharist does not stop with internal Church community. Those gathered are sent out with a mission of charity to the larger world. What, for de Lubac, was the relationship between explicitly Catholic or Christian unity and the transcendent destiny of the human race?

De Lubac approached this matter most directly through his reflections on the question of salvation outside the Church. On the one hand, he clearly held the belief that Christianity expresses God's ultimate revelation in a way that surpasses other religions or spiritual paths. On the other hand, within that framework, he emphasized the paradoxical nature of the multi-farious interrelationship between Christian unity and human unity. He eschewed facile resolutions to this tension. He stressed that the possibility of salvation outside the explicit Church is part of the Catholic tradition, and that this doctrine complements rather than contradicts the doctrine of the necessity of the Church (*Catholicism* 107-13).

There is more than a mere echo of de Lubac's position on this issue present in the text of *Gaudium et Spes*. De Lubac was on the subcommission that produced the first chapter of *Gaudium et Spes*.[26] The famous opening line of that document can be found in seminal form in *Catholicism*. *Gaudium et Spes* reads: "The joys and hopes and the sorrows and anxieties of people today, especially of those who are poor and afflicted, are also the joys and hopes, sorrows and anxieties of the disciples of Christ, and there is nothing truly human that does not also affect them."[27] In 1938, de Lubac had written: "Even in these times of intoxication mingled with anxiety, amidst the most pressing necessities, it is the role of the Christian, a man among his brother men, buoyed up by the same aspirations and cast down by the same anxieties, to raise his voice and remind those who forget it of their own nobility" (*Catholicism* 198). The entire introduction to *Gaudium et Spes* is a development of this theme. And the position that *Gaudium et Spes* takes on the relationship between the Church and the world is also that of *Catholicism*.[28] The world is characterized as an ambiguous place, one beset with problems and dangers, yet still as the fundamentally good historical arena in which the drama of human salvation is being played out. The de Lubacian dictum is proclaimed that the message of the Church does not fail to find an echo in the human heart. That the Church affirms and elevates whatever is good in human culture is declared both in *Gaudium et Spes* and in *Lumen Gentium*, and is also reflected in *Nostra Aetate's* position that "the catholic church rejects nothing of those things which are true and holy in these religions."[29]

The conclusion of *Catholicism* is a ringing endorsement of "social Catholicism," properly understood. That is, although de Lubac warned against any purely mundane approach that would threaten the transcendent character of the Church or reduce Christianity to a social program, he took pains to explain how social concern is integral to Christian salvation:

> There can be no question . . . of merely transposing into the natural order what faith teaches us about the supernatural world. . . .
> But an anxiety to make a clear distinction between the two orders, natural and supernatural, must not prevent faith from bearing its fruit. If in the upward direction a discontinuity between the natural and the supernatural is fundamental, there must be an influence in the downward direction. Charity has not to become

---

[26]See the references to de Lubac by Charles Moeller and Joseph Ratzinger in *Commentary on the Documents of Vatican II*, vol. V, ed. Vorgrimler, 63 and 145.

[27]*Decrees of the Ecumenical Councils*, ed. Norman P. Tanner (Washington, DC: Georgetown University Press, 1990) II.1069.

[28]De Lubac, *Catholicism*, 198.

[29]*Decrees*, II.969.

inhuman in order to remain supernatural; like the supernatural itself it can only be understood as incarnate. He who yields to its rule . . . contributes to those societies of which he is naturally a member. . . . The service of his brethren is for him the only form of apprenticeship to the charity which will in very truth unite him with them. . . . Whatever freedom he may justly claim for the details of his task, it is impossible for him not to aim at establishing among men relationships more in conformity with Christian reality. (*Catholicism* 203-4)

Integrally connected with this "social Catholicism" for de Lubac is the mystery of the cross. The final paradox is that the mystery of new life is bound up with the mystery of suffering and death.

Gustavo Gutiérrez cites de Lubac's retrieval of the historical and social elements of Christian salvation as one of the sources that provide a foundation for liberation theology.[30] Liberation theology builds upon the position that there are not two separated realms, the natural and the supernatural, with salvation belonging to the latter. Christian salvation must have roots in this world. Christian unity builds upon the interpenetration of the unity of the human race and the common destiny to which all are called.

Handing on Möhler's Legacy

Throughout the above discussion can be heard many echoes of the approach of Johann Adam Möhler. De Lubac refers explicitly to Möhler and the Tübingen school in *Catholicism* as a primary and seminal example of efforts at *ressourcement* and of appreciating revelation as the organic whole of God's plan as it develops in history (*Catholicism* 171). De Lubac self-consciously situated himself within this theological movement. Indeed, his retrieval of the Church Fathers, his conceiving of the Church as social and historical without neglecting the mystical, and his stress on a unity that embraces diversity all hearken back to Möhler. So too do his fight against individualism and egoism, his championing of an inclusive Catholic ideal, and his portrayal of Catholic truth not as a narrow-minded weapon but as a mystery that holds in tension various contraries.

De Lubac's work on the relationship between the natural and the supernatural can be read as a metaphysical vindication of Möhler's position on the reality of the Trinity over against that of Schleiermacher, for it

---

[30]Gustavo Gutiérrez, *A Theology of Liberation: History, Politics and Salvation*, trans. and ed. Sister Caridad Inda and John Eagleson (Maryknoll, NY: Orbis Books, 1973, rev. 1988 [Spanish orig. 1971]) 70.

provides an ontology that allows for speaking of knowledge of God in a historical and critical framework. That is, if Schleiermacher, realizing the historical character of Christian revelation, came to think that revelation tells us nothing about God in God's own self, de Lubac's dynamic, sacramental ontology lends support and depth to Möhler's belief that the doctrine of the Trinity does give access to truth about God, even though that truth remains beyond final comprehension.

The broad vision found in de Lubac's approach to the Church helps to bring together the sometimes tensive elements of the early and the later Möhler. De Lubac envisioned a Church that is both historical and mystical, both on a journey and containing within itself the destination. De Lubac could possibly be read as favoring the later Möhler over the early because of his strong christological focus and his relative neglect of pneumatology. I agree with Wood's assessment, however, that, although subordinate to the christological, the pneumatological element in de Lubac's ecclesiology remains strong.[31] The dimensions of ecclesiology associated with the pneumatological in Möhler's early work, such as organic unfolding, historical development, legitimate diversity, etc., are ever present throughout de Lubac's work.

Of all the points in de Lubac that are deeply reminiscent of Möhler, the deepest is his radical inclusiveness in conceiving of the Catholic spirit. For both of these theologians, Christians tend to be right in what they affirm and wrong in what they deny. Heresy lies not in being partial, but in being partial in a way that excludes alternatives. The Catholic spirit seeks to transcend false dichotomies in an often paradoxical both/and. Christians can be confident in the truth of their faith, though this truth remains beyond final comprehension.

Conclusion

De Lubac expressed a remarkably inclusive and comprehensive Catholic ecclesial vision. Those who develop contemporary versions of communion ecclesiology do well to draw inspiration from this aspect of his work. His specific positions on various issues, for example, the status of non-Christian religions, can be argued to be limited, time-bound, and debatable; the breadth of his understanding of catholicity, however, transcends his time. His appreciation of the Church as mystical revelation rivaled that of Journet; his attention to the engagement of the Church as mystery within the concrete affairs of history rivaled that of Congar; and his awareness of the Church as a social body working out a salvation with roots in this world helped to set that stage for liberation theology. Rare is the theologian who can perform with such range and reach.

---

[31] Wood, *Spiritual Exegesis and the Church*, 150-1.

FIVE

Communion and the Council

Karl Rahner and John Paul II

The Final Document of the Extraordinary Synod of 1985, in its assessment of the progress of the Church in the twenty years that had passed since the Council, cited as a problem the tendency of certain groups to read selectively the Council documents.[1] I have heard the message of the Synod summarized as such: Some interpreters focus on chapter three of *Lumen Gentium*, on the hierarchy, as the most fundamental text, and read all else in the light of it. Their post-conciliar vision remains that of an ancient institution that has perhaps oiled a few joints. Other interpreters focus on chapter two of *Lumen Gentium*, on the People of God, and read all else in the light of it. Their post-conciliar vision is that of a Church that has undergone a people's revolution in which social equality in the Church and in the world have become the only real issues. The bishops at the Synod were pleading for interpreters on all sides to see chapter one, on the Mystery of the Church, as primary, and to read chapters two, three, and all the rest in the light of it. Their post-conciliar vision is a Church awakened to a new sense of its origins in trinitarian love expressed through Christ and of the mission of both the hierarchy and the laity within the Church and within the world.

This call for a higher synthesis in the interpretation of Vatican II was echoed that same year in an essay by Hermann J. Pottmeyer. Pottmeyer found that "conservative" and "progressive" voices were finding it all too easy to justify their positions on the basis of the conciliar texts. He proposed that a common interpretative approach be based on "the Council's invitation to make the Church a *communio* and a sign of sal-

---

[1]Extraordinary Synod of 1985, "The Final Report," *Origins* 15 (19 December 1985) 448.

vation to the world."[2] He recognized the problem that after the Council positions were emphasized that highlighted the contrasts between the new teachings and the neo-Scholasticism that came immediately before. He suggested a new synthesis that combines both "progressive" and "conservative" statements from the documents in such a way that gives priority to the Council's progressive thrust but still takes very seriously the conservative remnants. Pottmeyer pointed out that it was expressly not the will of the Council Fathers to overturn Trent and Vatican I, and that the documents need to be interpreted with that in mind. He optimistically suggested that, as the Church develops and grows more confident in its new *communio* outlook, it will have an easier time reappropriating earlier understandings.

The higher synthesis based on the notion of *communio* as called for by both the Synod of 1985 and by Pottmeyer is a project that I support wholeheartedly. In fact, the initial motivation behind the research and the thinking that would eventually become this book has its roots in my reading of the Synod of 1985 final document and wanting to know more about this concept of "communion ecclesiology." I have come to agree that it is indeed the key to the Council, as well as the key to a better understanding of the Church today, one that can support continued renewal and reform.

But I have also become aware that differences in interpretation do not simply go away once communion ecclesiology arrives on the scene. For there are different versions of it, and even those with virtually identical versions might still encounter some differences in applying communion ecclesiology to the Council documents.

In this chapter I wish to explore briefly how the communion ecclesiology expressed in the documents of Vatican II encompassed all of the various forms of communion identified in the chart in chapter one and associated with the vision of de Lubac in chapter four. I will then examine the perspectives of Karl Rahner and John Paul II concerning how the documents are to be interpreted.

Communion in the Documents

The word "communion" appears throughout the Council documents. There are bonds of communion between God and Catholics, among various groups of Christians, between men and women, and among all human beings. The word stands in contrast to the neo-Scholastic drafts

---

[2]"A New Phase in the Reception of Vatican II: Twenty Years After the Council," in *The Reception of Vatican II*, ed. Giuseppe Alberigo, Jean-Pierre Jossua, and Joseph A. Komonchak, trans. by Matthew J. O'Connell (Washington, DC: The Catholic University of America Press, 1987 [French orig. 1985]) 29.

of the preparatory commissions. Bishop Emile de Smedt of Bruges summarized the failings of these documents by labeling them as clericalist, juridical, and triumphalist.[3] They reflected little of the *ressourcement* and virtually none of the *aggiornamento* that would characterize the work of the Council.

The documents of Vatican II used the word "communion" in various senses. Like de Lubac, the Council expressed a many-layered vision that avoided pitting against each other things that are potentially complementary. Perhaps interpreters of Vatican II should be requested to read some of de Lubac's work on paradox and mystery, if they have not already done so, before diving into the documents. In the following five sections, I draw upon the five forms of communion outlined in chapter one to try in an initial way to give a sense of the multi-dimensionality of the Council's approach to "communion."

Divine

Another word for "communion" is "love." Chapter five of *Lumen Gentium*, on the universal call to holiness, finds love to be at the heart of what the Church is. If Charles Journet's most basic complaint was that the Church is addressed in one treatise while grace and love are addressed in another, *Lumen Gentium* directly addresses that problem by putting love right in the center. There can be no consideration of what the Church is apart from a consideration of Christian discipleship. And the mark of the true Christian disciple is love. Love is described in terms of a trinitarian spirituality that seeks the will of the Father, the path of the Son, and the prompting of the Holy Spirit. The Church is most basically a communion of those who are bonded together through the love of Christ in relationship with the Trinity.

The connection between the Church and the Trinity is addressed already in chapter one of *Lumen Gentium*, "The Mystery of the Church." Rather than giving the Church a juridical definition, chapter one of *Lumen Gentium* expressed the origin of the Church in a dynamic narrative framework that links it with the plan of the Father, the founding by the Son, and the ongoing presence and mission of the Spirit. The Church is a communion of people bonded in trinitarian love. To participate in the Church is to share in the love of the three persons that is offered through Christ.

---

[3]Avery Dulles, *Models of the Church* (Garden City, NY: Image Books, 1974, expanded edition 1987) 39. See also the discussion in Giuseppe Alberigo and Joseph A. Komonchak, eds., *History of Vatican II*, vol. I (Maryknoll, NY: Orbis Books, 1995) 311-3.

Mystical

In chapter one of *Lumen Gentium*, the Church is approached not through juridical definition, but through images and symbols drawn from scripture. These images include the Church as a sheepfold, as a fishing net, as ground to be plowed, as living stones, and as the Bride of Christ. Preeminent among these images and symbols is that of the Church as the Mystical Body of Christ. In chapter seven, the Church is identified as the Communion of Saints, which includes not just those who have gone before us in death, but those who are still here on earth bonded together in communion through the love of God. Chapter eight of *Lumen Gentium* explores links between the Church and Mary.

This approach to scripture is iconic and typological. It is iconic in that it draws upon images in order to evoke a sense of the transcendent dimensions of the Church. It is typological in that it finds "types" of the Church in various things and persons in scripture. It is this approach, with roots in the Patristic authors, that has been so highly developed by Hans Urs von Balthasar (as will be examined in the next chapter).

Sacramental

The Church is said to be a sacrament in the very first paragraph of *Lumen Gentium*. Section eight goes on to say that the Church has visible and invisible elements, which coalesce to form one mysterious reality. In its commingling of the human and the divine, it can be compared to the mystery of the Incarnate Word.

The relationship between local churches (dioceses) and the Church universal is spelled out sacramentally in connection with the ongoing presence of Christ and in connection with the Eucharist. The Church is a communion of local churches. The bishop represents Christ in the diocese. The liturgy, especially the Eucharist, is presented as "the chief means through which believers are expressing in their lives and demonstrating to others the mystery which is Christ, and the sort of entity the true Church really is" (*Sacrosanctum Concilium* 2).

Each individual church, or diocese, with a bishop as its head, is "formed in the likeness of the universal Church." At the same time, though, "in and from these particular universal churches there exists the one unique Catholic Church. . . . This variety of local churches, in harmony among themselves, demonstrates with greater clarity the catholicity of the undivided church" (*Lumen Gentium* 23).

This focus on the local churches and their relationship to the Church universal has major implications for communion ecclesiology. First, it highlights the importance of a diversity that exists within a unity. The unity of the church is not to be understood simply as imposed from the top down, but is a harmony that arises from the playing of many varied instruments. The pattern of holding universal synods at regular intervals since Vatican II was intended as a means for mutual interchange among various segments of the Church. The bishop represents not just the concerns of the Church universal to the people in his diocese, but also the reverse.

Second, this conceptual shift promotes what the Council called "cultural adaptation" or what is now referred to more commonly as "inculturation." *Ad Gentes* spoke of how the gospel is like a seed that takes root in various types of soil and produces a variety of plants. The gospel exists always in inculturated forms, and great care must be taken not to impose unnecessarily an alien culture upon people who deserve to hear the gospel in a way that can preserve whatever is legitimate in their own heritage.

Third, the way that the universal-local relationship is spelled out has implications for Church authority. In order to balance off the one-sided emphasis on papal authority that took place because of the premature ending of that Council, Vatican II stressed the role of the bishops both as individual heads of dioceses and also considered together as a college with their brother bishop, the pope, as their head. In the diocese, the bishop, as the one who presides over the Eucharist, takes the place of Christ. He governs by a power proper to himself. He is not the vicar of the pope. Among his major roles is to be the symbol of unity.

The college of bishops is formed by the communion of bishops with each other in a way that represents the unity of the entire Catholic Church. That the Church taken as a whole is governed by the bishops is known as "collegiality." The pope remains the supreme head of the Church and the ultimate symbol of unity. Whether he governs the Church strictly as the head of the college of bishops or retains his own power in a way considered separately from the college has been a matter of some debate. But the role of the bishops was definitely clarified and strengthened in a way that emphasized their connection with the Eucharist and their representing the bondedness of local churches throughout the world in communion with each other. And many would interpret the role of the pope as also strengthened, because it is presented not just as a juridical office but also and more deeply as contextualized within the Church understood sacramentally as a communion.

In *Lumen Gentium*, then, the Church as sacrament is a communion of local churches, each local church itself being a communion in love of all the members. In and through that local eucharistic community, each member is connected with all other members, whether local or global, on earth or in glory, human or divine.

Historical

The second chapter of *Lumen Gentium* presents the Church as the People of God. The Church has a history rooted in the people of Israel.

As the messianic people of God, the Church is based on a covenant. As expressed in chapter seven, the Church is a Pilgrim Church, a Church on a journey, one that is not yet finished. All members of the Church are called to holiness, and share a fundamental equality on the spiritual level (8). The Church must travel the path of reform and renewal, as well as the path of poverty taken by its Founder (32).

Communion ecclesiology, when applied to a Church as a People of God and as a Pilgrim journeyer, gave the Catholic Church a new language in which to express its relations with the Orthodox and with Protestants. Non-Catholic Christians are said to be in partial communion. In *Unitatis redintegratio*, the Church is first described historically and organically as a communion in Christ and the Spirit. Rifts among Christians are thereby seen as disruptions of communion. Eventually large communities came to be separated from full communion with the Catholic Church. But the Catholic Church is able to recognize rights and wrongs on both sides of the disputes that led to separation, and to acknowledge in a positive sense that separated communities maintain some degree of communion with the Catholic Church. Their members are brothers and sisters in the Lord. They have the right to be called Christians. Their communities, through which the Holy Spirit is active, are means of salvation.

The vision of the Church journeying in history lends support to theologians and church leaders who emphasize the need for structural change on a practical level in order to meet the challenges of the modern age. Karl Rahner developed his ecclesiology along this path (as will be examined in the next chapter).

Social

Dignitatis Humanae (1) speaks of how all human beings share a fundamental dignity regardless of their nationality or religion. *Gaudium et Spes* (1) speaks of how Christians and all others share the same joys and hopes, the same sorrows and anxieties. It says that "God has a parent's care for every individual and has willed that all should constitute a single family, treating each other as brothers and sisters" (24). This solidarity extends to differences of gender, for *Gaudium et Spes* identifies the first form of communion as that between men and women. *Gaudium et Spes* refers throughout both to a basic human solidarity that already exists and to the call to a fuller and more explicit solidarity in Christ: "As the first-born of many brothers and sisters, after his death and resurrection he set up among those who accept him in faith and love a new communion of kinship, which is the Church" (32). The social justice concerns expressed in *Gaudium et Spes*, rooted in an anthropology of global human solidarity, are an integral part of Vatican II's communion ecclesiology.

Vatican II's communion ecclesiology thus addressed a broad range of issues. The word "communion" can be connected with all of the various forms of communion identified in chapter one of this text. Each form of communion receives not a casual mention but a strong endorsement. Any interpretation or appropriation of Vatican II must strive to be faithful to the breadth and depth of this vision of the Church.

Rahner: Vatican II as the Self-Actualization of the Church as a World Church

In an article published in 1979, Karl Rahner tried to articulate "an inner, essential connection among [the Council's] individual occurrences."[4] In doing so he pointed to an aspect that is an important dimension of communion ecclesiology, that the Council was "the Church's first official self-actualization *as* world Church."[5] Rahner explains how bishops from a wide variety of places throughout the world represented their local churches. This first of its kind gathering of the world-wide episcopate faced many new questions. Some questions dealt with inculturation, such as whether polygynous societies might have their social structure affirmed, or whether churches in Alaska might always have to use grape wine in the Eucharist. The question was raised about the use of the vernacular in liturgical celebrations. Moreover, the Church's responsibility toward the world understood as a global community arose as a major theme. The Council expressed a new openness to the great world religions and a new appreciation for the religious freedom of all. A stress was placed upon the universal salvific will of God.

Rahner saw the change represented by Vatican II as so significant that he compared its impact with that of the early shift from Jewish-Christianity to Hellenistic and later European Christianity. He thus named three great epochs in the history of the Church:

> Jewish Christianity
> Hellenistic and European Christianity
> The Catholic Church as a World Church

In this new "world Church," Rahner proposed, there is need for a pluralism of proclamation and a pluralism of liturgies. In terms of the Church's structure, there is a need for less Roman centralism and more collegiality. "Collegiality" in this context means above all that the authoritative processes of the Catholic Church be informed by a mutual

---

[4]Karl Rahner, "Towards a Fundamental Theological Interpretation of Vatican II," trans. by Leo J. O'Donovan, *Theological Studies* 40 (December 1979) 716.

[5]Ibid., 717.

flow of interchange between universal and local and vice-versa rather than being a uniform one-way street.

Rahner acknowledged the need for reappropriation of elements of the tradition, but he did not dwell on this point. He called instead for a Pauline boldness as the Church faces the ever more global future. His stress throughout was on the radically new, and how the changes associated with the Council represent an openness to a range of diversity that no one can as yet fully imagine.

John Paul II: Vatican II as a New Advent

A fresh testimony to the ongoing relevance of Vatican II is given by John Paul II in his 1994 "As the Third Millennium Draws Near."[6] This apostolic letter, which details preparations for the celebration of the year 2000, relies heavily upon the documents of Vatican II. Over fifty percent (22 of 41) of the letter's citations are to six of the Council's sixteen documents. It is not just the quantity, however, but the quality and force of the references that make them so integral and important to John Paul II's vision of the Church in the year 2000.

When he convoked the Council, John XXIII expressed his hope that Vatican II would result in a "new Pentecost."[7] In his vision, the Council would lead to a descent of the Holy Spirit upon a renewed Christendom, a kind of new beginning in which the fruits of the Spirit would be made manifest.

John Paul II's vision is similar to that of John XXIII in two important regards: first, he connects Vatican II with a central event on the church calendar, that is, Advent. Second, by choosing Advent he has selected a symbol for a new beginning. By associating Vatican II with Advent John Paul II does not negate the possibility of the Council eventually leading to a new Pentecost, but he implicitly places that Pentecost in the distant future. John Paul does not see Vatican II in itself as a complete Advent, but just as Advent's beginning; he sees the time since Vatican II as the continuation of that Advent that will lead to the celebration of Christ's incarnation in the year 2000. John Paul II calls the Council a "providential event whereby the church began the more immediate preparation for the jubilee of the second millennium."[8]

---

[6]John Paul II, *Tertio Millennio Adveniente* (As the Third Millennium Draws Near), *Origins* 24 (24 November 1994) 401-16.

[7]Pope John XXIII, "Pope John Convokes the Council," in Walter M. Abbott, ed., *The Documents of Vatican II* (New York: Guild Press, 1966) 709.

[8]John Paul II, *Tertio Millennio Adveniente*, 407.

John Paul II takes care to clarify that the developments of Vatican II are not simply new and original as if they had no history leading up to them. He emphasizes yet more, however, precisely the ways in which the Council was indeed a new beginning: "The Council's enormously rich body of teaching and the striking new tone in the way it presented this content constitute as it were a proclamation of new times" (20). The pope highlights the passage from Luke (4:16-30) in which Jesus reads from the scroll of Isaiah about the days of fulfillment when the blind will see and the lame walk. He interprets the coming millennium itself as representing a time of fulfillment, and recommends that "the best preparation for the new millennium . . . can only be expressed in a renewed commitment to apply, as faithfully as possible, the teachings of Vatican II to the life of every individual and of the whole church" (20).

John Paul II also regards the synods that have taken place since the Council as part of the preparation for the millennium. He notes that these synods "were born of the Second Vatican Council's vision of the church" (21). For John Paul II, Vatican II, far from being outdated and irrelevant to our current times, is producing fruits that have barely begun to ripen.

John Paul II's Ranking of Important Developments of the Council

Many a "top ten" list of the great achievements of Vatican II have been composed. These lists at times reveal as much about the concerns of the compiler as about the Council itself. Now, John Paul II does not come right out and say, "Here is my top ten." But passage 19 in "As the Third Millennium Draws Near" reads as a serial list of the achievements of Vatican II, and it takes but a little editorial license to carve out a list of the pope's "top thirteen" picks regarding the Council's accomplishments. It first has to be clarified, though, that for John Paul II, just as in the New Testament there are the two greatest commandments that surpass and include the other ten, so there are two main developments of the Council that represent an analogous summation. For John Paul II, the greatest principle of the Council was its affirmation that salvation comes through Christ, and the second is like it: that the salvation of Christ is mediated to us through the mystery of the Church, his body. All other developments of the Council need to be read in this light. With that framework ever in mind, I have carved from passage 19 a list of the pope's "top thirteen" that preserves much of his own wording:

1. A renewed discovery on the part of the Church of the depth of its identity as a mystery and as the body and bride of Christ.
2. The reaffirmation of the universal call to holiness.
3. The reform of the liturgy.

4. The renewal of church life on both the universal and local levels.
5. The promotion of various vocations, from those of the laity to those of religious, deacons, priests, and bishops.
6. The rediscovery of episcopal collegiality.
7. The openness to Christians of other denominations.
8. The openness to followers of other religions.
9. The openness to all people of our time.
10. The affirmation of religious liberty.
11. The affirmation of cultural diversity.
12. The attention to the means of social communication.
13. The authentic autonomy of earthly realities (understood as compatible with the absolute lordship of God).

It is notable that John Paul II's list contains many if not all of the developments of Vatican II most often highlighted by various Catholic reform movements. What differentiates the pope's list is its simultaneous stress on the Church as mystery and on strengthening the Church's internal and institutional elements. Catholic reform movements often tend to see these dimensions of the Church as opposed to each other. In John Paul II's vision, not only are these dimensions not opposed, but they are integrally related to each other such that the more "progressive" changes depend upon the existence of the more internal and institutional elements for their very authenticity. It is in this sense that John Paul II's approach to Vatican II attempts to be faithful to the Extraordinary Synod of 1985's call to move beyond selective readings that focus almost exclusively, on the one hand, on institutional matters or, on the other hand, on matters of progressive reform. Yet the pope's resolution is not a mere combination of themes, but more of a subordination of the progressive matters to concerns for the institution, which concerns are in turn subordinated to a regard for the mystical elements of the Church as a mystery.

The Council and Preparations for Celebration

As mentioned above, John Paul II believes that a renewed commitment to the application of Vatican II represents the "best preparation" for the new millennium. Although these practical applications do not reproduce lock step the Council's achievements as listed in passage 19, they do represent the overall spirit of John Paul II's interpretation of the Council.

A framing point of reference for all of John Paul II's suggestions is his strong call for the Church itself to travel the road of repentance and renewal. The pope closely follows Vatican II on this point when he states that the Church does penance because "she acknowledges as her own her sinful sons and daughters" (33). He discusses the sometimes poor historical record of the Church on the matters of tolerance and respect for religious freedom, but he also emphasizes the need for "a serious examination of conscience above all on the part of the church of today" (36). This call for repentance is one of the underlying themes of the entire document. As in the Old Testament, where penance was the appropriate preparation for the jubilee year, such is also the case with the coming jubilee.

Many of the points concerning which John Paul II calls for progressive reforms are expressed within this framework of a call to repentance. In fact, John Paul II seems to tie in the success of the goals of Church reform with the depth and sincerity of the penance that can be achieved. Foremost among these progressive goals is ecumenical unity. Although John Paul II does not promise full communion by the millennium, he gives the impression that such might be a possibility among some major groups.

Another element of progressive reform highlighted in the document is a renewed effort in openness to the modern world, including a stress on social justice, the option for the poor, religious freedom, and inter-religious dialogue. John Paul II discusses these points within the context of an assertion that Christians must examine their consciences concerning the reception given to Vatican II. Have the hopes of that Council to renew the world panned out? And if not, are not all Christians to accept the responsibility for that? The pope urges that sincere repentance over these matters could lead to strengthened progress concerning the Church's mission to the world.

In a way consistent with John Paul II's overall interpretation of the Council, these progressive reforms are in a sense qualified by an even stronger emphasis on both mystical and internal institutional concerns. This is especially true of two points: (1) a strong focus on the truth of salvation in Christ and (2) a continued appreciation of the transcendent mystery of the Church. Echoing *Veritatis Splendor*, John Paul II laments "the widespread loss of the transcendent sense of human life and confusion in the ethical sphere," as well as a "climate of secularism and ethical relativism" (36). He cautions that openness to the world and dialogue must be "accompanied by careful discernment and courageous witness to the truth" (36). Such dialogue calls for "a more lively sense of the importance of ecclesial obedience" as well as a deeper understanding of *Lumen Gentium's* depiction of the church as "founded on the activity of the Spirit, guaranteed by the apostolic ministry, and sustained by love" (47).

Such ecclesial concerns are complemented by a stress on the unique importance of Christ. John Paul II expresses "an urgent need for a synod on the occasion of the Great Jubilee in order to illustrate and explain more fully the truth that Christ is the one mediator between God and man and the sole redeemer of the world, to be distinguished clearly from the founders of other great religions" (38). Concerning interreligious dialogue, John Paul II warns that "care will always have to be taken not to cause harmful misunderstandings, avoiding the risk of syncretism and of a facile and deceptive irenicism" (53). The final citation of the document is to Vatican II's *Gaudium et Spes*, claiming Christ as the key to history, as the only name by which it is fitting that human beings be saved, as the light by which to illumine the various problems faced by the modern world (59).

John Paul II's overall approach to the Council is reflected in this ordering of priorities. Progressive reforms such as increased sensitivity to cultural diversity, ecumenical progress, religious freedom, the preferential option for the poor, and interreligious dialogue are to be pursued, but always humbly in a spirit of repentance, and with a strong affirmation of ecclesial structures and above all of the mystery of Christ and the Church.

Conclusion

For both John Paul II and Karl Rahner, Vatican II marks the beginning of the third great epoch of the Church. John Paul II dates the second epoch as beginning with the second millennium, which roughly marks the shift from a unified global Christianity to a Christianity in major schism. The effectiveness of the mystery of Christ and the Church in the world was damaged. The new millennium, which begins its preparatory phase with Vatican II, holds the promise of serious beginnings along the road of Christian unity. A Church more awakened to the mystery of Christ and strengthened in its essential structures will be more ready to meet the challenges of the modern world.

Karl Rahner dates the beginning of the Church's second epoch with the Hellenization of the Church, the shift from being a Jewish Church to being a Church identified most closely with the history of Western, European civilization. The shift signaled by Vatican II was that of becoming a world Church, a Church that embraces the process of inculturation itself as being more associated with the core of Christianity than any one particular culture.

Some obvious tensions exist between the views of John Paul II and those of Rahner. The pope emphasizes the need to preserve essential structures; Rahner emphasizes how radically flexible structures must be in order to address contemporary problems. For Rahner, a recognition of the Spirit present in the world is key to implementing Vatican II; for the pope the key is the recognition that salvation comes explicitly through Christ.

These are not small differences. They are not to be minimized. They reflect differences that will be discussed in more detail in the next chapter, which compares the views of Rahner and Hans Urs von Balthasar.

And yet I cannot help but suggest that their views can be read as complementary. That too is a topic for the next chapter and subsequent ones. For now, I wish only to say that a great danger in communion ecclesiology today lies in constructing versions that do not take with utter seriousness both of these interpretations of the Council.

SIX

Communion and Theological Method

Karl Rahner and Hans Urs von Balthasar

As the twenty-first century opens, any worthwhile short list of the past century's great Catholic theologians will include Karl Rahner, a German (1904-84) and Hans Urs von Balthasar, a Swiss (1905-88). They were fellow Jesuits, though Balthasar left the order and was eventually incardinated as a diocesan priest in Chur, Switzerland. They were friends and often mutual admirers who understood the work of each other well. They also had their differences, which at key moments were pronounced. There were tensions, especially for a time after Vatican II, when they worked together on the International Theological Commission. Balthasar's disagreements with Rahner were a factor underlying the development of the journal, *Communio*, which stands in reaction against what are perceived as the liberal tendencies of the journal *Concilium*.

Today, many who follow either of these theologians are suspicious and even intellectually hostile to the followers of the other. I will argue in this chapter that their positions are not by any means irreconcilable; in their differences, however, lies one of the great fissures in theological discussion today.

Before exploring those differences,[1] it will be helpful to set out a framework that will allow them to be tied back together in the end. I

---

[1] A good start at exploring their differences can be found in Stephen Fields, S.J., "Balthasar and Rahner on the Spiritual Senses," *Theological Studies* 57 (1996) 224-41. See also Rowan Williams, "Balthasar and Rahner," in *The Analogy of Beauty: The Theology of Hans Urs von Balthasar*, ed. John Riches (Edinburgh: T&T Clark, 1986) 11-34; Louis Roberts, "The Collision of Rahner and Balthasar," *Continuum* 5 (1968) 753-7; and articles from a symposium on nature and grace in Balthasar and Rahner in *Communio* 18 (1991) 207-80.

draw that framework from the French Jesuit Henri de Lubac (1896-1991), who himself belongs on any short list of great Catholic theologians of this century. De Lubac was Balthasar's teacher for Patristics, and a lifelong source of inspiration to him. He was also a friend and admirer of Rahner.

In his programmatic *Catholicism* (1938), de Lubac uses some musical imagery that captures the unity-in-difference of Rahner and Balthasar:

> The Church can play on this organ [the human being] because, like Christ, she "knows what is in man," because there is an intimate relationship between the dogma to which she adheres in all its mystery and human nature, infinitely mysterious in its turn. Now, by the very fact that she goes to the very foundation of man the Church attains to all men and can "play her chords" upon them.[2]

The various parts of this quote do not simply stand in opposition, but work together.

One part sounds like a main theme of Rahner's life work, that "there is an intimate relationship between the dogma to which [the Church] adheres in all its mystery and human nature, infinitely mysterious in its turn." Rahner explores the links between the self-transcendence of human beings and the infinite mystery of God. He emphasizes that the final revelation we encounter in Christ corresponds with what is in a deep sense already true about human experience in its ultimate depths. For Rahner, Christian revelation makes explicit and full that which has always been implicit in the human drama. Christian revelation is to some degree a process of self-discovery.

Another part of the quote from de Lubac, however, sounds more like a major theme in the life work of Balthasar, that "by the very fact that she goes to the very foundation of man the Church attains to all men and can 'play her chords' upon them." Balthasar was himself fond of using musical imagery, and conceived of Christianity as, among other things, a great symphony.

Even more important for Balthasar, however, is the image of a Church that plays a melody which is more wondrous and beautiful than any tune that human beings could have composed simply of their own inner resources. Balthasar emphasizes that Christian revelation consists in a love that shatters human expectations. Human beings may be instruments eminently suitable for the playing of the chords of revelation, but these chords of love have been revealed not through a process of self-discovery, but through Christ.

---

[2]Henri de Lubac, *Catholicism,* trans. Lancelot C. Sheppard (London: Burns and Oates, 1950; Universe Books edition, 1961 [French orig. 1938]) 15.

Rahner on Human Self-Transcendence and God

Rahner was not just an inventor of abstract theological concepts. Throughout his life he addressed practical matters that faced the Church. Much of his reflection on the relationship between God and human self-transcendence concerned the pressing question of who is a member of the Church and who is saved by Christ.

To transcend is to go beyond. Rahner held that as human beings we go beyond ourselves. This is especially observable when we are knowing, willing, and loving. When we strive to know, we don't just want to know what is comfortable for our own little world; we want to know the truth whatever it is. When we will, we do not simply will what is good for us; we will the good, whatever that may be. When we love, we do not simply love the desires that we project on to another person; we move outside of ourselves to love another for who he or she is. In these human operations we move in the direction of a world that exists beyond ourselves. In self-observation, we discover ourselves to be self-transcendent.

Rahner says more. As we move beyond ourselves to embrace the great mysteries of truth, goodness, and love, we are moving within the mystery of God. It is God who stands as the absolute mystery who provides an ultimate context that makes final sense of our striving and reaching beyond ourselves. According to Rahner, God is the *woraufhin* (endpoint, whither, that toward which) of our transcendence when we are moving beyond ourselves towards truth, goodness, and love. As human beings, we have a real link with God in this way. We have a real experience of God as this absolute mystery, though this experience is prior to the level of concepts.

Rahner called the level of experience prior to concepts the *transcendental* level. He called the level of concepts and clear categories the *categorical* level. He used this distinction to explain how many people who were not explicitly Christian could be considered implicitly Christian. It is possible, Rahner argued, that a person of another religion or an agnostic or even an atheist may reject God on the categorical level, but accept God on the transcendental level. That is, a person might say on the level of ideas, "I do not believe in God"; however, on the deeper, transcendental level this person may actively embrace the quest for truth, goodness, and love. In exercising one's self-transcendence and thus embracing the context of absolute mystery, one is actually embracing God, even though one might not know it. In his middle-range work Rahner called such a person an "anonymous theist." He later dropped the term as potentially misleading, but he never discarded the concept. He used also for a time the term "anonymous Christianity," for he held that anyone who lived a life based on goodness and love was really in a deep sense a Christian. In this way, Rahner was able to reconcile the

Christian belief that salvation comes ultimately through Christ with the fact that there are many exceptionally good people in the world who are not explicitly Christian.

Rahner's Limitations

There are limitations in how Rahner's approach has at times been implemented, especially by those who try to interpret him as offering an all-embracing "system" that fully captures the relationship between human beings and creation and the final mystery known as "God." A work like *Foundations of Christian Faith* might lend itself to such a reading in spite of the author's strong protests about the limitations of the book as representing a first level of reflection, as being highly selective by necessity, as not being a summary of his full work, and as being more comprehensive and systematic than his other works simply because of the nature of the topic.[3]

There is something of an irony in treating the work of Rahner, who helped to overthrow the overly systematic neo-Scholasticism of the seminary manuals by grounding Christian faith in absolute mystery, as itself being overly systematic. Yet the problem is there. Any teacher who has ever worked with Rahnerian material in the classroom knows how quickly diagrams on the board and outline summaries of points get turned into the next "system" of precisely how the universe is constructed. And then there are theologians, too, who criticize Rahner as one who will not allow God to be God but rather tries to contain God within a schema.[4] And of course there is the common charge, not without grounds, that Rahner does not take sin seriously enough (except when it comes to the institutional Church).

Some interpreters even think Rahner to have so regulated the interconnection between God and human consciousness as to have eliminated in any practical sense the need for an explicit profession of Christianity or even for explicit belief in God. His notions of the "anonymous Christian" and the "anonymous theist" seem to say that human goodness on its own is sufficient, even wonderful, though of course Rahner sees such goodness as residing in the activity of beings who are never "merely" human but who as human beings are preconditioned, as

---

[3]Karl Rahner, *Foundations of the Christian Faith: An Introduction to the Idea of Christianity*, trans. by William V. Dych (New York: Crossroad, 1982 [German orig. 1976]) xi-xv.

[4]Paul Molnar, "Can We Know God Directly: Rahner's Solution from Experience," *Theological Studies* 46 (June 1985) 228-61 and also Molnar's "The Function of the Immanent Trinity in the Theology of Karl Barth," *Scottish Journal of Theology* 42, no. 3 (1989) 367-99.

is all of creation, by grace. Why bother to be Christian, if Christianity is simply the fullest expression of what is already true otherwise, and if the transcendental drama of human salvation is already being worked out in the heart of every human being?

Anyone who truly studies Rahner will encounter an explicit Christian through and through, and the great majority of theologians who consider themselves to be Rahnerian are also explicitly Christian and Catholic. Still, a number of ex-Catholic or post-Catholic theologians love Rahner and have drawn upon his theology to legitimate their freedom from institutional ecclesiality. Even though Rahner himself worked within the Church and dedicated his entire work to addressing the practical problems that the Church faced in the modern world, and even though Rahner argued consistently and persuasively that Christianity is necessarily an ecclesial religion, it is still the case that justifying a non-ecclesial spiritual existence through a selective reading of his works is common and perhaps surprisingly easy to do.

Richard Lennan's defense of Rahner's ecclesiality in *The Ecclesiology of Karl Rahner* might be read as damning with faint praise his support for explicit Church membership:

> Given his constant reference to the Church's sinfulness, it might well appear that Rahner regarded the Church more as a hindrance than a support to faith. As a general principle of human behavior, however, he argued that we ought to reject what has been meaningful only when it can be replaced by something more meaningful [note to *Theological Investigations*, xii, 151]. Since those who abandoned the Church would have only an abstract God and an abstract Christ as projections of their subjectivity, even a burdensome ecclesial faith remained infinitely preferable.[5]

Whether because of, in spite of, or in ignorance of this argument, Rahner remains a steady favorite among those who are alienated from the institutional Catholic Church and yet who wish to continue to think of themselves as Catholic.

A Practical Ecclesiology

How much Rahner's actual texts truly play into the hands of those who use his work in such a manner is a matter of debate. Richard Lennan demonstrates convincingly that Rahner's life project was not the development of a lock-tight system, but rather the ongoing address-

---

[5]Richard Lennan, *The Ecclesiology of Karl Rahner* (Oxford: Clarendon Press, 1995) 181.

ing of the practical problems that faced the Church. The many volumes of the *Theological Investigations* reveal a theologian who developed his metaphysical speculations always in dialogue with present issues. For example, Rahner's notion of the "anonymous Christian" was developed as a way of explaining how the traditional concept of *extra ecclesiam nulla salus* could be maintained in a global situation in which Christians were beginning to experience themselves as a minority.[6] And his theology of the symbol was developed, at least in part, as a way of explaining how the Church could claim to represent Christ and yet still be imperfect.[7] His notion of the *Vorgriff* (the preapprehension of the meaning of an experience prior to its conceptual articulation) can best be understood as a way of explaining how the Church can hand on authentic teaching that is more than simply propositions.[8] Lennan shows throughout his book how Rahner's ecclesiology, rather than constituting an intractable system, itself shifted as the problems that Rahner addressed shifted. Surely there is a great deal of consistency in Rahner's approach from which a "system" can be teased out, but doing so distorts the whole by missing the critical importance for Rahner of the concrete ecclesial context out of which he was always working.

One of Rahner's deepest ecclesiological concerns was to articulate the balance of continuity and change in the Church. The Church needs to be continuous with its origins, but it must do so in a way that addresses the particular issues, or signs of the times, expressed in particular times and places. Lennan argues that in his early work, Rahner leaned most in the direction of the Church maintaining organic continuity with its origins. In his later work, without abandoning that concern, the balance of his attention shifted to how the issues at large in the world must determine the current and future direction of the Church. Rahner emerged as an advocate of significant change in the ways in which the Church of the future should be organized, such as the possibility that episcopal offices might be held by committees, that authority in general could be less centralized, that many personal decisions should be left to the consciences of individuals, and that what are now parishes might come more to resemble what we think of as dioceses.[9]

---

[6]Lennan, *Ecclesiology*, 38. For the direct source, see "Membership of the Church according to the Teaching of Pius XII's Encyclical, 'Mystici Corpus Christi,'" *Theological Investigations*, trans. Karl-H. Kruger, vol. 2, 1-88 (Baltimore: Helicon Press, 1963). Rahner does not use the term "anonymous Christian" in this essay, but the concept is clearly present.

[7]Lennan, *Ecclesiology*, 47. See also Rahner's "Theology of the Symbol," in *Theological Investigations*, trans. Kevin Smyth, vol. 4, 221-52 (Baltimore: Helicon Press, 1966).

[8]Lennan, *Ecclesiology*, 50.

[9]For an overview of Rahner's vision of the future of the Church, see Karl Rahner, *The Shape of the Church to Come*, trans. by Edward Quinn (New York:

Rahner also called attention to limitations of the Sacred Congregation for the Doctrine of the Faith's declaration on the admission of women to the priesthood, *Inter insignores* (1976), and pushed for further discussion of the matter.[10] Yet throughout his work Rahner stressed that changes should take place without threatening the existence of the Church's essential structures, such as the episcopal college, the papacy, the sacraments, and the three-fold hierarchical ministry, even as these might take different form.

Perhaps because of his practical orientation, Rahner was disinclined to dwell on ideal images of the Church such as the Body of Christ or the Bride of Christ or the Church as our Mother; Rahner emphasized more the Church in its journey in history. He is more likely to be found calling for the reform of the Church in its structures in response to practical questions than he is to be elaborating theologically what it means for the Church to be the Body of Christ or the Bride of Christ.

In his historical and practical emphases, Rahner's strengths abound. Those who read his work find grounds for appreciating the traditional Catholic focus on the goodness of the world and of human beings. Rahner is able to relate the Christian message to contemporary science, to a variety of cultures, and to other world religions. He is most helpful for giving frameworks that Christians can use for avoiding sectarian withdrawal from anything modern. Rahnerian Catholics tend to like Vatican II because it allowed for an optimistic engagement of the Church with the modern world.

Rahner, de Lubac, and Communion Ecclesiology

Did Rahner depart seriously from de Lubac in the area of theological anthropology? John Milbank, author of the oft-quoted *Theology and Social Theory*, claims that he did.[11] Since in this chapter I use de Lubac as the figure whose multi-dimensionality is able to bridge the methods of Rahner and Balthasar, I will address Milbank's claim that Rahner and de Lubac are incompatible.

De Lubac and Rahner were fellow Jesuits, friends, and mutual admirers. In de Lubac's 1965 book, *Le mystère du surnaturel*, which was a re-working of an article he wrote in 1949,[12] when he explains the criti-

Seabury, 1974 [German original 1972].

[10]Karl Rahner, *Theological Investigations*, vol. 20, 35-47.

[11]John Milbank, *Theology and Social Theory: Beyond Secular Reason* (Oxford: Basil Blackwell, 1990) 219-23.

[12]Henri de Lubac, "Le Mystèry du surnaturel," *Recherches de science religieuse* 36 (1949) 80-121. An English translation of this article is found in *Theology in History*, trans. Anne Englund Nash (San Francisco: Ignatius Press, 1996) 281-316.

cal point of how the grace that is offered to a concrete, historically determined person is truly free, he describes the graced character of such a determination. Then in a footnote he says, "It is what Karl Rahner today calls 'an abiding supernatural existential foreordained to grace,'" citing the first volume of Rahner's *Theological Investigations*.[13] De Lubac draws favorably upon Rahner's work at various key points, referring to "my profound estimation of Karl Rahner's theological work and my strong personal affection for him."[14] He disagrees with Rahner only twice, both times in a rather complimentary fashion. First, he thinks that one of Rahner's corrections to Thomism is found already in Thomas. Second, he disagrees with Rahner's estimation that he himself differs from Rahner concerning the matter of *"potentia obedientialis"*; de Lubac insists that Rahner has misread him, and that his own position is indeed in harmony with that of Rahner.

Milbank's attempt to sever Rahner from de Lubac must come under serious question in the light of de Lubac's own testimony. In particular, what Milbank alleges as their difference concerning *"potentia obedientialis"* merits closer examination. *Potentia obedientialis* is a scholastic concept that refers to the capacity of human beings, both before and after the Fall, to respond to God's grace. Rahner's main argument about this concept concerned the relation between the natural and the supernatural. He directed his argument toward an anonymous article, signed "D.," that had appeared in *Orientierung* in 1950.[15] Rahner argued that "D." was unable to resolve systematically the difficulties posed by trying to reconcile a system of "pure nature" with the absolutely free character of grace. A contradiction remained in that grace appears at the same time to be both "owed" and "not owed." Rahner's own strategy was to identify as a dimension of the human person a "supernatural existential," an orientation to transcendent mystery that does not belong to a "pure nature." "Pure nature" is then seen to be an abstraction, or what can be called a remainder concept. Rahner held that the absolute gratuity of grace as well as the always already graced nature of human beings can be maintained without contradiction in this new conceptual schema.

Rahner also mentioned de Lubac in that article, strongly qualifying any association between de Lubac's actual positions and those of "D."

D. belongs to the circle of those theologians who are usually grouped together (though some of them protest against it) as the school of "la nouvelle théologie." We are not concerned to decide

---

[13]Henri de Lubac, *The Mystery of the Supernatural*, trans. Rosemary Sheed (New York: Herder and Herder, 1967), 72, n. 4. The citation to Rahner is *Theological Investigations*, vol. 1, 312, n. 1.

[14]De Lubac, *The Mystery of the Supernatural*, 139, n. 36.

[15]*Orientierung* XIV (1950) 141-45.

whether and how far D.'s presentation really reproduces de Lubac's views accurately, which is D.'s intention.[16]

Later in the article, Rahner appropriated the concept of *"potentia obedientialis,"* making it not a negative notion within a concept of "pure nature," but rather a "supernatural existential" characterizing an already graced human being. He referred to *"potentia obedientialis"* as a concept "scorned by de Lubac."[17] De Lubac later responded that "I have never scorned the concept of *'potentia obedientialis'* except in the very sense in which [Rahner] himself resolutely rejects it."[18] In other words, de Lubac rejected *"potentia obedientialis"* only to the extent that it is understood within the framework of "pure nature"; in Rahner's supernatural existential he finds one particular articulation of the position that he himself had held all along.

Milbank reads Rahner as though he has simply taken the scholastic two-tier system and replaced it with a transcendental two-tier system.[19] He holds that in contrast with de Lubac and Balthasar, who follow Blondel in recognizing a supernatural dimension to actual concrete persons and events, Rahner reduces the supernatural to a dimension of an abstract analysis of a universal human consciousness. Milbank holds further that Rahner, when faced with the need to relate this abstract analysis to actual, historical revelation, encounters a new form of extrinsicism that he can only resolve by making revelation an external expression of what is already always true anyway.

In my own reading, however, it is Milbank who reifies what for Rahner is, on the one hand, a completely abstract and formal concept such as "pure nature" and, on the other hand, a dynamic, not fully objectifiable dimension of human existence such as the "supernatural existential." Milbank turns Rahner's transcendental "method" into a lock-tight cosmic "system." He ignores, moreover, the extent to which Rahner's transcendental analysis begins by exploring what must be true about human beings, given the specific character of Christian revelation. In a related way, Milbank does not attend to Rahner's continual awareness that God is not simply the philosophical endpoint of a human trajectory, but remains always the absolute mystery in which human creatures have their being and who has been revealed unsurpassably in the person of Jesus Christ.

---

[16]Rahner, *Theological Investigations*, vol. 1, 303.

[17]Ibid., 315.

[18]De Lubac, *The Mystery of the Supernatural* 139, n. 36.

[19]Though he differs on some points, Milbank appears to draw heavily for his interpretation of Rahner from Balthasar's *The Theology of Karl Barth*, trans. John Drury (New York: Holt, Rinehart and Winston, 1971 [German orig. 1951]) 241-4, and also from *Love Alone*, trans. Alexander Dru (New York: Herder and Herder, 1969 [German orig. 1963]). Hereafter in text as *Love*.

I do not want to deny all differences whatsoever between de Lubac and Rahner on the matter of *"potentia obedientialis."* Max Seckler argues that, although their intentions are in league, they do not resolve the problem of "pure nature" in the same way.[20] Seckler finds de Lubac to follow St. Thomas more closely on the existence of a natural desire to see God, though he acknowledges that after seven centuries of theological development it is a matter of speculation as to whom Aquinas might agree with now. He attributes de Lubac's minimizing of differences between himself and Rahner to de Lubac's irenic spirit.

In my opinion, the technical judgments that Seckler makes about their differences are true. But de Lubac's embrace of Rahner was more than just a personal inclination toward irenicism. De Lubac can fully agree with Rahner's "supernatural existential" and with his transcendental method because there is a welcomed place for it in de Lubac's multi-dimensional approach. De Lubac's method is broader and more inclusive than that of Rahner; it is not a contrary alternative. De Lubac can feel comfortable rejecting *"potentia obedientialis"* when operating within a framework that acknowledges a Thomistic "natural desire to see God," and he can feel comfortable accepting a transposition of *"potentia obedientialis"* into a "supernatural existential" when operating within a framework of transcendental Thomism. These approaches are distinct, but not necessarily contradictory. De Lubac had a remarkable capacity to translate from one framework to another. Rahner's approach can fit within de Lubac's approach, although, as I argue below, so can that of Balthasar.

Milbank forces a choice between Rahner and de Lubac. He does have his finger directly on real difficulties in Rahner, especially given the way that Rahner is sometimes misappropriated to diminish the importance of specifically Christian revelation. Rahner fails to give adequate attention to the ideal dimensions of the mystery of the Church that Balthasar so develops. But Milbank takes Rahner's weakest points, objectifies them, and uses them to attribute to Rahner a "system" that in the end is un-Rahnerian. In doing so he misses the positive ways in which Rahner can be interpreted as carrying forward certain dimensions of de Lubac's legacy, dimensions that are not strongly present in Balthasar.

Balthasar and the Way of Love

The germ of Balthasar's disagreements with Rahner can be found in his 1950 *The Theology of Karl Barth.* Here Balthasar already expressed

---

[20]Max Seckler, "*'Potentia obedientialis'* bei Karl Rahner (1904-1984) und Henri de Lubac (1896-1991)," *Gregorianum* 74, no. 4 (1997) 699-718.

misgivings about Rahner's use of the category of *potentia obedientialis*. Even more tellingly, though, Balthasar's description of Barth's critique of Catholicism foreshadowed his own later criticisms of Rahner:

> By now Barth's objection to Catholicism should also be clear: he accuses it of possessing an overarching systematic principle that is merely an abstract statement about the analogy of being and not a frank assertion that Christ is the Lord. This principle presupposes that the relationship between God and creature can already be recognized in our philosophical fore-understanding (of natural theology). This means that God's revelation in Jesus Christ seems to be merely the fulfillment of an already existing knowledge and reality.[21]

In an earlier chapter I argued that one major root of communion ecclesiology can be found in Johann Adam Möhler's both adopting and reacting against the positions of Schleiermacher (and other figures). Another major root can be found in Balthasar's both adopting and reacting against the positions of Karl Barth, whose own theology represents an outright rejection of Schleiermacher.[22] Schleiermacher represents the "turn to the subject" at the core of much modern theology, an approach that accepts the basic shift associated with Descartes and Kant and then tries to align it with a Christian vision. In line with Barth, Balthasar rejected strongly any theology that tries to fit Christianity within the context of a prefabricated philosophical system. Barth and Balthasar both emphasized the objectivity of revelation, its transcendent character as coming from God and not from human beings, and the beauty of revelation with its own self-authenticating power.

Balthasar departed from Barth in his championing of Catholicism. Barth argued that Catholicism itself, being based on the concept of the "analogy of being," was tied to a philosophical stance taken prior to the hearing of the Word, and therefore idolatrous, even the anti-Christ. He proposed in its place an "analogy of faith." Balthasar followed Erich Przywara in assessing the analogy of being as the opposite of idolatry, as being an articulation of a truth that flows from revelation itself, and as being the only way to respect how God is present and active and revelatory yet still hidden and mysterious and incomprehensible.[23] He sees

---

[21]Balthasar, *The Theology of Karl Barth*, 37. I use here the translation from Edward T. Oakes, *Pattern of Redemption: The Theology of Hans Urs von Balthasar* (New York: Continuum, 1994) 56.

[22]See Oakes' chapter on Balthasar and Barth in *Pattern of Redemption*, 45-71.

[23]See Oakes' chapter on Balthasar and Przywara in *Pattern of Redemption*, 15-44.

Barth as being too beholden to the traditional Protestant lack of appreciation for the independence and goodness of the world.[24]

Balthasar saw in Rahner one who has taken the "turn to the subject" along the trail blazed by Kant and Schleiermacher. In contrast, he saw himself in line with Goethe:

> First I would like to say that I consider Karl Rahner to be, on the whole, the strongest theological power of our time. And it is evident that he is far superior to me in speculative power. In 1939 we worked together on a plan for a new work in dogmatics . . . which later became *Mysterium Salutis*. But our starting points had actually always been different. There is a book by [Georg] Simmel called *Kant und Goethe*. Rahner has chosen Kant, or if you prefer, Fichte: the transcendental starting point. And I—as a Germanist—have chosen Goethe, [who stressed] the figure: this indissolubly unique, organic, self-developing form (I am thinking of Goethe's *Metamorphosis of Plants*). This form [is] something that Kant, even in his aesthetics, never really dealt with.[25]

Goethe rejected the turn to the subject with its bifurcation of subjectivity and objectivity. He sought the unity of subject and object in the appearance itself, in the form.[26] There is an objectivity in which the subject can be caught up, captured, even enraptured. It is this direction that informs Balthasar's aesthetic theology of revelation with its stress on beauty and newness.

In *Love Alone*, Balthasar contrasted his own theological method both with the traditional "cosmological method" that collapsed with the coming of the Enlightenment and with the "anthropological method" he associates with Rahner, though Rahner is not named in that particular book. Balthasar depicted Kant and Schleiermacher as reductionists, and he said that Fichte, because he seemed to suggest that absolute subjectivity was to be found in the transcendental structure of human beings, was charged with atheism in a way that "was not unfounded" (*Love* 29). From these roots, said Balthasar, sprang Modernism, which judged everything, including God's revelation, according to how it enhanced the life of the individual. Balthasar portrays the Rahnerian anthropological method as being unable to overcome being mired in these subjectivist origins.

Whereas Balthasar admitted that subjective appropriation has

---

[24]Oakes, *Pattern of Redemption*, 65.

[25]The quote is taken from Oakes, *Pattern of Redemption*, 72-3. It is Oakes' own translation of a passage from "Geist und Feuer: Ein Gespräch mit Hans Urs von Balthasar," *Herder Korrespondenz* 30 (1976) 75-6.

[26]See Oakes' chapter on German Idealism, esp. 81 and 94.

always been an important element in Christian life, he objected fiercely to the view that Christian revelation can be brought under the judgment of human, subjective criteria:

> No one [in the traditional outlook] had ever seriously proposed finding the criterion for the truth of revelation in the heart of pious individuals; nor had there been any attempt to measure the depths of grace by the abyss of human need and sin; the content of dogma had never been judged by the excellence of its influence upon man. (*Love* 35-6)

Balthasar's own position is that revelation, whose sole purpose is the glorification of divine love, is self-authenticating:

> God's word must interpret itself and it wishes to do so. And if it does, then one thing is clear from the outset: it will not be found to contain what man has thought out for himself about himself and God, whether *a priori* or *a posteriori*, whether readily or after infinite pain, whether from the first or in the course of a long evolution. (*Love* 41-2)

Balthasar thus contrasted his own approach with transcendental method. He called it "the way of love." It is based on an aesthetic appreciation of the objective beauty of revelation.

Balthasar presented the way of love as a mean between the extremes of an extrinsicism that relies on blind faith and an immanentism that relies on subjective criteria. He stressed the pure gratuity of love, a love that is recognized because of its entrancing beauty. It is a love that is most appropriately imaged in the groom/bride relationship. It is a love that calls for an unconditional commitment, including even the willingness to give one's life. Because love desires no reward other than love itself, the life of contemplation has an edge over the life of action. The love that comes to be known through revelation does more to lay bare one's previous lack of love than to confirm something that one already knew. One who encounters such love experiences the love itself as its own authentication.

For Balthasar, Christian "conversion" is not simply a series of developments through which a person grows as it were from the inside out; in the New Testament, "the central act in all conversion is this rising into the awareness of one's reality which is called into being by the encounter with Jesus."[27] Conversion entails an encounter with a revelatory reality beyond oneself, and not one which simply confirms what one could have

---

[27]Hans Urs von Balthasar, "Conversion in the New Testament," *Communio* 1 (Spring 1974) 53.

figured out on one's own if one had simply looked deep enough inside.

Balthasar's focus on the otherness, objectivity, and beauty of revelation allowed him to probe deeply and imaginatively the content of Christian revelation as expressed in scripture and in the writings of the Church Fathers. Following Barth, Balthasar compared revelation to a great symphony whose melody needs to be heard in a way that transcends any particular rendition in a particular medium. He explored it further as a drama, a complex and exhilarating love story, in which the sinful souls of human beings are courted by divine love. He believed that the drama ends ultimately in universal salvation, for in the final analysis, though human freedom remains a reality, the love of God is irresistible. It will hunt one down even in the darkest corner of hell. This latter belief was inspired in Balthasar not only by Origen but also by Adrienne von Speyr, especially in her vision of Holy Saturday.[28]

For Balthasar, the mystery of the Church can best be apprehended through a meditative, typological analysis of persons encountered in the scriptures who represent symbolically various dimensions of the reality of the Church. As Larry Chapp explains Balthasar's position, the Church ultimately takes its identity from Christ; it has both an identity and non-identity with him.[29] The Church furthermore finds its identity in the personal missions of its individual members. Key figures in scripture typify particular missions in distinctive ways.

According to Balthasar, the Church has its beginning at the foot of the cross when Jesus entrusts Mary to John.[30] Mary represents the Church in its ideal, immaculate sense. She is the Mother of Christ who is transformed into the Bride of Christ and the Mother of all Christians. In a certain sense John is there as a surrogate for Peter, but in another sense the origin of the Church in the Mary-John relationship signifies the being of the Church as a communion in a way prior to the development of its institutional, hierarchical form. Balthasar's position is expressed by John Saward:

> By bequeathing [Mary] to John, Jesus unites the heavenly Church, perfected in advance, with the still struggling earthly Church. In

---

[28]Balthasar wrote that his own life's work cannot be separated or considered apart from the work of von Speyr. See *Our Task: A Report and a Plan*, trans. by John Saward (San Francisco: Ignatius Press, 1994 [German orig. 1984]) 1.

[29]Larry S. Chapp, "Who Is the Church? The Personalistic Categories of Balthasar's Ecclesiology," *Communio* 23 (Summer 1996) 322-38.

[30]Balthasar's ecclesiological reflections on Mary, John, and Peter are found in various places throughout his work, especially in *The Office of Peter and the Structure of the Church*, trans. Andree Emery (San Francisco: Ignatius Press, 1986 [German orig. 1974]); *The Christian State of Life*, trans. Sister Mary Frances McCarthy (San Francisco: Ignatius Press, 1983 [German orig. 1977]); and *Our Task*, 124ff.

other words, the visibly organized pilgrim Church on earth, in all its imperfections, has been entrusted by its Head to care for and protect the purity and the sanctity of the original, ideal Church. John's mission is to be the link between Mary and Peter and thus between the Church as holy and immaculate and the Church as hierarchical and infallible.[31]

The Church is thus for Balthasar a communion in which are linked together its ideal and its historical dimensions. The spiritual communion precedes what will emerge as necessary institutional elements.

One of Balthasar's most important contributions to a contemporary communion ecclesiology is the ability he opens up to consider the Church in terms of images, often dramatic ones, that express its ideal side. If Rahner developed an important dimension of de Lubac's *Catholicism*, that of "an intimate relationship between the dogma to which she [the Church] adheres in all its mystery and human nature, infinitely mysterious in its turn,"[32] Balthasar developed another crucial dimension. The next sentence in *Catholicism* reads, "Now by the very fact that she goes to the very foundation of man the Church attains to all men and can play her chords upon them." De Lubac himself used the metaphor of music to describe the role that the Church plays in relation to human beings; for de Lubac the melody that is played comes from explicit Christian revelation. De Lubac is able to explore the meanings of the Body of Christ, the Bride of Christ, and the Church as our Mother in a way that Rahner does not pursue. Balthasar has this range, and in offering it he continues the legacy of the later Möhler, of Journet, and of one important strain of the legacy of de Lubac, a dimension of the Church as mystery that was especially significant in chapter one of *Lumen Gentium*.

This approach to the Church has its own danger of being misused. It can support the mystification at times engaged in by Church leaders who justify their institutional intransigence by a simplistic appeal to "mystery." It is an approach that perhaps some theologians of the twentieth century have had their reasons to avoid. But the zeal for institutional reform should not deprive Christians of the ability to appreciate the Church in its glory, so that they can say along with de Lubac:

The Church which lives and painfully progresses in our poor world is the very same that will see God face to face. In the likeness of Christ who is her founder and her head, she is at the same time both

---

[31]John Saward, *The Mysteries of March: Hans Urs Von Balthasar on the Incarnation and Easter* (Washington, DC: Catholic University of America Press, 1990) 78; quoted in Oakes, *Pattern of Redemption*, 261.

[32]De Lubac, *Catholicism*, 15.

the way and the goal; at the same time visible and invisible; she is at once the bride and the widow, the sinner and the saint.[33]

Balthasar may not be the best theological voice available when it comes to the relation of the Church to various cultures, to science, to other religions, or to the plight of the poor.[34] But if communion ecclesiology must address also the majesty of faith, its drama, its wonder, its beauty, its freshness, its being beyond all expectations, and perhaps above all its intimacy, then the perspective of Balthasar is crucial to say the least.

Can It All Fit Together?

De Lubac holds the key to reconciling the views of these theological giants. He was himself a master of paradox, one who avoided any simplistic reduction of the Christian mystery to this or that side. Yet de Lubac also rejected the path of taking bland middle positions that simply avoid extremes. Instead he retrieved from the Church Fathers the *complexio oppositorum*, the dynamic holding in tension of contrary points. In the spirit of de Lubac, I suggest that it is not a contradiction, but a *complexio oppositorum*, to hold simultaneously that:

1. revelation transcends human capacities in such a way as to shatter human expectations, and

2. revelation so corresponds to what is already true about the human condition as to provide a shock of recognition that it is on some deep level what we knew all along.

Balthasar himself believed that in the final analysis the differences between himself and Rahner were more complementary than otherwise. In the fall of 1977, in a talk given at the Catholic University of America, Balthasar outlined three schools of thought in theology: the transcendental approach of Rahner, his own focus on the beauty and objectivity of revelation, and the social Catholicism of de Lubac which is currently being manifested in liberation theology.[35] He presented all three approaches as important, legitimate, and potentially complementary. He reiterated, of course, his objection that Rahner has diffi-

---

[33] Ibid., 27.

[34] A sympathetic and insightful exploration of Balthasar's limitations can be found in Larry S. Chapp, *The God Who Speaks: Hans Urs von Balthasar's Theology of Revelation* (San Francisco: International Scholars Publications, 1996) 215-33.

[35] Hans Urs von Balthasar, "Current Trends in Catholic Theology and the Responsibility of the Christian," *Communio* 5 (Spring 1978) 77-85.

culty articulating the need for an explicit, historical Christianity and that some of his pupils have taken this weakness to radical extremes. He argued, characteristically, that "God . . . communicates and actually demonstrates such unheard-of things that man feels not satisfied but awestruck by a love which he never could have hoped to experience." He spoke of how liberation theology "often becomes self-seeking and confused," and could use some help in clarifying its genuine claims.

Yet Balthasar points out approvingly that all three schools of thought have been advances beyond neo-Scholasticism. And in the end his criticisms are phrased encouragingly. He says that "the transcendental school of thought will be criticized only if the historical facts of revelation are not given sufficient expression, and liberation theology will be criticized when it comes close to giving absolute priority to the political dimensions." His clear implication is that he has confidence that these approaches can sidestep their potential pitfalls. In summing up his position he states:

> In conclusion I might point out that the three theological directions outlined here do not contradict each other in their positive aspects. They complement each other, in that each contributes something which the others do not stress sufficiently or are in danger of forgetting. None of the three sets itself up as absolute, but all recognize the whole of "*Catholica.*"[36]

Balthasar knew full well that Rahner's manner of taking the turn to the subject rests as much on a rejection of the subjectivism of Kant and Schleiermacher as it does on an acceptance of certain aspects of their starting points. He also knew that Rahner insisted throughout his life on the necessity of an explicit Christian revelation without which we could not come to know categorically that which we would otherwise experience only transcendentally. Finally, Balthasar knew that both Rahner's approach and his own do not in themselves deal adequately with the horror of human suffering caused through the type of social injustices widespread in Latin America or by the incredible yet real atrocities of the Holocaust.

Rahner was himself quick to point out the limitations of his own approach and its need to be complemented by other approaches. He reported that he took very seriously J.B. Metz' criticism that his work needs a fuller political and social dimension.[37] Late in his life, when

---

[36]Balthasar, "Current Trends," 85.

[37]Karl Rahner, "Introduction," in James Bacik, *Apologetics and the Eclipse of Mystery: Mystagogy according to Karl Rahner* (Notre Dame: University of Notre Dame Press, 1980) ix-x.

asked whether transcendental anthropology truly constituted the "nutshell" of his theology, Rahner responded:

> Transcendental anthropology does correctly characterize my theology, but under the following two presuppositions: (1) that a religion which is essentially historical, and which has become historical, also carries within itself elements which are not necessarily deducible a priori, but are accepted as concrete historical facts and (2) that I hope I see this and to some extent incorporate it into my theology. By no means do I claim that transcendental anthropology is the only possibility. . . . I would say that there are few philosophical, anthropological, and theological problems more difficult than the relationship between transcendentality and history. Consequently, I'm not surprised if someone wants to point out that my theology doesn't adequately handle this difficulty. I certainly don't suffer under the delusion that I have spoken the final, adequate, and totally incontestable word on this matter.[38]

These qualifications give evidence not only of Rahner's own awareness of the particularity of his own positions, but also of his desire that the gap between his own approach and that of Balthasar be spanned.

Today some followers of Rahner and some followers of Balthasar take their mentors' positions to extremes that involve the wholesale rejection of the other. Yet Rahner and Balthasar themselves, with strikingly different starting points and emphases, both achieved a high degree of the *complexio oppositorum* for which de Lubac called.

---

[38]Karl Rahner, *Faith in a Wintry Season: Conversations and Interviews with Karl Rahner in the Last Years of His Life*, ed. Paul Imhof and Hubert Biallowans, English trans., ed. Harvey D. Egan (New York: Crossroad, 1990 [German orig. 1986]) 21-2.

SEVEN

Communion and the Common Good

Joseph Ratzinger and the Brothers Himes

Many of the points of theological tension that exist between the approaches of Rahner and Balthasar can be discovered operating in the work of a wide range of contemporary Catholic theologians. In this chapter, I examine such tensions as they emerge in a comparative study of, on the one hand, Joseph Cardinal Ratzinger and, on the other hand, Michael Himes and Kenneth Himes.[1] I focus on the respective ways in which they treat the concept of the "common good" within a framework of communion ecclesiology. Ratzinger has been strongly influenced by Balthasar; the Himeses have been strongly influenced by Rahner.

My main concern here is to consider the extent to which these contrasting approaches to communion ecclesiology and the common good can be considered to be distinctively "Catholic." Ratzinger and the Himeses both argue that there is a particularly "Catholic" approach to the relationship between the Church and society, and in fact each presents their own approach as representative. Underlying my exploration of their positions stands the goal of finding frameworks of inclusion that can bring together a Balthasarian and a Rahnerian theological approach within a Catholic framework. Surely Ratzinger and the Himeses are thinkers independent enough to escape simplistic identification as being either "Balthasarian" or "Rahnerian"; understood broadly, however, the influence is strong enough in each case to examine fruitfully some significant parallels.

If Ratzinger and the Himeses are right that there is a particular Cath-

---

[1] For the Himeses' thought I rely exclusively upon Michael Himes and Kenneth Himes, *Fullness of Faith* (New York: Paulist Press, 1993). Hereafter in text as *FF*. For Ratzinger's thought I rely mainly on Joseph Cardinal Ratzinger, *Church, Ecumenism, and Politics*, trans. Robert Nowell (New York: Crossroad, 1988 [German orig. 1987]). Hereafter in text as *CEP*.

olic approach to issues of Church and society, one might expect to find some deep similarities between them. And indeed there are. Both Ratzinger and the Himeses contrast a distinctively Catholic theology and anthropology with a Lutheran Reformationist approach. Both express a tension between a Catholic vision and the Enlightenment. Both use terms and concepts associated with "communion ecclesiology" to articulate the meaning of the Church understood as a sacrament. And finally, both find in the Catholic tradition resources for constructing a "Catholic" approach to social theory and the common good that challenges modern thought. These deep similarities between Ratzinger and the Himeses are not just structural. There are remarkable areas of overlap in the particular ways they construct a Catholic vision of the human person and a Catholic vision of a good society.

Some serious divergences in their positions can also be found. These divergences mainly concern how to cast the relationship between Church and world and how to balance caution and optimism when working for the common good. Yet this study will claim that where their streams of thought diverge there is uncovered in-between much fertile ground for discussing what constitutes a Catholic vision of the common good and the Church's relationship to it.

PART I: AREAS OF CONVERGENCE

Five Positions Taken by Both Ratzinger and the Himeses

1. The Catholic theological tradition and its consequent social teaching provide a wealth of resources for constructing a much-needed public theology.

That the Himeses take this position needs little justification; it is the main theme of *Fullness of Faith*. The Himeses use David Hollenbach's definition of "public theology" as "the effort to discover and communicate the socially significant meanings of Christian symbols and tradition" (*FF* 4).[2]

That Ratzinger takes a similar position needs to be established. In *Church, Ecumenism, and Politics* Ratzinger argues for a public theology of similar definition. This is apparent when he discusses the Sacred Congregation for the Doctrine of the Faith's (CDF) second document on liberation theology, *Libertatis conscientia*.[3] He argues forcefully for

---

[2] David Hollenbach, "Editor's Conclusion," in "Theology and Philosophy in Public: A Symposium on John Courtney Murray's Unfinished Agenda," *Theological Studies* 40 (1979) 714.

[3] CDF, "Instruction on Christian Freedom and Liberation," *Origins* 15 (17 April 1986) 713-28.

the integral relationship between the document's theological sections and its social sections. He complains of Christians who have privatized their faith: "From original sin to redemption the whole traditional construction seems to them far too irrational and unreal for them to introduce it into public discussion" (*CEP* 258). But, he holds, the traditional construction of Christianity with its comprehensive understanding of the human person does need to be linked with a political vision, which is precisely what he thinks the CDF instruction does.

Ratzinger is not at all backing down here on his oft-repeated insistence that Christianity itself offers no specific economic or political or social program. And the Himeses are in agreement that "It is not for the church to devise a blueprint for society" (*FF* 64). The Himeses insist that Church leaders should teach specifics "with a becoming modesty in their claim to final wisdom on a topic" (*FF* 103). But Ratzinger and the Himeses also agree that on an appropriately general level of principle and even application the Catholic tradition has a word to proclaim about public policy.

> 2. Much blame for problematic aspects of modern Western thought can be laid at the doorstep of Martin Luther.

Ratzinger identifies the major problem with Luther's approach as his individualistic understanding of faith in which personal assurance of salvation is the decisive element. Luther's insistence upon "faith alone" relegates love to the profane world of works, and his call for "scripture alone" eliminates the need for tradition. But above all, argues Ratzinger, Luther's radical personalization of the faith reduces the church to the merely congregational, in contrast to the Catholic notion of Church that emphasizes divine institution and connectedness throughout the generations. In this way, Luther severs the link between the Church and the transcendent and finds a link exclusively in the relationship between the individual and God (*CEP* 110-5).

The Himeses claim the main problem with Luther's anthropology to be his pessimistic stress on sin, and they are in strong agreement with Ratzinger concerning the problems of individualism and privatization. Indeed, they find the economic individualism of contemporary liberal capitalism to be a secular working out of Luther's theology (*FF* 30-2). Their premise is that Luther's pessimistic anthropology leads to a Hobbesian social theory based on the belief that human beings are incapable of transcending their self-interest. Even Adam Smith's economics, which posits that allowing people to pursue their self-interest will work out for the best, is based upon a pessimistic Lutheran view of the human. The Himeses hold that a Catholic vision balances self-interest with the capacity for altruism, and that human beings can be expected to contribute directly to the common good without relying exclusively on an invisible hand. And Ratzinger would concur, at least in large part:

A correct vision of mankind . . . must start from a relationship in which everyone remains a person and free and is bound to the other precisely as such. It must be a doctrine of relationship and search for a type of relationship which is not an attitude of using people as means towards ends but a self-giving of persons. (*CEP* 262)

It is a traditional Catholic strategy in apologetics to find in Martin Luther a point where things begin to fall apart, and then to counter with Trent's relative optimism and the reconnection of faith with love, works, and tradition. And one does not have to operate with a counter-Reformational Catholic view to raise serious claims in this regard. I do question, though, whether a post-Vatican II Catholic view could make so much out of the impact of Luther's errors on modern thought without giving extensive treatment to the positive impact that Luther's thought has had on the modern world and on the Council. Also, it strikes me as a large oversight that neither Ratzinger nor the Himeses mention either John Calvin or Max Weber's classic text, *The Protestant Ethic and the Spirit of Capitalism*.[4] Despite these misgivings, my point remains that both Ratzinger and the Himeses share a similar "Catholic" reading of the history of the modern world.

> 3. A contemporary Catholic vision needs to be articulated over against Enlightenment philosophies concerning the individual, the community, freedom, reason, and the transcendent.

Both Ratzinger and the Himeses acknowledge things they appreciate about the Enlightenment: namely, the separation of church and state, the development of democratic forms of government, and the focus on human rights. Yet Ratzinger suggests that the Enlightenment has no moral foundation of its own, and that whatever is good in these developments really stem from Christianity:

> Even the ethics of the Enlightenment which still holds our states together lives on the after-effects of Christianity, which provided it with the foundations of its rationality and its internal cohesion. When the Christian foundations are removed completely nothing holds together any more. (*CEP* 217)

The Himeses at times seem more sincere than Ratzinger in their praise of Enlightenment contributions. Like Ratzinger, however, they expressly wish to support political democracy while using a Catholic

---

[4]Max Weber, *The Protestant Ethic and the Spirit of Capitalism*, trans. Talcott Parsons (New York: Scribner, 1958 [German orig. 1904]).

vision to challenge its underlying philosophies of individualism and self-interest (*FF* 37).

Both Ratzinger and the Himeses tend to reify the Enlightenment and attribute to it a truncated view of the human person. They attack its individualism that denies the importance of community. They attack its narrowing down of human reason to the instrumental and the practical while relegating matters of faith and morals to the private sphere. And they attack its concept of freedom as being free from all constraint without recognizing that true freedom is made possible through connectedness with tradition and through participation in community.

Ratzinger and the Himeses both characterize the development of Western thought after the Enlightenment as a series of challenges to universal reason that lead to various localisms, nationalisms, and irrationalisms. Ratzinger refers to Schelling, Rousseau, Saint-Simon, and Herder as weaving a romantic path to narrow nationalism and ultimately to forms of thought that place the irrational on an equal plane with the rational (*CEP* 22-8; 153).[5] The Himeses give a recounting of how from Kant through Vico to Herder, the critique of pure reason gives way to cultural and national particularisms (*FF* 138-41). Both tend to read modern developments as natural extensions of Enlightenment thought.

4. Communion ecclesiology provides a theological framework for articulating a Catholic view of the human person over against the Enlightenment view.

Ratzinger and the Himeses both draw heavily upon concepts associated with communion ecclesiology when articulating the relationship between the Church and society. Both argue consistently for the social nature of the human person, and both find the Catholic grounding for this view in the communion of the Trinity. Ratzinger argues that since the triune God is a community, we who are made in the image and likeness of God must have a communal dimension to our beings (*CEP* 31). He finds in the Trinity a call to give up "the lie of independence in all relationships" (*CEP* 274). The Himeses, similarly, find in the Trinity a community of self-giving love that underscores the human experience that "to exist is to be in a network of relationships" (*FF* 57).

For the Himeses, freedom is most properly the freedom to accept God's free gift of grace (*FF* 76-7). It is actualized politically through

---

[5]For an earlier discussions of the Enlightenment, Modernity, and Marxism, see Joseph Ratzinger, *The Meaning of Christian Brotherhood*, trans. W.A. Glen-Doeple (San Francisco: Ignatius Press, 1993 [German orig. 1960] 14-8, as well as Joseph Ratzinger, *Introduction to Christianity*, trans. J.R. Foster (New York: Herder and Herder, 1970 [German orig. 1968] 30-47.

one's most fundamental right, the ability to participate in a community which allows one to be self-giving (*FF* 61). The human community to which we are called is a reflection of our experience of communion with God through Christ (*FF* 163). The Church is a sacrament both of unity with God and of the unity of all humankind (*FF* 164). The Himeses follow Virgil Michel in seeing in the communion of saints "a telling analogy for the way that earthly society should be structured" (*FF* 165).

For Ratzinger, the most basic freedom is the freedom to be transformed in Christ, which entails membership in Christ's Mystical Body. Membership in the Church translates into political freedom for the individual, who answers in conscience first of all to God, not to the state. The importance of individual freedom of conscience for Ratzinger becomes clear in his allusions to the problem of the Third Reich and the need for individuals to stand up against the government. Yet such individual witness is made possible first of all through participation in a Church that transforms one's "I" into a "We" (*CEP* 127). And the witness of conscience is directed not primarily toward the establishment of individual rights, but against the totalitarian state that would interfere with traditional patterns of organizing life (*CEP* 185-6). For Ratzinger, political freedom consists in the freedom to have just laws and time-tested social norms that help to regulate life. Like the Himeses, he connects freedom both with participation in community and with acceptance of the giftedness of life:

> Considered biblically freedom is something other than indeterminacy. It is participation, and indeed not just participation in some particular social structure but participation in being itself. . . . freedom is identical with exaltation of being, which admittedly only makes sense if exaltation of being is really exaltation: the gift of life and being given in love. (*CEP* 198)

Both Ratzinger and the Himeses draw further upon the notion of community to argue that human reason extends beyond the merely technical and utilitarian to encompass the moral, the metaphysical, and the aesthetic. Ratzinger stresses that human judgment is not confined to what individuals can reproduce in a laboratory, but includes traditional standards that have developed historically and organically within the context of communities (*CEP* 155; 185). The Himeses argue that values are not simply individual choices but reflect community norms and goals that need to be debated in the public sphere (*FF* 5-8). Both Ratzinger and the Himeses cite a Catholic vision as supporting neither an abstract favoring of universal reason nor a particularist reliance on local preferences, but an appropriate balance between the universal and the local (*FF* 149; *CEP* 115-6). Reason as well as freedom thrives not through the rejection of tradition and community, but through one's participation in them.

To the extent that the authors agree about communion ecclesiology, they provide a credible grounding for a Catholic vision of the human person that counters what they portray as the Enlightenment view. As will be discussed below, the authors diverge considerably concerning how these concepts relate to the church-world distinction. It is their divergences on this point that will raise questions concerning a Catholic vision.

5. The common good emerges from the dynamic interplay of social forces which include altruistic behaviors on the part of individuals and groups self-consciously directed toward achieving a good society.

The Himeses consistently use the term "common good." Ratzinger does not. I will use "common good" when referring to both of their visions of a just society. Yet one shared characteristic is that their "visions" do not involve specific blueprints or elaborately designed schemes. For both, the precise details of what constitutes the common good are not determined *a priori*. Instead, the common good takes shape within a society due to the dynamic interplay of social forces under the right conditions.

According to both Ratzinger and the Himeses, the common good is not to be dictated by a master planner. It cannot be adequately achieved in a totalitarian state that does not respect the freedom of human beings. On the other hand, however, both Ratzinger and the Himeses stress that the common good cannot be addressed adequately by focusing mainly on the rights of individuals over against the community. Both hold that a purely *laissez-faire* approach to social and economic matters represents not the best of all possible worlds but an abdication of moral and political responsibility. The social forces that dynamically create the common good must include individuals and groups that act conscientiously not simply out of self-interest but also out of altruistic concerns.

Both Ratzinger and the Himeses accept a fundamental separation of church and state. Both emphasize the limitations not only of the rights of the state and of the church, but also of the rights of individuals. Both find a significant missing ingredient in modern social recipes to be a focus on the importance of various levels of community that serve as intermediaries between the individual and the state. Such communities can include the family, the church, the neighborhood, the union, the small business, the club, the political group, and any number of voluntary associations.

The Himeses develop this position systematically as a "communitarian" social theory (*FF* 33-8). They call communitarianism "the 'deep theory' of Catholic social thought" (*FF* 170). What distinguishes communitarianism from liberal individualism is precisely its giving priority to the common good (*FF* 39). Yet the Himeses reject the radical form of communitarianism that denies individual rights whatsoever. In accord with their reading of Catholic social teaching, they opt for a moderate form of communitarianism that still values individual rights strongly as it contextualizes those rights within a concern for the community (*FF* 45-6).

The Himeses present communitarianism as the Catholic alternative to Enlightenment social contract theory. Rather than seeing individuals alone possessing rights prior to the existence of the state, communitarianism sees both communities and individuals possessing rights prior to the state. Communities have the right and the obligation to pursue the common good. The foremost right of individuals is to participate in a meaningful way in the life of the community. All other human rights are derivative from that right, and hence are themselves ultimately connected with the common good. In a communitarian framework, individuals and groups work toward the common good not just by seeking their own self-interest or by relegating moral questions to the realm of the personal, but by relying upon a combination of reasonably limited self-interest, public debate about standards, and the altruistic pursuit of what is perceived to be the common good of all.

Although Ratzinger does not use the term "communitarianism," he expresses explicit support for a wide range of positions associated with a moderate communitarian stance. His stance on individual human rights within the context of community is similar to that of the Himeses. Moreover, he strongly defends the importance of small communities and traditional modes of social organization over against the anonymous authoritarian state. He laments the Enlightenment's destruction of "the manifold ways in which society was formerly shaped and organized with their pockets of freedom" (*CEP* 186). He identifies the basic cell of freedom as the family. The local church and the Church universal also constitute a special zone of freedom. Even the state itself can become an organ of freedom if its sees its own limited role as formulating laws that protect traditional communities from arbitrary interferences (*CEP* 261). Individuals are called to be socially motivated not simply by self-interest but by duty and love, even to the point of martyrdom. True freedom is manifested in the willingness to bear the cross (*CEP* 198).

Ratzinger articulates an organic view of social development that underlies his support of traditional communities. He argues: "The traditions from which reason offered emancipation had in fact also been the tried and tested methods for regulating the ways in which human beings shared their lives" (*CEP* 185). He refers to the "vital spark of organic historical reality" that is missing from the contrived plans of social reformers (*CEP* 215). Yet what is needed according to Ratzinger is not a Romantic longing for the past nor an effort to anachronistically recreate old structures. Medieval society had its own problems with the political hegemony of the Church and the vulnerability of communities to the arbitrary whims of individuals. What is needed, rather, is an appropriate relationship between a state that knows its own limits, a church that knows its own limits, and a community-oriented culture that builds upon the values of freedom, reason, and the transcendent as traditionally understood (*CEP* 163). According to Ratzinger, having the right kinds of institutions is of crucial importance for the well-being of society, but having the right kinds of moral customs is even more important (*CEP* 253-4).

The Himeses also warn against a Romantic yearning for a pre-industrial society. They call for a political rather than a sentimentalized concept of communitarianism (*FF* 34-35). For the Himeses as for Ratzinger the concept of the common good is dynamic. It is not the restoration of a golden past. In its particulars, it emerges from within the interplay of social forces when the conditions are right. In sum, these conditions include a culture compatible with a Catholic vision of the human person, a proper relationship between church and state, and individuals and groups committed to working altruistically for the common good.

I find that, to the extent to which they agree, the authors provide a notion of the common good that can credibly be called "Catholic." Their view of the common good is in line with the tradition of papal social encyclicals that promotes an undefined but well-located position between liberalism and socialism. On this point, however, arise serious divergences concerning utopianism and social action that will be discussed below.

PART II: AREAS OF DIVERGENCE

Divergences Concerning the Characterization of Modern Thought

The differences between Ratzinger and the Himeses concerning modern thought begin with their depictions of Luther. For Ratzinger, the main error of Luther was his individualistic personalization of faith that ultimately cut the Church out of the equation. This set the stage for the relegation of faith and morals to the private sphere. The Church, the bearer of the transcendent, was severely hampered in its ability to have a proper influence on the modern world.

According to Ratzinger, in the absence of the transcendent various schemes to create a perfect society have arisen. Because social reformers cannot distinguish between heaven and earth, they propose to transform the earth into a heaven. They see all sin as structural and try to eliminate it through social engineering. The solution to the problems associated with the Enlightenment is to renew respect for the transcendent, which enters the world through Christ and through the Church. When what is out of human control is placed in God's hands, and when proper concepts of freedom and reason are restored, then human beings can have the courage to accept the limitations of what is possible and achieve a modest social good.

The Himeses likewise lament the privatization of faith and morality and call for a Catholic understanding of the human person, but they themselves find the major error in Luther to be his pessimistic anthropology, his belief in total depravity, that leads eventually to the Hobbesian belief that human beings cannot be expected to transcend their own narrow self-interests. The Himeses' solution to the problems of the Enlightenment, then, is to recapture a relatively optimistic Catholic anthropology that will awaken citizens to their responsibilities in the social sphere and call them to combat unjust structures such as the relative inequality between the rich and the poor.

Ratzinger's own operative anthropology is much closer to the Himeses than it is to Luther's, but he does not make an issue of Luther's pessimism. Like the Himeses, he thinks that human beings can be called upon to make sacrifices, but as a rule he stresses caution over optimism when talking about social progress.

Divergence Concerning Communion Ecclesiology

As demonstrated above, Ratzinger and the Himeses both operate with a sacramental vision of the nature of church known as communion ecclesiology. But Ratzinger applies these relational and non-juridical concepts most directly to the explicitly institutional Catholic Church in its local and universal manifestations. The Himeses barely pause on the institutional Church before quickly passing on to the Church as a symbol of the unity of all humankind.[6] For the Himeses, the Church is presented most fundamentally as the reality of solidarity among all human beings which is recognized and celebrated in the explicit Catholic Church. The Himeses stress that in its deepest sense the Mystical Body of Christ includes everybody.

This is not to say that the Himeses in any way devalue the institutional Church. Throughout *Fullness of Faith*, they reflect seriously and respectfully on official Church teaching. But their regard for the world and its

---

[6]For a critique of the Himeses on this point, see Michael J. Baxter, "The Non-Catholic Character of the 'Public Church,'" *Modern Theology* 11 (2 April 1995) 243-58.

own dimension of transcendence allows them to apply the concepts of communion ecclesiology in an analogous sense directly to the world itself. The concepts of Trinity, grace, incarnation, and the Communion of Saints speak to how a society should be structured because the world is already in itself a place of grace, sinful but redeemed in Christ.

Ratzinger scarcely refers to human solidarity and makes no ecclesial claims about it. For Ratzinger, "the Church is the occurrence of human history being drawn into the sphere of the divine" (*CEP* 118). It is the Church that makes the transcendent present to a secular world. The secular world is defined by its withdrawal from the transcendent to form its own legitimate sphere of human freedom. Ratzinger views secular society as the realm of human making, whereas the Church represents that which humans could not achieve on their own, the revelation that is encountered as coming from outside of human control.

Ratzinger does not devalue the world any more than the Himeses devalue the Church. He speaks of the goodness of creation and of the importance of achieving the most just society possible. But he does not attribute transcendence directly to the social world. For him, communion with God through Christ is manifested foremost in the explicit community of the Church, whereas for the Himeses the Church makes explicit what is already in a deep sense true about the world.

One upshot of this difference is that Ratzinger considers the Church as the bearer of the transcendent to constitute a sacrosanct zone that is above the criticisms leveled by modern thinkers. In *The Ratzinger Report*, he reflects:

> For a Catholic . . . the Church is indeed composed of men who organize her external visage. But behind this the fundamental structures are willed by God himself, and therefore they are inviolable. Behind the *human* exterior stands a *more than human* reality, in which reformers, sociologists, organizers have no authority whatsoever.[7]

Although Ratzinger acknowledges the good in modern developments that grant religious freedom and that recognize the relative autonomy of the state, he does not otherwise emphasize the positive impact of modern developments on Church teaching or on Church reform. The Himeses, in contrast, are quite explicit about how Catholic teaching has shifted in this century, particularly in regard to how it spells out its concerns for human dignity, equality, and participation (*FF* 42-5). These shifts reflect that, in the Himeses' view, the impact between Church and modern culture has not been a one-way street.

---

[7]*The Ratzinger Report*, with Vittorio Messori, trans. by Salvator Attanasio and Graham Harrison (San Francisco: Ignatius Press, 1985) 46.

Their respective attitudes toward the world is also reflected in how they treat mysticism. When Ratzinger speaks of mysticism, he tends to associate it with early monasticism and the flight from the secular world (*CEP* 249-51). The Himeses stress more the valuing of all creation by Augustine and the nature mysticism of Francis of Assisi. For them, mysticism is associated more with an appreciation of one's connectedness with the world through a realization of one's creatureliness and poverty than with a flight from the world (*FF* 110-2).

Divergence Concerning the Common Good

The Himeses approach the common good as something that Christians and all citizens should work toward with hope and optimism. They identify relative inequality as the world's main social and economic problem. They claim that this problem is structural, and that Christians are called to act in concert with an option for the poor. They make some very specific suggestions about the implications of Catholic communitarianism for public policy, including public support for private schools and for the arts, entitlement programs that require recipient responsibility, and work sabbaticals for parents. Their main dialogue partner is liberal capitalism, and against its *laissez-faire* attitude they argue that moral action must be taken.

Ratzinger approaches the common good very cautiously as the limited good that can be achieved by people who stop trying for utopia and instead accept what is possible. He repeatedly warns his readers not to set their hopes too high. He makes no mention of gross economic inequalities or of an option for the poor, and he argues against views that would analyze all social problems as structural. He refrains from making overly specific suggestions concerning public policy. His main dialogue partners are Nazi totalitarianism and Marxist communism, and against such utopian attitudes he argues that social limitations must be accepted.[8]

These differences in the overall thrust of their approaches are significant. Ratzinger emphasizes the acceptance of how little is possible. The Himeses urge the recognition of how much is possible.

For both Ratzinger and the Himeses, the key question for public theology concerns what the Church, both hierarchy and laity, has to say to the world. For Ratzinger, however, the Church, as the place where the transcendent enters the world, must warn the world about its own pre-

---

[8]Even in Ratzinger's latest reflections on social issues in the wake of the collapse of Marxist economies, Marxism remains a major dialogue partner. See Joseph Ratzinger, *Turning Point for Europe?*, trans. Brian McNeill, C.R.V. (San Francisco: Ignatius Press, 1994 [German orig. 1991]).

tensions to wholeness, and must urge the world to accept what is humanly possible while it looks beyond itself for its ultimate fulfillment. For the Himeses, the Church, as the sacrament of the unity of humankind, must call the world to recognize what is already in a deep sense true about itself, and out of that recognition work for the transformation of social structures so that it might more fully become what it already is.

Conclusion

It is difficult to judge to what extent these important differences are ones of degree or of kind. Yet I find in these differences as much or more ground for exploring what constitutes a Catholic vision as I find in the authors' similarities.

I have identified two major differences of Ratzinger and the Himeses as their positions on church and world and on utopianism. I now wish to say something about how these differences might be mediated within a Catholic vision.

I am presupposing here that a "Catholic" vision represents an inclusive "both/and," that it strives for the higher ground above contrasting positions, and that Catholic thinkers such as Ratzinger and the Himeses will tend to be correct in what they affirm and run into problems in what they ignore or exclude. This is not to say that a Catholic vision cannot exclude anything; surely it can and must draw lines concerning what falls outside acceptable alternatives. But minimally a Catholic vision must make room for a wide range of alternatives that legitimately find their grounding within the tradition.

The first difference to be considered concerns how the Church as communion is to be understood as a sacrament. I wish to draw here upon the distinction from Thomas Aquinas' *Summa Theologiae* that I mentioned in chapter one. Aquinas speaks on the one hand of sacraments such as Baptism, Confirmation, and the Anointing of the Sick, whose grace represents something incommensurable with what human beings can achieve within their own lives. They rely for their material on external bodily substances such as water and oil. Aquinas speaks on the other hand of sacraments such as matrimony and reconciliation in which the grace given is more in proportion with what human beings are naturally inclined to achieve on their own. The matter of these sacraments are perceptible human actions, such as the interiorly prompted repentance of the sinner.[9] It seems that Ratzinger considers the Church to be a sacrament more in the first sense, and the Himeses more in the second sense. Perhaps the Himeses might want to argue with

---

[9] *Summa Theologiae*, part III, q. 84, a. 1.

Thomas concerning whether even the first set of sacraments grants grace in ways proportional to human capacities. I suggest that the Church, as the sacrament of sacraments, needs to be understood as somehow encompassing both of Aquinas' senses, and that any position that emphasizes one sense to the exclusion of the other would be less than Catholic. In my judgment, Ratzinger and the Himeses could learn from each other on this point.

A related difference is Ratzinger's preference for connecting mysticism with flight from the secular world compared with the Himeses' preference for nature mysticism linked with a solidarity in poverty with all creatures. The flight from the world appears to be well paired with Ratzinger's view of the Church as a zone of transcendence over against a world defined by its lack of transcendence. Nature mysticism seems well suited to the Himeses' embrace of the world with its inherent sacramentality. Yet can anyone constructing a Catholic vision seriously choose one of these approaches to the exclusion of the other? Do not both have their place within the Catholic tradition?

The remaining difference is that of Ratzinger's anti-utopianism versus the Himeses' social activism. Does one more than the other reflect a Catholic vision? Ratzinger could perhaps point to Michael Novak for support in casting anti-utopianism as a Catholic position.[10] Yet the Himeses could point to the argument of Karl Rahner that there is inevitably a dynamic relationship between utopia and reality in the Christian understanding of existence.[11]

It is quite possible to view Ratzinger and the Himeses' positions as containing contrasting emphases that are potentially compatible within a Catholic framework. Much depends on the meaning of "utopian."[12] If "utopian" means the embrace of totalitarian programs, then the Himeses are not utopian. If it means that one disagrees with the famous statement paraphrased from Voltaire's *Dictionnaire Philosophique* (1764), "Don't make the best the enemy of the good," then the Himeses are not utopian. If it means that one is radically uncompromising and prophetically rejecting of all that is not perfect, then the Himeses are not utopian.

The Himeses can only be characterized as utopian, in my opinion, if one takes the meaning of that term from sociologist Karl Mannheim's *Ideology and Utopia*.[13] According to Mannheim, ideological forms of

---

[10]Michael Novak, *Freedom with Justice: Catholic Social Thought and Liberal Institutions* (San Francisco: Harper and Row, 1984) 16-38.

[11]Karl Rahner, "Utopia and Reality," *Theology Digest* 32 (Summer 1985) 139-44.

[12]For a discussion of different meanings of "utopia" used in theology, see Dennis M. Doyle, "Utopia and Utopianism," *New Catholic Encyclopedia*, vol. 18 (Washington, DC: The Catholic University of America, 1989) 527-9.

[13]Karl Mannheim, *Ideology and Utopia*, trans. by L. Wirth and E. Shils (Lon-

thought are dedicated to maintaining the *status quo*. Utopian forms of thought are dedicated to working for positive social change. Only in this Mannheimian sense, which is not addressed by Ratzinger, can the Himeses be considered to be "utopian."

This Mannheimian meaning of utopia has been adopted by Gustavo Gutiérrez in his *Theology of Liberation*.[14] Ratzinger has accused liberation theologians of being utopian because of their reliance upon Marx.[15] The Himeses, however, are far from being Marxists. It is probable that the reason why the Himeses never mention Marxism in their entire work on Catholic social thought is because they consider it to be irrelevant.

Many of the differences between Ratzinger and the Himeses are due to their differences in context. When one applies Catholic social teaching mainly to Marxism, one will end up anti-utopian. When one applies it to liberal capitalism, one will be more inclined to wake people from their moral apathy to work for social change. The Himeses do not propose any utopian blueprint, and could accept Ratzinger's statement that "Catholic social teaching is not aware of any utopia but rather develops models of the best possible way of shaping society" (*CEP* 272). Ratzinger, on the other hand, would likely approve of the Himeses' use of Hollenbach's definition of the common good as that "measure of the communion of persons that is achievable in society"[16] (*FF* 45).

Both Ratzinger and the Himeses share the position that the common good is something that emerges from the dynamic interplay of social forces that must include public debate of moral standards and the altruistic contributions of individuals and groups. Within parameters set by that principle, whether one tends to approach the common good more cautiously or optimistically constitutes a significant but not irreconcilable difference. I propose that a Catholic view needs to include both meanings of "utopian" discussed above, rejecting utopianism in the sense associated with Voltaire and accepting some form of it in the sense used by Mannheim.

I do not deny that the differences between the positions of the Himeses and Ratzinger are real and important. Given that they reflect the deep tensions discussed in the last chapter between the positions of Rahner and Balthasar, the Catholic vision that would mediate such ten-

---

don, 1936 [German orig. 1929]).

[14]Gustavo Gutiérrez, *A Theology of Liberation*, trans. Sister Caridad Inda and John Eagleson (Maryknoll, NY: Orbis Books, 1973, revised 1988 [Spanish orig. 1971]). A related use of "utopia" can be found in Gregory Baum, *Religion and Alienation: A Theological Reading of Sociology* (New York: Paulist Press, 1975) 99-107 and 274-92.

[15]Ratzinger, *The Ratzinger Report*, 186-8.

[16]David Hollenbach, "The Common Good Revisited," *Theological Studies* 50 (March 1989) 70-94.

sions would have to be broad indeed. But I have tried to argue that such a broad vision is worth considering. Where the views of Ratzinger and the Himeses converge, they present an interesting but limited expression of a Catholic vision. Where they diverge, they present poles that a truly Catholic vision must encompass. A communion ecclesiology suitable for our times must include them both.

EIGHT

Communion, Reform, and Liberation

Hans Küng, Leonardo Boff, and the CDF

Hans Küng and Leonardo Boff both approach the Church from the bottom up. They offer versions of communion ecclesiology that stress the dynamic character of the Church as the people of God and the priority of charism over structure and institution. Both theologians have been censured by the Sacred Congregation for the Doctrine of the Faith (CDF).[1] Approaches "from the base" receive explicit negative attention in the CDF's "Some Aspects of the Church Understood as a Communion."[2] Yet Küng and Boff's ecclesiologies at times elaborate upon dimensions of ecclesiology concerning which the CDF's own document could be stronger. To the extent that Küng and Boff ignore or minimize other dimensions necessary for a communion ecclesiology, their own approaches are partial and in need of challenge. Still, what they have to contribute is rich in importance.

I do not wish to speak of Küng and Boff as if their positions are the same. Their overall theologies have many significant differences, with Küng's roots in a contemporary appropriation of Reformation-style theology and Boff's roots in liberation theology. Important elements of their underlying ecclesiologies, however, are deeply similar. Boff's stress on pneumatologically inspired charisms as the basis of the Church has trace-

---

[1]For CDF criticisms of Küng, see *The Küng Dialogue: Facts and Documents* (Washington, DC: United States Catholic Conference, 1980). A collection of documents with commentary more favorable to Küng is Leonard Swidler, ed. *Küng in Conflict* (Garden City, NY: Image/Doubleday, 1981). For CDF criticisms of Boff, see "Doctrinal Congregation Criticizes Brazilian Theologian's Book," *Origins* 14 (April 4, 1985) 683-7. Vatican comments on the two silencings of Boff are found in *Origins* 15 (May 30, 1985) 18 and *Origins* 21 (May 30, 1991) 42.

[2]CDF, Some Aspects of the Church Understood as a Communion," *Origins* 22 (25 June 1992) 108-12.

able roots in Küng. Küng is by far the most frequently cited theologian in Boff's *Ecclesiogenesis*.[3] In recent years Küng has incorporated into his thinking a deep concern for global justice.[4] My contention in this chapter is that, although limitations of their ecclesiologies need to be taken into account, both Küng and Boff have a significant contribution to make to an overall vision of communion ecclesiology. The CDF document, while offering important doctrinal correctives to Küng and Boff, manifests its own particular slant and selective emphasis.

The inclusion of Küng's and Boff's voices takes on special importance in light of Vatican II's thrusts in the directions of ecumenism and social justice. There was something breathtakingly ecumenical, not only about the actual positions articulated in the documents, but also about the Council's spirit of openness and willingness to strike out in new directions. The same is true of Vatican II's treatment of the Church–world relationship. That the Council's spirit of openness can and has been exaggerated by some constitutes a fair judgment. But this fact grants no one license to ignore that spirit. Küng's radically reforming thrust and Boff's deep concern for justice belong in the Catholic Church today as ways of staying honest to certain dimensions of Vatican II.

Yves Congar, in a review of Küng's *The Church* that was in many ways highly critical of Küng's basic approach, called the work "great" and "original," characterized by "an attitude of complete loyalty and honesty with regard to the facts and texts historically considered." He heralded the book as one that "inaugurates a new series of ecumenical research, approaching with freshness and audacity the questions that most divide Christians." He judged that "Küng's constructive contribution is extremely rich," citing among other achievements that Küng "reinserts a spiritual anthropology into ecclesiology." Congar emphasized finally, "I would reject any use of my criticism as an excuse to neglect Küng's immense contribution."[5]

Küng's Contribution to Communion Ecclesiology

Küng's *The Church* (1967) put forth a postconciliar vision that depicted the Church in the early Christian centuries as a charismatic movement of followers of Jesus. Küng's portrait of a dynamically

---

[3]Leonardo Boff, *Ecclesiogenesis: The Base Communities Reinvent the Church*, trans. Robert Barr (Maryknoll, NY: Orbis Books, 1986 [Portuguese orig. 1977]).

[4]Hans Küng, ed., *Yes to a Global Ethic*, non-English articles translated by John Bowden (New York: Continuum, 1996 [German orig. 1995]).

[5]Yves Congar, "Bulletin D'Ecclésiologie (I)," *Revue des Sciences Philosophiques et Théologiques* 53 (October 1969) 693-706. I use here an unpublished translation by R. B. Williams, O.P.

emerging Church guided by the presence of the Spirit is reminiscent of the early Möhler in *Unity in the Church*, though perhaps taken to the extreme the later Möhler feared. The clarity and the passion of the writing, which remains even in the English translation, contributed to the popular and scholarly influence of the work.

The ecumenical force of *The Church* comes through in Küng's view of Jesus Christ as the primary source of revelation, of scripture as the primary expression of Christ's gospel, and of ministerial offices as always in the service of the people of God, never above it. Küng sees the Church as not itself the kingdom of God, but as its herald.[6] It is a "sinful and pilgrim Church" (*Church* 33). The Church is the eschatological community of salvation (*Church* 81). The basic underlying structure of the Church is charismatic; that is, it is based on the gifts given to the community by the Spirit (*Church* 179-85).

Küng takes the position that the "catholic" Church is significantly broader and more inclusive than the Roman Catholic Church. The way he articulates this stance puts him at odds with official Roman Catholicism. Some of his positions stand directly in tension with *Lumen Gentium*. In that document, the Church is the seed of the kingdom (LG 5). Statements about the Church's sinfulness tend to be ambiguous (LG 8). An emphasis is placed upon the need for charisms to be subjected to apostolic authority as expressed in the office of bishops (LG 7).

Küng's contributions to communion ecclesiology lie not so much in what he neglects or denies as in what he affirms. He affirms a Church comprised of disciples of Jesus. He affirms a Church in which the people of God are informed by the Spirit. He affirms a Church that changes in history and that must address the issues of our time. He affirms a Church that must acknowledge its own failings. He affirms a Church called to live out a spirit of humility and service. To the extent that communion ecclesiology involves a growth beyond an overly juridical approach to an emphasis on community through Christ and the Spirit, Küng has a significant contribution to make. Dry as dust versions of communion ecclesiology that spend more time defending institutional structures than seeking out the Spirit amid the people can benefit much from Küng's prodding.

Küng's Deficiencies

Yet Küng himself tends to be dichotomizing and one-sided. He emphasizes charism over against the hierarchy. He has seemed to enjoy tweaking the noses of Church officials in public. More importantly, his version

---

[6]Hans Küng, *The Church* (Garden City, NY: Doubleday, 1967 [German orig. 1967]) 96. Hereafter in text as *Church*.

of communion ecclesiology lacks essential dimensions. In *The Church in Anguish: Has the Vatican Betrayed Vatican II?*, Küng calls for an interpretation of Vatican II that emphasizes the Church as a communio, pluralism in unity, collegiality, ecumenism, and *aggiornamento*.[7] The meaning that Küng gives to "communio," however, shares little in common either with the CDF's meaning or the range of meanings in common theological discussion. Küng restricts "communio" to meaning basically a Church that strives to be egalitarian in its authoritative style. The term for Küng has little to do with the Church as trinitarian, as the Mystical Body of Christ, or as the Communion of Saints. Küng's call for *aggiornamento* is not balanced by an equal call for *ressourcement*.

As Yves Congar pointed out in his review of Küng's *The Church*, Küng not only takes the un-Catholic position of scripture alone, but he finds a canon within the canon of scripture such that he gives priority to early Pauline texts, especially to Corinthians.[8] He tends to treat later developments, even those expressed in the New Testament, as corruptions. This view is contrary to that of Möhler, who affirmed the normativity not just of scripture alone but of the way that the scriptures were received by the Church Fathers and of the way that Church structures and doctrines developed organically in the early centuries. As Congar put it, ". . . interpretation continues in history, with the assistance of the Holy Spirit. This is Tradition, including the major interventions of the pastoral magisterium. . . . Küng does not deny this, but in our opinion he does not take enough account of it."[9]

The approach that Küng took in *The Church* is carried to even further extremes in *Christianity: Essence, History, Future*.[10] Küng continues to object to any positing of an ideal essence of the Church that is disconnected from its actual historical manifestations, including its many dark abominations (such as persecution of Jews). Küng does not directly acknowledge the role of the Holy Spirit in the development of any church structures or doctrines. He holds that structures and doctrines emerged functionally for practical reasons, usually more political than religious or spiritual. Küng will only talk about the so-called real Christianity that exists within the history of this world, and draws its essence from that. He says, "The real essence of Christianity comes about in its perversion." Küng explains:

---

[7]Hans Küng and Leonard Swidler, eds., *The Church in Anguish: Has the Vatican Betrayed Vatican II?* (San Francisco: Harper and Row, 1987 [German orig. 1986]) 14-7.

[8]Congar, "Bulletin D'Ecclésiologie (I)" 697-8.

[9]Ibid., 700.

[10]Hans Küng, *Christianity: Essence, History, Future*, trans. John Bowden (New York: Continuum, 1995 [German orig. 1994]). Hereafter in text as *Christianity*.

In all the negative factors at which criticism of the church rightly takes offence and which an idealistic admiration happily disguises, we do not simply have the expression of an historical "form" of Christianity. That would be to trivialize the evil in Christianity. Is the positive to be identified with the abiding "essence" and the negative with the fleeting "form"? No, inconvenient though this is, we also have to take seriously the negative element in the church, the perversion of Christianity. And this perversion of Christianity conflicts with its essence, although it is dependent on it. It is not the legitimate essence of Christianity but its illegitimate essence, not its authentic essence but its perverted essence. As a dark shadow this perversion runs alongside the essence of Christianity through all historical forms. (*Christianity* 9)

Küng holds that the only teaching that defines the authentic essence of Christianity is belief in Jesus. A church is simply a community of those who believe in Christ. Each local church fully represents the whole Church. There is no doctrine of the Trinity in the New Testament, and so churches are not to be bound by it. Non-Chalcedonian, monophysite churches should be recognized as being fully Christian. The development of christological and trinitarian dogma that was expressed at Chalcedon in 451 was politically motivated and controlled by the emperor. It is this weak formulation of doctrine, claims Küng, that made Christianity so powerless in the face of Islam with its simple teaching of one God brought by a prophet in line with the prophet Jesus. Such are positions that Küng holds.

Küng holds further that the manner in which the papacy developed in Roman Catholicism represented "Roman power politics in the name of the apostle Peter" (*Christianity* 310). Roman Catholicism developed as a political system, opposed by the Orthodox and by the Reformers, and in discontinuity with the earlier Christian Church. Küng ends his book with a call for a global humanistic ethic in the name of Christianity. He assures his readers that the Spirit still maintains the community of believers, though often in spite of the errors of the leaders. Küng's demystification of the Church represents, in my judgment, a Protestant-style extreme. The Roman Catholic Church is for him purely a human and political reality, not in any way theological in itself.

Yet one would be hard pressed to deny that within his not always consistent[11] perspective Küng points out many things that are all too true. His work can be read as a development of a line in de Lubac's *Catholicism*: "Catholicism has unfortunately at times been narrow, in

---

[11]Catherine Mowry LaCugna points out the inconsistency of Küng's use of "tradition" in *The Theological Methodology of Hans Küng* (Chico, CA: Scholars Press, 1982) 197-8.

direct opposition to what it is supposed to be."[12] It can be read as a concrete rendering of Balthasar's admission that "there is no end of Christian abominations."[13] Balthasar himself, in an essay highly critical of Küng, acknowledged nonetheless, "With regard to many of the subjects that are raised one says with a sigh of relief: 'At last things are being called by their proper name.'"[14] Küng, however, holds that these admissions of those he judges to be idealizers such as de Lubac and Balthasar are not enough, because they do not do anything to bring about needed changes in the Roman system.

In spite of Küng's at times negative impact, his approach can serve as an important corrective to versions of communion ecclesiology that tend to overstress the ideal to the neglect of the concrete historical. Also, his approach can help to counteract uses of communion ecclesiology that mystify believers and legitimate power structures without effective reference to the mystery of Christian revelation. His work, moreover, serves as a challenge to those who identify the "catholic" and the "Roman Catholic" without sufficient nuance. Küng's work, despite its one-sidedness and exaggerations, raises questions that help bring to consciousness some of the real problems in the Church today, problems as real as the divisiveness that he and others, both those with him and those against him, help to sustain.

Boff's Contribution to Communion Ecclesiology

It is somewhat unfortunate that Boff wrote his major books on ecclesiology[15] within a significantly different frame of reference than his book on Mary[16] and his book on the Trinity.[17] The former

[12]Henri de Lubac, *Catholicism*, trans. Lancelot C. Sheppard (London: Burns and Oates, 1950 [French orig. 1938]) 169.

[13]Hans Urs von Balthasar, *New Elucidations*, trans. Sister Mary Theresilde Skerr (San Francisco: Ignatius Press, 1996 [German orig. 1979]) 282. As quoted in Oakes, *Pattern of Redemption*, 321.

[14]Hans Urs von Balthasar, "The Task Imposed by Our Heritage," in *Hans Küng: His Work and His Way*, ed. Hermann Häring and Karl-Josef Kuschel, trans. Robert Nowell, 65-6 (Garden City, NY: Image/Doubleday, 1980); orig. from *Civitas* 23 (1967-68) 450-4.

[15]Leonardo Boff, *Church: Charism and Power*, trans. John W. Diercksmeier (New York: Crossroad, 1985 [Portuguese orig. 1981] and Leonardo Boff, *Ecclesiogenesis: The Base Communities Reinvent the Church*, trans. Robert R. Barr (Maryknoll, NY: Orbis Books, 1986 [Portuguese orig. 1977]).

[16]Leonardo Boff, *The Maternal Face of God: The Feminine and Its Religious Expressions*, trans. Robert R. Barr and John W. Diercksmeier (San Francisco: Harper and Row, 1987 [Portuguese orig. 1979]).

[17]Leonardo Boff, *Trinity and Society*, trans. Paul Burns (Maryknoll, NY:

express positions very similar to those of Küng, and have all of Küng's power and promise as well as all of his deficiencies. The latter engage Boff on topics of popular devotion and relationality that draw more directly upon his Latin American heritage and have more natural points of intersection with other versions of communion ecclesiology.

Many of the positions that Boff takes in *Church: Charism and Power* hearken back to Küng. The Church has most fundamentally a charismatic structure: "Charism is more basic than the institution."[18] The Church is guided by the Spirit, and so, instead of being bound to past positions, is called to make new decisions in response to new situations. The events through which the Church commingled with the Roman Empire in the fourth century constitute only a story of corruption, not of growth in the Spirit. The present-day hierarchy abuses human rights within the Church, especially those of women and of dissenting theologians. The powers at large in the Church today need to be converted from the power of domination to the power of love.

Boff's Küngian approach in his explicitly ecclesiological works classifies as a version of communion ecclesiology because of its focus on community as a means to move beyond juridicism.[19] The strong emphasis on the Spirit and on charism represents one important thrust of Vatican II. Unfortunately, Boff also continues Küng's tendency to dichotomize charism and institution, to bait the hierarchy publicly, and to underplay many dimensions of the Church that are essential to communion ecclesiology's fuller vision. I refer here not only to the hierarchical dimensions, which Boff acknowledges always with a twist of displeasure, but also to the aesthetic and ideal dimensions of what it means to be Church, that mysterious dimension of the Church that finds expression in images and symbols drawn from the scriptures.

Boff departs from the early Küng in these ecclesiological texts in his strong stress on social justice. (Küng makes great strides on this point in his later works.) For Boff, the change from the power of domination to the power of love must include a dimension of social transformation. To "liberate" the people within the system without changing the social structures that oppress them would be the equivalent of "liberating" people within a prison. Yes, their conditions are improved, but they are still imprisoned. Truly to liberate people would be to transform the social and economic structures that bind

---

Orbis Books, 1988 [Portuguese orig. 1986]). Hereafter in text as *Trinity*.

[18] Boff, *Church: Charism and Power*, 159.

[19] See especially Boff's discussion of the contrast between a juridical model and a community model in Boff, *Ecclesiogenesis*, 23-33.

them.[20] This link between ecclesiology and justice is critical to any complete vision of communion ecclesiology. Whether or not one buys Boff's particular presuppositions about what would constitute social and economic liberation, the link between communion within the Church and the social and economic implications for life in the world are given serious treatment by him.

Boff on Mary and the Trinity

Strikingly little of the language of love and spirituality and intimacy and relationality makes it into Boff's works on ecclesiology when compared with his works on Mary and the Trinity. These latter works are permeated with basic communion ecclesiology words and concepts. *The Maternal Face of God* and *Trinity and Society* reveal Boff's faith and theology to be much more deeply multi-dimensional than displayed in his more Küngian works. In these works Boff is more concerned with mining and articulating and exploring the riches of the Christian tradition than with questions about who makes decisions and how the structure of the Church should be conceived. For all of their anti-institutionalism, *Church: Charism and Power* and *Ecclesiogenesis* remain mired within the sphere outlined by the juridical abuses against which they are railing. The works on Mary and the Trinity, in contrast, manifest the same strong focus on social liberation, but add to that a theological and devotional liberation by tapping more deeply into the depths of the Christian faith.

In *The Maternal Face of God*, Boff adds to his incisive analytical abilities an expression of his strong belief in the person of Mary and in her traditional privileges. Not all of his interpretations are "traditional," and the links that he forges between Marian theology and liberation are fresh and dynamic. Yet the reality that one is confronted here by an author who is a serious Catholic believer is palpable. And this reality carries over in that book to the way that Boff speaks about the Church:

> The Church is that portion of humanity that has explicitly accepted the gift of salvation in Jesus Christ: the *communitas fidelium*. Mary stands in a unique relationship with this humanity that has directed its life toward the following and discipleship of her Son in the power of the Spirit. Just as she engenders Christ, she continues to engender Christians. And they are engendered in the same power of the Spirit dwelling within her. That is why Mary is proclaimed Mother of the Church. But that is not all. The entire Church, the community of the

---

[20]Boff, *Church: Charism and Power*, 135.

faithful and the people of God *in via*, is invited to live divine grace more purely, and with a greater determination, and thus to actualize the new being inaugurated in the persons of Mary and Jesus. This is the basic calling of the Church.[21]

One wonders if this passage had appeared instead in *Church: Charism and Power*, and if the style and tone of the rest of the work were adjusted accordingly, how different Boff's overall ecclesiological vision might sound.

The language of communion is also very prominent in *Trinity and Society*. The very premise of the book is that the Trinity constitutes a perichoretic communion that provides a model for how Church and society should be conceived. Boff's deep beliefs and religious sensibility come through:

> We are not condemned to live alone, cut off from one another; we are called to live together and to enter into the communion of the Trinity. Society is not ultimately set in its unjust and unequal relationships, but summoned to transform itself in the light of the open and egalitarian relationships that obtain in the communion of the Trinity, the goal of social and historical progress. If the Trinity is good news, then it is so particularly for the oppressed and those condemned to solitude. (*Trinity* 158)

Somewhat in contrast to Boff's more explicitly ecclesiological works, *Trinity and Society* emphasizes the relational and grace-filled dimensions of the Church while still making clear the link between ecclesial communion and social justice. The Church is the "sacrament of trinitarian communion," called to uproot injustices within itself and within the world. For Boff, "The universe exists in order to manifest the abundance of divine communion" (*Trinity* 237).

The CDF on "Some Aspects" of Communion Ecclesiology

The CDF, in naming the 1992 document on communion ecclesiology, "Some Aspects of the Church Understood as a Communion," signaled its intention that the relatively brief text not be taken as a complete expression of communion ecclesiology in all of its dimensions. The purpose of the document was not to attempt to give a balanced, overall account of all of the aspects of communion ecclesiology; rather, it was to highlight selectively elements that the CDF judged to be neglected or ignored in current theological discussion. If it was

---

[21]Boff, *The Maternal Face of God*, 164-5.

intended to achieve a long-range balance, it was not by being balanced itself but by loading up one side of the scales in a situation where the scales were perceived to be loaded in the opposite direction.

For the most part, the document raises issues critical to the Catholic tradition and is theologically sound in what it affirms. A possible exception to this, in my opinion, is the way the CDF configures the relationship of the Church universal with the local churches, giving clear and exclusive priority to the former. I find more tenable the position of Joseph Komonchak that the relationship between the Church universal and the local churches is a more complex one of mutual interdependency in which each arises out of the other.[22] The importance of this issue is not to be underestimated. It has strong implications for church authority, inculturation, and ecumenism.

One way to try to understand the CDF's approach to communion ecclesiology is to ask: What does it rule out? The CDF's use of communion ecclesiology can be compared with the function of Chalcedon's teaching that Jesus is one person with two natures, human and divine. Although its teaching does not carry anything like the weight or the authority of Chalcedon, it is in some senses similar in form and style. Chalcedon's teaching does as much to spell out negative boundaries that should not be violated as it does to spell out positively how Jesus is to be understood and imagined. The teaching could be presented as saying: Do not speak of Jesus as if he were not fully divine; at the same time, do not speak of Jesus as if he were not fully human. The doctrine leaves open many possible ways to understand and imagine Jesus as long as the basic boundaries are not crossed. But it clearly rules out any understandings that would constitute a denial of either Jesus' full humanity or of his full divinity.

I will formulate the points addressed by the CDF in "Some Aspects" as negative principles. I want to be clear that this is not the way these principles appear in the document, but a way of trying to get at their implications. I divide them into categories that try to bring out some of the weighting and selectivity of the document:

Points Highlighted and Stressed as Correcting Current Errors

1. Do not speak of the Church as though it were simply a human means of organization that is not intrinsically bound up with God and revelation.
2. Do not speak of the Church as though it concerns only people currently living and does not, as the communion of saints, provide real links with those who have died before us.
3. Do not speak of the Church as though it were simply a feder-

---

[22]Joseph A. Komonchak, "The Local Church," *Chicago Studies* 28 (1989) 320-35.

ation made up of local churches without recognizing the sense in which the Church universal, born at Pentecost, precedes all local churches.

4. Do not speak of the church as though the Eucharist were not intrinsic to it.
5. Do not speak of the Church as though the episcopacy were not intrinsic to it.
6. Do not speak of the Church as though its unity and diversity are mutually opposed rather than complementary.
7. Do not speak of the Church as though the Petrine ministry were imposed from without rather than representing a constituting principle of each local church as such.
8. Do not speak of the Catholic Church as though it were incomplete in its very essence as are other churches.

Thus, the CDF document on communion ecclesiology rules out approaches to the Church that are reductionistic; that ignore the transcendent or mystical elements of the Church; that downplay the role of the Church universal, the Eucharist, and the episcopacy; and that deny the special status of the pope or of the Catholic Church.

There are yet other elements in the document that, while not necessarily being directed at current errors, help to lay out the fundamental context of what communion ecclesiology is. These points are very important in the document, close if not equal to the first eight. I again phrase them negatively in terms of what they rule out:

Points That Lay Out the Basic Context

9. Do not speak of the Church in a way that denies its core as being the personal union of each human being with the divine Trinity.
10. Do not speak of the Church as though its inner unity can be considered completely apart from a larger human solidarity.
11. Do not speak of the Church in a way that disregards its foundations in scripture and in the patristic witness.
12. Do not speak of the Church in such a way that denies either its present pilgrim status or its eschatological fulfillment.
13. Do not speak of the Church in a way that denies the central role of Mary at its heart.

There are yet more points that express elements of communion ecclesiology that are acknowledged or mentioned or alluded to or conceded, but not specially affirmed or stressed or highlighted. I consider these to be "Other Aspects" of communion ecclesiology, ones that in another context could potentially receive fuller treatment:

Points Acknowledged or Mentioned or Conceded

14. Do not speak of the Church as though it were completely transcendent with no concrete, historical, and changing dimensions, including the ways in which its doctrines, sacraments, and authoritative structures have been expressed.
15. Do not speak of the Church as though local churches were simply particular manifestations of a pre-existing Church universal, without also emphasizing the sense in which they have their own completeness.
16. Do not speak of the Church as though its unity were static and given solely from its hierarchical nature without attention to the dynamic interplay between the local churches and the Church universal.
17. Do not speak of the church as though other ecclesial bodies do not share some degree of communion with the Catholic Church through the unity of the Holy Spirit.
18. Do not speak of the Church as though its journey toward the eschaton does not include integrally the current social concerns of human beings.

The range of concerns expressed in these eighteen points represents in a reasonably full manner concerns associated with communion ecclesiology. These concerns are of staggering importance. However, the selection, proportion, and nuance of the way these points are expressed reflect also particular concerns of the CDF at a particular time in history.

The CDF is evidently more distressed at this time about theological positions that underplay the Church universal than those that underplay the local churches; about those that deny the transcendent dimensions of the Church than those that deny its historical concreteness; about those that minimize the status of the Catholic Church in relation to other churches rather than those that overemphasize it; and about those that threaten the internal structure of the Church than those that stress its interrelatedness with the world.

The larger tradition of communion ecclesiology, however, has been to stress simultaneously the balance and synthesis among all of these elements of the Church. The CDF's own document serves as an illustration of Ratzinger's point that particular versions of communion ecclesiology can differ in what is stressed or highlighted. The CDF document is accurate in what it implies that communion ecclesiology rules out; it could potentially be followed up, however, by a balancing document stressing the *Other Aspects* of communion ecclesiology, emphasizing more than in the present document elements such as points fourteen through eighteen listed above.

The CDF Critique of Boff[23]

How does Boff appear under the lens of the CDF's version of communion ecclesiology? In 1985 the CDF published a list of complaints about Boff's *Church: Charism and Power*.[24] A re-examination of that document reveals that at every point the charges can be boiled down to claims that the principles of the CDF version of communion ecclesiology have been violated. The document identifies the underlying issue as Boff's praxis approach to truth. If truth can in no sense pre-exist experience, then truth must emerge anew in each concrete situation. If such were the case, then the Church universal with its Deposit of Faith could not be recognized as prior to any particular local church. Base communities, such as the politically activist prayer groups of Latin America, could then be taken to be the initiating cells of "Church."

In the view of Cardinal Ratzinger and the CDF, however, base communities, although they contain "ecclesial elements," cannot be called "Church" in the proper sense. This is because base communities do not belong in a full sense to the Church's essential constitution that requires a global network of eucharistic communities united through the bishops that regulate them. Base communities can potentially represent partisan concerns that might exclude people of different political persuasions. For Ratzinger, "Church" in the full sense of the term would have to be open in principle, for example, to both a Nicaraguan Contra and a Sandinista of good faith. At least to the outside observer, it does not appear that base communities are always open in this regard.

The CDF document on *Church: Charism and Power* also complained about what it labeled Boff's "ecclesiological relativism." Boff is charged with holding that Catholicism and Protestantism each represent an incomplete mediation of Christianity and that each needs the other for a dialectical fullness. This position is taken to be in contradiction to *Lumen Gentium's* statement that the "Church of Christ . . . subsists in the Catholic Church" (8). In other words, Vatican II articulated the position that the Catholic Church has a certain fullness that other churches lack. Other churches are thus not in full communion with the Catholic Church. On a practical or concrete historical level the Catholic Church may be lacking, but in an essential or ideal sense it has the fullest possi-

---

[23]Studies of the Boff-CDF relationship are Harvey Cox, *The Silencing of Leonardo Boff: The Vatican and the Future of World Christianity* (Oak Park, IL: Meyer-Stone Books, 1988) and Mark Delisi, *Ecclesiological Divergence and Convergence: A Study of How the Congregation for the Doctrine of the Faith and Leonardo Boff Understand the Hierarchy* (Dayton: University of Dayton Master's Thesis, 1993).

[24]Sacred Congregation for the Doctrine of the Faith, "Doctrinal Congregation Criticizes Brazilian Theologian's Book," *Origins* 14 (4 April 1985) 683-7.

ble set of tools for salvation. From this point of view, because Boff implies that the Catholic Church is essentially incomplete like any other denomination, he appears to be in violation of the CDF's principles.

A further complaint of the CDF concerned what they perceive as Boff's reductionist treatment of the sacraments in *Church: Charism and Power*. Boff offers a Marxist analysis of the role of the hierarchy as the sole possessors of the means of production of grace. The CDF charges that the sacraments and the hierarchy that administers them should never be analyzed as if they were simply human instruments that could be detached from the order of grace.

Charges can and have been made elsewhere that Boff has violated other Catholic principles in his understanding of "transcendence" and in his flat assertion that "charism is more fundamental than the institution."[25] The CDF document on *Church: Charism and Power*, however, does not focus directly on these issues. It ends with a complaint that Boff's denouncing of the Church's hierarchy and institutions goes far beyond the bounds of legitimate criticism.

Is the CDF Right about Boff?

Insofar as Boff tends to launch generalized criticisms of the hierarchy, and insofar as his Church as sacrament of the Holy Spirit appears to move solely from the bottom up, the CDF has had some legitimate grounds for raising questions about Boff's ecclesiology. Boff's portrayal of a Church of the people which, through the base communities, will grow within and eventually replace the old, dying institutional Church, is one-sided and acerbic. Though Boff may have many grounds, both personal and social, for feeling as he does, some of his writings are excessively anti-institutional.

As I have argued, however, the CDF's version of communion ecclesiology has its own limitations. Certain of Boff's strengths, such as his awareness of the Church as the people of God and his emphasis on the link between ecclesiology and justice, lie in the areas where the CDF appears weakest. At Vatican II new concepts regarding history, human freedom and dignity, the relation between the Church and world, the importance of social justice, and the need to dialogue seriously with contemporary movements burst on the scene. Each of these concepts has its own distinguished history leading up to its official recognition and embrace.

Some of Boff's positions on the particular issues that the CDF criticizes can be defended. For example, when Boff speaks of Catholicism and Protestantism as both being incomplete mediations

---

[25]Leonardo Boff, *Church: Charism and Power*, 159.

of Christianity, each needing the other for its fulfillment, Boff is not necessarily contradicting the teaching of *Lumen Gentium* that the "Church of Christ . . . subsists in the Catholic Church," as the CDF would have it. Boff is speaking simply on the level of historical praxis. He refuses to engage in any speech that he considers essentialist. Boff has arguable philosophical reasons for doing so. In traditional Catholic teaching, the Catholic Church *is* incomplete *in practice*; it is only when considered "essentially" that the Church is said to have a fullness of the means of salvation. Boff does not openly deny this; he just thinks it unhelpful to use the essentialist speech necessary to talk about it.

The CDF's rejection of Boff's praxis approach because of certain potential implications is simply too cut and dried. The same is true of Boff's "Marxist" analysis of the sacraments in terms of production and consumption. Of course, taken by itself, such an analysis is "reductionist." But placed within the context of a dialogue in which other, deeper dimensions of the sacraments are also highlighted, such an analysis is interesting and even illuminating.

The CDF displays a tendency to subordinate Vatican II's progressive concerns to the Council's more traditional concerns about inner church community and structure. The CDF's selective reading of Vatican II reveals itself in the footnotes of "Some Aspects of the Church Understood as a Communion." The Dogmatic Constitution on the Church receives thirty-three citations; the more progressive Pastoral Constitution on the Church in the Modern World receives only one, as a general reference among others in the first footnote.

In particular, the CDF's version of communion ecclesiology underplays the structural contribution of local churches in favor of stressing the power of the Church universal. It does this by claiming an unqualified priority, ontologically and temporally, of the Church universal in relation to local churches. Such a position, however, is a bit like insisting that the chicken came before the egg. Joseph Komonchak argues that any attempt to pinpoint the relationship between local churches (dioceses) and the Church universal as one of priority over the other misconstrues the entire problem.[26] *Lumen Gentium* stated that the Church universal arises in and out of the local churches.[27] If Roman authority constitutes part of the essential structure of the Church, then so does diversity and true inculturation. Karl Rahner's argument that the main achievement of Vatican II was the shift from being a Euro-

---

[26]Komonchak, "The Local Church," 320-35.

[27]*Lumen Gentium*, 23. In "Some Aspects," the CDF references this quote, and then complements it with one from John Paul II concerning "the churches formed in and out of the church." Quoted on p. 109 of "Some Aspects" from "Address to the Roman Curia," *Acta Apostolicae Sedis* 83 (1991) 745-7.

pean to a world Church needs to be taken seriously.[28] Boff's theology, for all of its limitations, should be appreciated for its contribution on this count.

A version of communion ecclesiology that strives for more of a balance between the Church universal and the local churches could place more emphasis on progressive aspects of Vatican II. It could be used not just to defend centralized authority but also to champion the need to respect cultures and customs, the need to work for justice, and the need to consult the faith of the entire Church when making important decisions. Under the lens of a more balanced version of communion ecclesiology, Boff's theology would appear quite different. It would still look very particular, very partial, still in need of some challenge and balance. But it might appear less as a heretical denial of essential truths about the structure of the Church and more as a somewhat one-sided affirmation of other crucial elements of that structure. It presents important and useful emphases of which other versions of communion ecclesiology stand in need.

Serious questions can thus be raised about the CDF's opinions concerning Boff's positions. On one level, it is fair to say that to the extent that the CDF is correct about Vatican II and communion ecclesiology, there are legitimate grounds for suspecting that Boff needs to do some hard thinking about whether certain elements of his theology are truly "Catholic." On a deeper level, however, the CDF's particular version of communion ecclesiology, though technically correct on many important points, suffers from a distinct imbalance. It is true that the Council protected the essential structures of the Church; but it is also true that the Council called for serious dialogue with the developing world and its philosophies. What is the proper response to a theology that questions the essential structures of the Church not because it is against the Church but because it is suspicious of anything "essential?"

It is a sad irony that communion ecclesiology, which developed as a tool to overcome an overly juridical concept of the Church, can be put to the technical, juridical use of silencing one of the most inspiring theologians of the Catholic Church today. After being silenced by the CDF for a year in 1985, and then again in 1991, Boff officially announced his resignation from the priesthood and the Franciscan Order on June 28, 1992.[29] Although the comparison some defenders of

---

[28]Karl Rahner, "Towards a Fundamental Theological Interpretation of Vatican II," trans. Leo J. O'Donovan, *Theological Studies* 40 (December 1979) 716-27.

[29]Leonardo Boff, *The Path to Hope: Fragments from a Theologian's Journey*, trans. Phillip Berryman (Maryknoll, NY: Orbis Books, 1993), especially the added "Letter to My Companions on the Journey of Hope," trans. Francis Pimentel-Pinto, 123-9.

Boff make between silencing and the racks and thumbscrews of the Inquisition is ludicrous, nonetheless, as a technique silencing stands in contradiction to legitimate values in the modern world and adds fuel to the fire of those who characterize the Vatican as hopelessly regressive and domineering.

Although several of the challenges raised by the CDF to the ecclesiology of Leonardo Boff were important ones, a more balanced approach to communion ecclesiology on their part might have led to a deeper appreciation for the positive elements of Boff's approach and a more balanced assessment of his work. Boff in particular might be helped if the CDF would pay greater and more positive attention to the dynamic and essential role of local congregations, to the inner unfolding of love within Christian communities, to the concrete, historical dimensions of the Church, to the interconnection between ecclesial well-being and social concerns, and to the role of the hierarchy as holding together legitimate diversity rather than suppressing it.

Conclusion

Catholic theologians such as Küng and Boff need to be included in any conversation concerning what might constitute a full vision of communion ecclesiology expressive of the teaching of Vatican II. Their own versions are lacking, to be sure. On some important points their positions stand in tension with official Catholic teaching. Yet on those points where they get it right, they often get it very right. Communion ecclesiology, to be true to the Council, must maintain a historical dynamism, a sense of the people, a fostering of charisms, a willingness to be self-critical, and a dialogical spirit through which communication and development are anything but a one-way street. These elements need to be promoted with more of a sense of respect for the hierarchy; but promoted they need to be.

Küng represents a whole set of theological positions associated with the Reformation and with contemporary theological appropriations of it. It is better, I believe, to have such voices inside the Roman Catholic Church rather than outside. Vatican II represented the Catholic Church's coming to grips with the Reformation in an open manner that had been unheard of for four hundred years. A case could be made that within the Council's documents, many positions associated with the Reformers did function in positive ways; they were not so much rejected as they were appropriated in a contextual manner. Examples are Luther's teaching on the priesthood of all believers, his emphasis on scripture, and his focus on the Church as a community. The CDF needs to be careful that, when it rejects positions such as Küng's, it does not unwittingly marginalize positions and dynamics important to the Council. Above all, Küng's challenge that to be "catholic" is larger than being "Roman Catholic" needs to be continually reckoned with in an honest and open-minded fashion. Admittedly, Küng also takes many positions that from a Roman Catholic standpoint are out and out erroneous and will never be made compatible with official Church teaching.

Boff, to the extent that he follows Küng, also provides some Reformation-style positions. Where Boff moves beyond Küng, however, I think he provides substantive positions that should be considered constitutive of any attempt to articulate a full vision of communion ecclesiology. Where he speaks of the communion of the Trinity and communion with Mary, there are many potential links with the CDF's approach. Where he speaks of the connection between communion and justice, he is providing needed emphasis on elements fundamental to any ecclesiology worthy of Vatican II.

NINE

Communion on the Borders

Elizabeth A. Johnson and Roberto Goizueta

Communion ecclesiology by definition embraces a significant degree of diversity. Its unity is not to be a mere uniformity imposed from above. The Church universal is formed in and out of local churches, just as local churches are formed in and out of the Church universal. Communion ecclesiology, to be what it is supposed to be, must be traceable not only in the mainstream and the establishment and among the well-heeled, but also on the margins and the borders and among the poorly shod. In this chapter I examine recent works by two Catholic theologians who identify themselves as operating on the margins: feminist theologian Elizabeth A. Johnson and U.S. Hispanic theologian Roberto Goizueta. I explore the extent to which concerns associated with communion ecclesiology, such as *ressourcement*, trinitarian spirituality, iconic awareness, and a relational vision of the Church might be found in these works.

The categories of "communion" and "relationality" are central to the works we will consider. Johnson's *She Who Is* offers a feminist perspective on talk about God.[1] Her more recent *Friends of God and Prophets* is a contemporary retrieval of the image of the "Communion of Saints."[2] Goizueta's *Caminemos con Jesús* offers a U.S. Hispanic perspective on fundamental questions in theology.[3] Each of these books manifests the combination of being both representative of an identifiable approach

---

[1]Elizabeth A. Johnson, *She Who Is: The Mystery of God in Feminist Theological Discourse* (New York: Crossroad, 1996). Hereafter in text as *SWI*.

[2]Elizabeth A. Johnson, *Friends of God and Prophets: A Feminist Theological Reading of the Communion of Saints* (New York: Continuum, 1998). Hereafter in text as *FGP*.

[3]Roberto S. Goizueta, *Caminemos con Jesús: Toward a Hispanic/Latino Theology of Accompaniment* (Maryknoll, NY: Orbis Books, 1995). Hereafter in text as *CCJ*.

and yet groundbreaking in its own right. Each book can serve as a good test case of whether the category of "communion ecclesiology" can be useful for understanding voices on the margins.

I will be especially interested in a comparison of these voices with figures associated with communion ecclesiology. Because Hans Urs von Balthasar is so associated with the contemporary communio movement, I will pay special attention to connections with his work. I will also bring into the discussion the document on communion ecclesiology of the Sacred Congregation for the Doctrine of the Faith (CDF) in order to explore whether Johnson and Goizueta might offer something of value to complement the congregation's approach.[4]

Elizabeth A. Johnson's Catholic Feminist Approach

Johnson's *She Who Is* and *Friends of God and Prophets* can both legitimately be read as contributing to a Catholic theology of communion. In terms reminiscent of Zizioulas's *Being as Communion*,[5] Johnson claims that "being in communion constitutes God's very essence" (*SWI* 227).[6] Johnson finds a relatedness at the heart of all reality, "a mystery of personal connectedness"(*SWI* 228). The Triune God emerges in the conclusion of *She Who Is*, as the indicator that relatedness, mutuality and equality, and the outpouring of compassionate, liberating love lie at the core of all. The "isolated patriarchal God of the Enlightenment" is overcome by a community in diversity whose mutual interaction can be imaged as a *perichoresis*, like a joyous, revolving dance (*SWI* 220-1). Understood in this way, the Trinity can function "as a model of mutual love stressing the equality of all persons" (*SWI* 196). In *Friends of God and Prophets*, Johnson explores the Communion of Saints as "a Christian symbol of profound relationship" (*FGP* 7). She names the Communion of Saints finally as "the experience of persons connected to one another in virtue of being connected to the sacred mystery at the heart of the world" (*FGP* 262). To be a person is to be a person in relationship; relationship is understood as being ontological, not as an add-on to a previously complete reality. Johnson detects not a detached, above-it-all God, but a God who is related, a compassionate God who suffers.

Johnson's approach is similar to the combination of *ressourcement*

---

[4]Sacred Congregation for the Doctrine of the Faith, "Some Aspects of the Church Understood as a Communion," *Origins* 22 (25 June 1992) 108-12.

[5]John Zizioulas, *Being as Communion: Studies in Personhood and the Church* (Crestwood, NY: St. Vladimir's Press, 1985).

[6]Johnson does not cite Zizioulas in *She Who Is*, but she does cite theologians whose work evidences contact with Zizioulas, such as Catherine Mowry LaCugna and William Hill. See also *FGP*, 193-4.

and *aggiornamento* associated with Henri de Lubac.[7] De Lubac himself, in *Catholicism*, was exceedingly clear that any *ressourcement* must be performed very critically. There is much in the Church Fathers that cannot simply be retrieved without a lot of hard sorting and editing.[8] And de Lubac also argued explicitly that any retrieval must take place in dialogue with the particular questions of a particular time. Johnson is not merely going beyond a scholastic synthesis to retrieve scriptural and patristic sources, but she is reading the entire range of Christian sources with the intention of working through its patriarchal garb toward a revelation of a God of mutuality and equality. She employs the feminist hermeneutical key of asking how a particular source of revelation contributes to "the emancipation of women toward human flourishing" (*SWI* 30). She thus uncovers a sometimes hidden communion of relationality and mutuality interwoven in traditional sources.

Although Johnson does not dwell for long on the Church either as spiritual community or as institution, she can be read as one who applies the categories of trinitarian communion and the Communion of Saints directly to the human community without a strong emphasis on the explicit mediation of the Church. Most current versions of communion ecclesiology begin with the Church and then move on to consider the world. In contrast, and in a way I find similar to the Himes brothers, Johnson finds Trinity, community, relationality, and the grace that leads to human flourishing already present in the world. She explores deeply the implications of communion for human solidarity. Furthermore she tackles the critically important issue of the communion between women and men, which *Gaudium et Spes* called, "the first form of the communion of persons"(12), yet which is often neglected in current versions of communion ecclesiology. In *Friends of God and Prophets*, Johnson explicitly emphasizes the inclusive extension of communion not only to all human beings who are currently alive, and not only to all who have died, but also to "other living creatures, ecosystems, and the whole natural world itself" (*FGP* 240).

A Balthasarian Critique and Appreciation of Johnson

Johnson cites Balthasar several times in *She Who Is* and once in *Friends of God and Prophets*, always favorably, though in one instance she adds to one of his insights the feminist position that maleness is not

---

[7]For an exploration of these terms, see M. D'Ambrosio, "*Ressourcement* Theology, *Aggiornamento*, and the Hermeneutics of Tradition." *Communio* 18 (Winter 1991) 530-55.

[8]Henri de Lubac, *Catholicism*, trans. Lancelot C. Sheppard (London: Burns and Oates, 1950 [French orig. 1938]) 173.

constitutive of the essence of the Christ (*SWI* 164, n. 25). It seems to be part of Johnson's theological method to cite all of her sources as positively and favorably as possible, even those with which she obviously has some disagreements. She does not directly criticize Balthasar, though given her analysis of the patriarchal difficulties that come from men's theological speculations concerning gender, one suspects that she could have done so. I am thinking in particular of the way that Johnson speaks of the limitations and oppressiveness of romantic idealizations of motherhood and of constricting women's roles by confining them symbolically to motherhood and virginity (*SWI* 176). But the majority of Johnson's references draw upon Balthasar, quite accurately, as a defender of the ultimate incomprehensibility of God, as a promoter of the analogical nature of God-talk, and as one who supports hope in a universal salvation (*SWI* 107, 11; *FGP* 191-2).

The spirit of the "hypothetical" critique I am about to formulate can best be gleaned from Balthasar's *Love Alone*.[9] I find also Benedict Ashley's critique of Johnson to be cast in a Balthasarian fashion. Ashley associates Johnson's methods with a Rahnerian approach, and he criticizes her for holding "women's flourishing" to be the ultimate criterion of truth. Ashley rejects Johnson's radical egalitarianism, her stress on the unknowability of God, and what he takes to be her "docetic" Christology.[10]

I will point out a few general lines along which any Balthasarian critique might travel. Johnson could be depicted as one who commits the cardinal sin of subjecting the revelation of God to merely human, subjective criteria. She could be taken as one who places a feminist vision of radical egalitarianism over and above the word of God. She explores at length the implicit presence of the Holy Spirit in the world and in human experience before ever treating the explicit presence of the Spirit in Christianity. She could be accused of minimizing the extent to which the sources of revelation themselves, although always as bearers of the melody and not the melody itself, reveal the melody through their very concrete particularities. To edit out anything as non-revelatory that may appear patriarchal may prevent one from appreciating ways in which distinctive gender roles can be liberating. Revelation is not to be authenticated according to whether it matches our own ideas of what we think it should be. More authenticating would be the evidence that revelation itself has shattered one's categories, has brought to bear the unexpected, has taught one the true meaning of love.

I want to be clear that I am in no way claiming that Balthasar himself

---

[9]Hans Urs von Balthasar, *Love Alone*, ed. and trans. Alexander Dru (New York: Herder and Herder, 1969 [German orig. 1963]).

[10]Benedict Ashley, *Justice in the Church: Gender and Participation* (Washington, DC: Catholic University of America Press, 1996) 189-206.

would have said these things specifically about Johnson, though I have to suspect that a few of them might have crossed his mind in her regard. But to simply leave it at that would represent a one-sided reading of Johnson that would not be characteristically Balthasarian. I raise these charges because as I point to areas of convergence between Johnson and Balthasar, I do not intend to suggest that a full reconciliation of their positions would be easy or even possible. But I do find connections between the two that are real and important and that reflect concerns commonly associated with communion ecclesiology.

Although Johnson's critique of the Kantian turn to the subject is not as final as Balthasar's, she maintains her distance from that turn, citing its restriction of theological knowledge to human phenomena and its inattention to what Metz has called the "Alps experience" of being enraptured by the beauty of nature. And, although it is true that Johnson can be read as holding feminist criteria over and above Christian revelation, she could also be read more sympathetically and with some accuracy as using the impact on women's flourishing as a tool for freeing scripture and tradition from cultural baggage that binds them, in order to unleash their transcendent, revelatory power. Johnson uses her feminist criterion, not simply to stand over and judge the sources, but as a standpoint from which to enter into the sources and open up what they have to offer. In spite of obvious differences, it is quintessentially Balthasarian to mine the tradition in a way that upsets conventional understandings.

It is in her playful and adventurous exploration of images that Johnson is most reminiscent of Balthasar. And although she draws upon extra-ecclesial human experience perhaps more significantly than Balthasar would like, when she turns her attention to the tradition, she meets some of Balthasar's most important criteria. She is trinitarian to the core, and in her christology she reads the event of Jesus always against the background of the Old Testament. She is interested not in abstracting images from their historical context, but in exploring "the whole theological significance of what transpires in the Christ event" (*SWI* 167). She finds in the New Testament a Jesus who shatters our pre-conceived categories about what the mystery of God's love is like (*SWI* 169). And she discovers a Spirit who is both immanent and transcendent, one who is "not amenable to human manipulation or exploitation" (*SWI* 145). Her reading of the Communion of Saints includes a prayerful listening to stories of typical personages in scripture such as Hagar and Mary Magdelan (*FGP* 144-50). Her feminist retrieval of traditional sources involves a fresh reading of biblical images as applied to God such as Sophia and Mother.

Johnson's description of the *perichoresis* of the Trinity has something of a Balthasarian flare:

> Casting the metaphor in yet another direction, we can say that the eternal flow of life is stepped to the contagious rhythm of spicy salsas, merengues, calypsos, or reggaes where dancers in free motion are yet bonded in the music. (*SWI* 221)

In a recent article, Johnson names approvingly a wide range of the types of metaphors that are increasingly being used to talk about God. Again, the Balthasarian flavor is evident:

> God is like a master theatrical improviser in live performance, amplifying and embroidering each theme as it presents itself; like a choreographer composing steps in tandem with the creative insights of the whole dance troupe; like a composer of a fugue, starting with a simple line of melody and weaving a complex structure by endlessly folding it back upon itself; like a jazz player, inspired by the spirit of the audience and the night to improvise riffs upon a basic melody; like a designer who sets the rules of a game that includes wildcards and then lets it play.[11]

What is common here between Johnson and Balthasar is not just their penchant for exploring images in connection with divine revelation but their particular manner and style of doing it. Their appropriation of traditional images is creative and daring and fascinating. They treat stories from scripture not just as providing examples of revelation but as expressing revelation in and through their concrete, particular details. Their exploration of stories and images is for them not simply an application of theology, but constitutes the very doing of theology.

Johnson is obviously deeply influenced by Rahner in emphasizing the presence of grace in the world in a manner not always at every moment explicitly linked with Christianity. Like Rahner, Johnson uses a method that correlates Christian revelation with the contemporary cultural situations of human beings. Like Rahner, the "pastoral" theologian, Johnson never fails to tie her metaphysical speculations to practical questions that human beings face. But more than Rahner, however, and in the direction of Balthasar, Johnson allows the study of the concrete particularities of Christian revelation expressed in scripture to have a determinative and grounding impact on her theological understanding. When Johnson is mining and gleaning from the scriptures, she is not simply finding examples of what is true always and everywhere about the graced character of existence in relation to a God who is absolute mystery. This is not to say that this characterization would be completely fair to Rahner either, and in fact it is not. It is to say, how-

---

[11]Elizabeth A. Johnson, "Does God Play Dice? Divine Providence and Chance," *Theological Studies* 57 (1996) 17-8.

ever, that Johnson is less susceptible to such a charge because of the way that she listens to the concrete details of scriptural stories and incorporates them into her theological vision. Rahner has a tendency to explore symbols more concretely in homilies than in theology; for Johnson such exploration is more basic to theology itself.

Balthasar is known for a certain liberty, even a purposeful looseness, in his interpretation of images and in his openness to new revelatory insights mediated by the human imagination when sufficiently open to the transcendence of the Word. This opening up of the universe of religious images over against academic approaches that often tend to be dry and mundane is a project in which Balthasar and Johnson share. As Johnson puts it, "Sister scholars uncover alternative ways of speaking about divine mystery that have long been hidden in Scripture and tradition" (*SWI* 5). It is a key element in the development of a communion ecclesiology that pays serious attention to the mystery of God.

Roberto Goizueta's U.S. Hispanic Catholic Approach

Like Elizabeth A. Johnson's recent books, Roberto Goizueta's *Caminemos con Jesús* can be read as a contemporary Catholic theology of communion. At first glance it might appear to contain elements in sharp contrast to a Balthasarian approach, for Goizueta offers what could be labeled a theology of liberation. In the final analysis, however, the points of comparison with Balthasar are very strong. Goizueta's perspective as a U.S. Hispanic theologian, which he defines in many ways as "in-between," serves also as a corrective to some Latin American versions of liberation theology. This corrective, I will argue, moves distinctly in the direction of Balthasar.[12]

Comparison with Liberation Theology

Goizueta's liberation approach is most evidenced in his final chapter where he argues passionately for a preferential option for the poor. The universality of God's love calls for the recognition that, if God truly loves all, God must have a special concern for those who are suffering and impoverished. Without justice, which must include the overcoming

---

[12]In a recent article, Goizueta acknowledges a possible parallel with Balthasar's aesthetic approach, but he remains very cautious about Balthasar's lack of a strong grounding in the option for the poor. See Roberto S. Goizueta, "U.S. Hispanic Popular Catholicism as Theopoetics," in *Hispanic/Latino Theology: Challenge and Promise*, ed. Ada María Isasi-Díaz and Fernando F. Segovia, 261-88 (Minneapolis: Fortress Press, 1996) 267, n. 21.

of economic oppression, there can be no authentic pluralism based on a dialogue of equal parties.

Goizueta, however, while recognizing that liberation theology itself exists in many forms, gently criticizes those versions that he thinks tend to be too influenced by Enlightenment concepts of rationality and by Marxist concepts of praxis. For some, liberation becomes too exclusively limited to the material realm and is seen as something that can be produced or achieved by human action. As Goizueta puts it, "To reduce human action to social transformation is to reduce it to productive activity, which is to reduce it to technique; and to reduce human action to technique is to reduce the human person to but a passive object, a mere instrument of production" (CCJ 84). Some liberation theologians, moreover, have tended to undervalue popular religion. As Goizueta makes these critiques, he acknowledges that many liberation theologians have been growing beyond these difficulties, and he quotes theologians such as Gustavo Gutiérrez, not as examples of the problems but as examples of how liberation theologians have themselves been wrestling in positive ways with these issues.

Still, Goizueta holds that his own U. S. Hispanic standpoint offers a distinctive perspective. Some of that distinctiveness lies in:

1. his treasuring of popular religion;
2. his clear affirmation of a positive link between popular and institutional expressions of religion;
3. his giving central place to beauty and to a theory of aesthetics;
4. his inclusion of not just material deprivation but also cultural alienation among the forms of poverty to be addressed;
5. his focusing not just on economic liberation but also on liberation as the fostering of personal relationships among human beings with God.

This focus on relationships provides the main connection between Goizueta's theology and communion ecclesiology. Like Johann Adam Möhler in *Unity in the Church*, Goizueta places his initial emphasis on the relationship among God and human beings that exists within local liturgical communities. The unity in the Church is first of all the bondedness in love that values rather than erases diversity. In a way reminiscent of Möhler's depiction of a love that grows organically as it expands to create more communities, Goizueta focuses on the love that exists in concrete, particular, local communities. He finds connections with the universal grounded always in the ability of local communities to recognize commonalities in and through their own particularities.

To illustrate this last point, Goizueta poses the question of how one can come to know what marriage is (CCJ 97). It would not be by engaging in as many marriages as possible in order to arrive at a universal notion abstracted from one's many experiences. The way, rather, would be to enter as deeply as possible into one marriage, and to come to know the universal through the experience of the particular. From the depth of one's own marital relationship one can recognize commonalities with other marriages, and thus come to know more profoundly what marriage is.

Like Zizioulas (with Möhler still in the background), Goizueta sees the Trinity as representing the communal nature of God; "personhood" is not prior to community but is achieved within it. The model holds true also for human relationships. Goizueta argues against the tendency of the dominant U.S. culture to see individuality as a primary reality that exists prior to any relationships. In Goizueta's U.S. Hispanic perspective, community precedes individuality. Authentic individuality is achieved only within the context of a community which precedes one and from which one draws one's identity. True freedom is found not in a struggle to be a completely autonomous self-made person, but only in relationships. From the particularity of his own perspective, Goizueta, like Elizabeth A. Johnson, affirms Zizioulas' understanding of "being as communion." Interrelatedness as persons lies at the very heart of reality.

Like Möhler and de Lubac, Goizueta promotes an inclusive "both/and" approach to what it means to be Catholic. But his initial point of entry to this position is not the inclusiveness of the patristic authors, but rather the cultural experience of U.S. Hispanics as being always "in-between." U.S. Hispanics live in-between the communities of their past and the communities of their present, in-between being exiles and being aliens, in-between being Latin American and "American," in-between being marginal and having opportunities, and in-between anger and gratitude. This experience, claims Goizueta, has led U.S. Hispanics not to being either-or dichotomizers, but to being people of the "both/and," people who are as bridges and whose instincts lean toward inclusion. It is an approach sensitive to analogy and paradox and sacrament, a way of being Catholic.

Goizueta's sacramental approach to faith, his focus on inculturation, and his stress on social justice show many similarities with the work of de Lubac. De Lubac was a pioneer who forged links between the sacramental and social aspects of Catholicism. It is true that Goizueta does not explore ideal images that represent the Church universal as does de Lubac. Yet the Church universal, considered in its relational aspects, does play a significant role in Goizueta's work as the Communion of Saints. He does not dwell on the Communion of Saints as an abstract theological concept, but he describes concretely how, in U.S. Hispanic perspective, one's community is comprised not just of those alive now but also of those who have gone before us in death.

Goizueta illustrates how, for Hispanic Catholics, two persons who dwell in the very center of the community are Jesus and Mary. When Hispanics in San Antonio act out the Passion, they are truly walking along with Jesus. It is really Jesus who is being nailed to the cross as they look on. When an Hispanic woman kisses the feet of Jesus on a cross, she is really interacting with Jesus. When Hispanics celebrate the feast of Our Lady of Guadalupe and recount her story, they know that they are accepted as fully dignified human beings by this blessed lady. One cannot know one's own identity as an Hispanic Catholic without being in relation with Jesus and Mary, who are sacramentally and thus really present through ritual and story. For Goizueta, such concepts as the Church as the Communion of Saints or the Church as the Body of Christ are not abstract idealizations but concrete descriptions that arise from a phenomenology of the U.S. Hispanic experience.

The Jesus who is thus present is one who knows what it is to suffer, and into whose suffering the poor can enter. The Mary thus present is one who loves the poor and who helps them to recognize their dignity as her special ones. Goizueta, who is in many ways grounded in liberation theology, on this point distinguishes his approach from that of many liberation theologians by insisting that this sense of personal dignity is not necessarily attached to a socially transforming practice. It is a dignity that has its own intrinsic value.

Some Parallels with Balthasar

Goizueta, in a move that might be described as an Hispanic Catholic *ressourcement*, illustrates the intrinsic value of human dignity by drawing upon the aesthetic theory of the Mexican philosopher José Vasconcelos. There are some interesting parallels between the philosophy of Vasconcelos and the theology of Balthasar. Over against positivist and reductionist philosophies popular in Mexico in the opening years of the twentieth century, Vasconcelos held that aesthetics is the key category for interpreting human action.[13] In the "special pathos of beauty" can be found a principle that unifies the intellectual, the moral, and the aesthetic (*CCJ* 91). The experience of beauty entails an "empathic fusion" of subject and object by which the subject becomes caught up and loses himself or herself in the experience. Such aesthetic union is the basis of love, in which people lose themselves in a union that transcends each. The human desire for aesthetic union is in itself "the yearning for communion with the divine nature" (*CCJ* 94). As with

---

[13]Readers interested in the role of beauty in a U.S. Hispanic approach to theology will want to read Alejandro García-Rivera, *The Community of the Beautiful: A Theological Aesthetics* (Collegeville, MN: Michael Glazier, 1999).

Balthasar, God, love, and beauty present themselves through objective forms that captivate the being of the subject. Aesthetics must precede ethics. Where Balthasar held that contemplation was superior to action, Vasconcelos found a priority for play, recreation, and celebration in relation to practical action.

Goizueta uses these points from Vasconcelos to critique the tendency among liberation theologians to settle for the Marxist meaning of *praxis* as socially transforming activity. When measured against the classical understanding of *praxis* in Aristotle, this definition of practical activity sounds as though it better fits *poesis* or even the more specific *techne*. Goizueta argues that *praxis* in Aristotle had to do not with making (*poesis*) or technical activity (*techne*), but with activity done for its own sake. He gives the example of the difference between making a guitar and playing a guitar. The activity of making a guitar is *poesis*; the activity of playing a guitar is *praxis*. The playing of a guitar has an intrinsic value that can be appreciated without reference to some practical external goal.

Goizueta detects in the Marxist meaning of *praxis* a reductionism that subordinates the dignity of persons and the meaning of celebrations to the achievement of political ends. Those who cannot contribute to liberation can come to be perceived as useless. Goizueta is not at all opposed to the transformation of unjust political structures, and indeed the bulk of his book bears out his commitment to such projects. He holds, however, that concern for beauty and concern for justice must be combined. He does this by arguing that the aesthetic dimension of human action is always mediated by the ethical-political; it is lived out within the ethical-political as the deepest sense of the ethical-political. The dignity and the love that constitute the deepest dimensions of human lives are lived out always within concrete social contexts. It is important that these contexts reflect as much as possible this dignity and this love in a real way. But the aesthetic dimension of human activity is never to be reduced to or subordinated to the ethical-political. It is distinct, prior, and even superior.

Goizueta's corrective to liberation theology can serve as one response to the call made by Balthasar himself in the 1977 lecture at the Catholic University of America referred to in chapter six.[14] In this reconciling talk, Balthasar spoke of three theological methods—the anthropological approach, liberation theology, and his own "way of love"—as limited but potentially complementary approaches, each needing the other for its completion. Goizueta holds that where the main concern for Latin American liberation theologians is Justice, the corresponding concern for U.S. Hispanic theologians is Beauty.

---

[14]Hans Urs von Balthasar, "Current Trends in Catholic Theology and the Responsibility of the Christian," *Communio* 5 (Spring 1978) 77-85.

Goizueta's reliance upon Vasconcelos' aesthetic theory to carve out a realm that is sacrosanct and not to be subordinated to those dimensions of reality studied by the social scientists parallels Balthasar's reliance on Goethe (and also on Barth) to identify the objectivity of the aesthetic form as that which draws the subject outside of himself or herself. The overlap with Balthasar is striking when Goizueta says:

> When one travels, for instance, through the Rocky Mountains, one is caught up into their majesty and splendor. The extraordinary vistas raise the hairs on the back of one's head and send a chill down the spine. Such a reaction is not merely arbitrary and subjective, but an appropriate subjective response to an external, objective reality: the overwhelming natural beauty of the mountains. Not only a "meaningful experience," aesthetic, or empathic fusion is also a revelation of self-transcending truth. (*CCJ* 161)

Balthasar himself described liberation theology sympathetically and suggested that criticism be limited to the point where "it comes close to giving absolute priority to the political dimensions."[15] That is precisely the point at which Goizueta provides his corrective, one based on aesthetic theory.

Goizueta treats Hispanic ritual and narrative in ways that are perhaps not unlike Balthasar's treatment of scripture, patristic writings, and the visions of Adrienne von Speyr. There is a strong confidence in the revelatory power present in the form, and a freedom to allow the imagination to engage these forms with a trust that the revelatory power will guide it. And when attending to their respective sources, both Goizueta and Balthasar place heavy emphasis on the celebration of the Triduum and on the person of Mary. Goizueta's U.S. Hispanic approach and Balthasar's aesthetic theology share much indeed.

Points of Comparison with the CDF's Statement

Several points of intersection have been uncovered between the theologies of Johnson and Goizueta and a range of concepts commonly associated with communion ecclesiology. Both theologians focus on the connection between relationality in God and relationality among human beings. Both operate with an explicitly sacramental appreciation of life. Both engage in a style of *ressourcement* theology. Both value an aesthetic approach to theological sources. And both affirm the positive links between popular, local religion and the Church universal. Yet one wonders how their approaches might line up with the vision of

---

[15]Ibid., 41.

communion ecclesiology expressed in the CDF's "Some Aspects of the Church Understood as a Communion."

One suspects that if either Johnson or Goizueta tried to produce an official-style document on communion ecclesiology, their starting points would run counter to those of the CDF. They would likely stress the local and the particular so strongly that the institutional elements of the Church universal might seem relatively neglected. Neither has any opposition to the institutional elements of the Church universal, and in fact they both seem to see them as functioning, at least potentially, in a positive and complementary fashion within the very fabric of popular, local religion. But as the CDF emphasizes the priority of the Church universal, Johnson and Goizueta tend to emphasize the priority of the local and the particular.

Still, a strong point of comparison could be developed starting with the CDF's notion of the "mutual interiority" characteristic of local churches that provides the basis for recognizing the common faith that exists among them. The document states:

> In order to grasp the true meaning of the analogical application of the term *communion* to the particular churches taken as a whole, one must bear in mind above all that the particular churches, inso-far as they are part of the "one church of Christ," have a special relationship of "mutual interiority" with the whole, that is, with the universal church, because in every particular church "the one, holy, catholic, and apostolic church of Christ is truly present and active."[16]

What this means is that each particular church contains micro-cosmically within itself the entire Church universal. One example the document gives of this is that the office of the papacy is not simply exterior to each particular church, but exists as an intrinsic dimension.

Although Johnson and Goizueta would come at "mutual interiority" from a different direction than that of the CDF, the kernel of a potential synthesis is present in the concept. Recall Goizueta's example of how one comes to know what "marriage" is through the experience of one's own marriage and the recognition of analogical elements in other mar-riages. For the CDF to highlight "mutual interiority" is to open for con-sideration the potential fruitfulness of approaches that begin from the local and the particular, even as the CDF denounces movements that are said to arise from the base in opposition to the institutional ele-ments of the Church universal.

The strongest potential intersection between Johnson and Goizueta and the CDF's focus on communion ecclesiology lies in their emphasis

---

[16]CDF, "Some Aspects," 9.

on the relational aspects of the Catholic faith and their ability to link the experience of intimacy and solidarity in small forms of community with the universal elements of God and the shared tradition. If communion ecclesiology is to be recognized as the one, basic Catholic ecclesiology, then it must include this major thrust in Catholic theology today that focuses on context, social location, and the process of inculturation. It is understandable that the CDF document would take the Church universal and Church unity as its central concerns; the equally important matters of diversity and the role of local churches, however, cry out for more attention. It is precisely in this critical aspect of communion ecclesiology that Johnson and Goizueta have valuable contributions to make.

TEN

Communion and Ecumenism

Jean-Marie Tillard, John Zizioulas, and Miroslav Volf

Until this chapter, with the one major exception of Friedrich Schleiermacher, I have treated communion ecclesiology as an inner-Catholic affair. Although such a limited discussion is both justifiable and necessary, the nature of communion ecclesiology itself calls for further ecumenical considerations. In this chapter I will examine some convergences and divergences in the positions of three theologians, Jean-Marie Tillard, John Zizioulas, and Miroslav Volf, who represent respectively the Roman Catholic, Orthodox, and Free Church traditions. Tillard is a foremost contemporary exponent of communion ecclesiology in the Catholic Church. Zizioulas, the Metropolitan of Pergamon and, along with Tillard, a longtime contributor to the Faith and Order commission of the World Council of Churches, is a foremost contemporary advocate of communion ecclesiology in Eastern Orthodoxy. Volf, who comes originally from the former Yugoslavia, has recently written a substantial book on communion ecclesiology from the perspective of a Free Church Protestant. He wrote this book, *After Our Likeness*, as his *Habilitationsschrift* under the direction of Jürgen Moltmann at the University of Tübingen.[1] Volf includes under the term "Free Church" a variety of denominations including Baptists, Congregationalists, Quakers, and Pentecostals.

In the discussion that follows, I will show how communion ecclesiology can function both to articulate deeply shared views among theologians representing the major churches as well as to clarify significant points of difference. These three thinkers all express a vision of the

---

[1]Miroslav Volf, *After Our Likeness: The Church as the Image of the Trinity* (Grand Rapids, MI: William B. Eerdmans, 1998). Hereafter in text as *After*.

Church as a communion modeled on the relations among the three persons in God. Their versions of communion ecclesiology differ concerning the relative status of the individual Christian believer, the local church, and the Church universal.

Each form of communion ecclesiology that we have examined has entailed a retrieval of the patristic witness concerning the nature of the Church. Möhler was a patristics scholar. *Unity in the Church* was basically a study of the organically developing Church as witnessed in the writings of the Church Fathers. One of the main points that differentiated Möhler from Schleiermacher is that the former looked not just to scripture but to scripture as received by the Church in the early centuries as normative for Christianity.

Many of the significant twentieth-century figures associated with communion ecclesiology, such as Yves Congar, Henri de Lubac, Jean Danielou, Hans Urs von Balthasar, Jean-Marie Tillard, and John Zizioulas, have likewise been patristics scholars. Their approaches to studying the Church involve a *ressourcement*, a return to the sources. They go behind overly systematic, ahistorical, ideological renderings of Christianity to retrieve a dynamic and lively vision that informed Christian consciousness in its centuries of birth. As a point of focus in this chapter, I will emphasize how, in constructing their versions of communion ecclesiology, each of the three authors being considered in some way retrieves elements of the patristic witness.

The Patristic Vision according to Tillard

For Tillard, the underlying vision of communion ecclesiology represents a catholic identity that resided within the context of the life of the early Church. It can be accessed through official texts, but the vision itself is something deeper, that which informed the actual life of the community.

Tillard surfaces several characteristics of the Church in this early shared vision. He sums up a few of them on the first page of *Church of Churches*: "One belongs to one community of salvation, coming from God, joined to the Promise, born of faith, entrusted with faithfully protecting the content of the Good News."[2] Built into this vision, then, are presuppositions about unity; about revelation; about covenant; about faith; and about authority. Communion ecclesiology, for Tillard, involves the examination and retrieval of these elements of the Church.

One important way that Tillard explores these elements is through a

---

[2]Jean-Marie Tillard, *Church of Churches: The Ecclesiology of Communion*, trans. R.C. DePeaux (Collegeville, MN: Liturgical Press, 1992 [French orig. 1987]) 1. Hereafter in text as *Church*.

consideration of how the story of Pentecost in Acts was interpreted by a wide range of patristic writers. He finds in the patristic use of Pentecost something of an encapsulation of what the early vision of the Church was. Tillard acknowledges that it is debatable to say that the Church was "born" at Pentecost, but one can at the very least find there a highly privileged manifestation of the Church.

Tillard highlights the tendency of the Church Fathers to read the story of Pentecost over against the story of the Tower of Babel. This emphasis reveals something of Tillard's own method. As Tillard points out, the historical-critical approach to scripture indicates that the author of Luke-Acts most probably did not have the Tower of Babel story in mind while composing the story of the Pentecost. Such a point might incline some contemporary biblical critics to see in the patristic reception a misreading of the text, one that does not reflect the mind of the original author. For Tillard, though, what is important is not just the meaning intended by the biblical author, but the way that a text was received and interpreted by the early Church as part of the larger canon. In line with Möhler, Tillard rejects any "scripture alone" approach in favor of an approach that finds tradition to be also a major expression of revelation.

Many patristic authors saw in Pentecost a counterpoint to the confusion and dispersion represented by the Tower of Babel. That which had been dispersed is reassembled, not in a way that suppresses differences, but in a way that achieves a communion amid diversity. In contrast to Babel, where one unifying language was shattered, many languages were made as one through the power of the Holy Spirit in the apostolic witness. Thus were manifest three essential elements of the Church: the Holy Spirit, the apostolic witness, and the communion through which the diversity is contained within a unity. These three elements correspond respectively with the Church's holiness, its apostolicity, and its oneness. One finds already in this analysis ways in which Tillard's communion ecclesiology stands opposed to any approaches that reduce the Church to a merely human means of organization; that deny the existence of its authoritative structures; or that downplay the need for an actual unity.

In addition to the Church being one, holy, and apostolic, Tillard detects in the story of Pentecost the Church's catholicity. All nations are present symbolically at Pentecost: "We are Parthians, Medes, and Elamites. We live in Mesopotamia, Judea, and Capadocia, Pontus, the province of Asia, Phyrgia, and Pamphylia, Egypt, and the regions of Libya around Cyrene. There are even visitors from Rome—all Jews, or those who have come over to Judaism; Cretans and Arabs, too" (Acts 2:9-11). As a oneness manifested in diverse cultures, the Spirit-filled gathering at Pentecost is already simultaneously a Church universal and an inculturated church.

This position can be read as a counter-point to the CDF's granting of a clear and exclusive priority to the Church universal over the local churches both ontologically and temporally. It can be also be read, then, as support for Joseph Komonchak's stress that each arises out of the other; that is, the Church universal arises in and out of the local churches, and the local churches arise in and out of the Church universal.[3] *Lumen Gentium* itself held both, and at least on the surface sounded more like Komonchak than the CDF on this point. In "Some Aspects," the CDF gives the teaching of *Lumen Gentium* a certain slant. The CDF seems to "concede" that the Church universal arises in and out of the local churches; it affirms and emphasizes that the local churches arise from the Church universal.

Tillard's reading of Pentecost challenges the CDF's slant. This is not to say that there is not a way in which the apostolic reception of the Spirit can be considered as prior to the Church, but that at the very moment the Spirit is expressed as the apostolic witness, there are receivers of that witness, and those receivers represent in nascent form the local churches. The Church as manifested at Pentecost may indeed precede all other manifestations of local churches, but it symbolically contains already within itself the local churches out of which the Church universal arises. That is, at Pentecost the Church is already both universal and local; the gospel is inculturated from the moment of its utterance-reception. There is no Church universal that is not also to be found inculturated in local churches. Tillard is thus able to affirm certain points that are often associated with Protestant and Free Church traditions, such as the importance of each individual Christian's confession of faith and the constitutive role of the local church.[4]

The Church as Tillard finds it in the Church Fathers is both eschatological and historical. It is eschatological in that it makes real the Promise; it fulfills what has been awaited. But it does so not abstractly but in concrete historical events and in real communities. As Tillard puts it: "The Church is born inseparable from the human drama as such" (*Church* 9). This holding-in-tension the historical and the ideal is an important characteristic of communion ecclesiology in the tradition of Möhler, and is also in line with *Lumen Gentium* and the CDF's "Some Aspects."

---

[3]Joseph A. Komonchak, "The Local Church," *Chicago Studies* 28 (1989) 320-35. See also Joseph A. Komonchak, "The Church Universal as the Communion of Local Churches," in *Where Does the Church Stand? Concilium*, vol. 146, 30-5 (Edinburgh: T&T Clark, 1981).

[4]This is especially true in Tillard's recent work, *L'Eglise locale: Ecclésiologie de communion et catholicité* (Paris: Cerf, 1995), in which he treats in depth several themes associated with a congregationalist understanding of church. See the extensive review by David Carter, a Methodist, in *One in Christ* 32 (1996) 378-85.

Tillard relies upon the Body of Christ image to articulate the new possibility for human existence opened up by Christ and represented in the Church. It is a new life made possible through the Cross, the Resurrection, and the Spirit. This new possibility for human existence entails the taking up of the isolated "I's" of human beings into a solidarity which affirms them and connects them as the one Body of Christ in the image of the Trinity. Yet within this solidarity, unique "I's" are not absorbed but remain within a plurality that does not erase singularity. Although the doctrine of the Trinity will not be formally worked out until the fourth and fifth centuries, Tillard sees the Christian life as it emerges in the Church's beginning as mirroring the image of "the trinitarian God whose nature is proclaimed by Christian faith" (*Church* 18).

According to Tillard, the Church as understood by the patristic writers is not simply an ethical organization or a band of those who follow Jesus, but is in its very nature a communion. It consists in communities throughout the world gathered by the Spirit and rooted in the Trinity. It is truly in its very nature the Body of Christ. As such the nature of the Church is connected in an integral way with the Eucharist. It is in the Eucharistic celebration, says Tillard, that the Church is fully itself (*Church* 105).

Linked with the celebration of the Eucharist is the office of the bishop at the center of life in the local church. Tillard carefully acknowledges that the history of the episcopacy cannot be traced in detail but sees in it the evolution of apostolic links. The ordained ministry is in the service of communion; its role is to guarantee that *aggiornamento* takes place in line with the words and deeds of Jesus. The Church Fathers recognized in the bishop the icon of Christ, though this identification was more cultic and sacramental than simply juridical.

Tillard makes several qualifications concerning bishops that are ecumenically appropriate: that the episcopacy is a service; that the bishop cannot exist without the local church; that the hardening of a basically legitimate lay-clergy distinction has been regrettable;[5] that many ministries in the Church are guaranteed by the apostolic witness; that the role of the bishop as icon needs to be understood against the background of the anthropology of the early centuries, not as an idolatry; and that ministers, though they have power over the life of faith, have no power over the freedom of the act of faith, and that faith itself ultimately comes only from God. Yet these qualifications do not lessen Tillard's resolve that the episcopacy as it evolved represents the will of God as the shape that the Spirit gives to eucharistic communities.

Tillard affirms also an essential role for the papacy amid several

---

[5]For a discussion of this point in the work of both Tillard and Kenan Osborne, see Brian Staudt, "The Lay-Cleric Distinction: Tragedy or Comedy?" *Church* 12 (Fall 1996) 47-50.

strong qualifications. The Church is founded on the apostles, not on a super-apostle; the pope exercises not dominion but power, being more like a choir director than an army general; interventions should be kept to a minimum; subsidiarity, the exercise of authority on the most local levels possible, is to be encouraged; and any future unity will be not just a return to the past, but will retain multiple traditions. Beyond these qualifications, though, Tillard holds strongly that the papacy is of divine institution; that it has an important function of unity; that it serves the deposit of faith; that only in the Roman Church is communion in its fullness; and that the role of the Roman Church is providentially willed by God.[6]

The approach of Tillard has many obvious parallels with that of Möhler. The best way to explore the nature of the Church is through a patristic retrieval. The Church is most basically a communion of human beings with God, patterned upon the life of the Trinity. Not simply the human reception of revelation, the Church is part of what has been revealed. It is the Body of Christ. The nature of the Church is expressed most fully in the Eucharist. The episcopacy has evolved as that which maintains the apostolic witness. The papacy, a gift and service to the Church, is a sign of unity.

The Patristic Vision according to Zizioulas

Zizioulas' approach to communion ecclesiology overlaps with that of Tillard in many important ways. Both of these theologians emphasize that there is a shared vision in the early Church that needs to be retrieved. Reminiscent of Möhler, this vision includes:

1. The Church is most basically a communion.
2. The life of the Spirit present within the Church gradually develops various external structures and modes of expression.
3. The Church is both historical and eschatological; it is from God and yet present amid the struggles of this life.
4. The Church is truly the body of Christ.
5. The reality of the Church is most fully expressed in the Eucharist.
6. The Eucharist comes to be intimately linked with the bishop in the local church.

---

[6]Tillard's most comprehensive study of the papacy is Jean-Marie Tillard, *The Bishop of Rome* (Wilmington, DE: Michael Glazier, 1983 [French orig. 1982]). His recent reflections on the papacy in ecumenical context can be found in Jean-Marie Tillard, "The Ministry of Unity," *One in Christ* 33 (1997) 97-111.

7. The bishop represents unity within the local church as well as unity with the Church universal.

8. The papacy, properly understood and carried out, could function as an important service of unity.

There are also, however, some important differences between Tillard and Zizioulas. Tillard addresses broadly the issues underlying both the East-West and the Catholic-Protestant split. Zizioulas is more specifically focused on the East-West split from the perspective of the East. Perhaps the most important difference is that for Tillard, the patristic witness that needs to be appropriated today consists mainly in a presupposed vision that informed a wide range of writers of both East and West over the entire first millennium of Christianity; for Zizioulas, it consists mainly in a philosophical/theological synthesis that was attained gradually in the writings of Athanasius and the Cappadocian Fathers, all Eastern, and confirmed in the christological and trinitarian doctrines of Nicaea and Chalcedon. In line with these differences, Tillard draws upon Augustine as one among many Church Fathers who express the underlying vision of communion ecclesiology; Zizioulas sees in Augustine a point in which the West took a wrong turn by placing priority on the concept of the openness of God over the relational aspects of the three persons in God.

For the most part these differences reflect what one might expect when comparing visions from Western Roman Catholicism and from Eastern Orthodoxy. On one important matter of method, however, Tillard and Zizioulas engage in a somewhat surprising East-West role-reversal; Tillard bases his research mainly in an exegesis of scriptural and patristic texts, whereas Zizioulas tends to be more philosophical and systematic.

Despite these several significant differences, I find the similarities in Tillard and Zizioulas to be much more profound. Although Tillard speaks from within a tradition that affirms the papacy and Zizioulas does not, both theologians argue that a reformed papacy, properly understood and carried out, can potentially function as a sign of unity for all Christians. And, although Zizioulas speaks from within a tradition that has placed great stress upon the ecclesiality of the local church, both theologians agree on the local church's importance as well as on the need for local churches to have concretely expressed connections with the Church universal through the episcopacy. From a purely theological perspective, a comparative reading of Tillard and Zizioulas can inspire realistic hopes concerning the future of Catholic and Orthodox relations.

Zizioulas focuses his primary attention on how Christian life and communion came to be expressed philosophically and theologically in the writings of the Greek Fathers that culminated in the doctrines of

Nicaea and Chalcedon.[7] He holds that the exact thing that the Greek Fathers were able to achieve was a philosophical synthesis that uncovers relational being as the very core of all reality and existence. Everything is personal at the core. The Christian God is a relational community. How Christians come to grips with that revealed truth and express it doctrinally is for Zizioulas the main issue underlying the patristic vision of the Church.

Yet Zizioulas is fond of pointing out that those who contributed the most to the patristic synthesis were not the academic theologians of the Church such as Justin Martyr, Clement, and Origen, but rather the pastoral bishops such as Ignatius, Irenaeus, and Athanasius. What they drew upon in their thinking was not abstract speculation but ecclesial experience, above all the experience of the eucharistic assembly. It was here that they learned that God could be known only through personal relationships and personal love. What emerges is a distinctively Christian philosophy that identifies being with life, a life of communal relationship.[8]

Zizioulas describes vividly how at the eucharistic assembly, in addition to the embodied members of the congregation, there are present the Communion of Saints and the triune God. The experience encompasses both history and its eschatological fulfillment; though performed in time, the ritual gives Christians a real foretaste of eternal divine love.

From this eucharistic experience springs an awareness of God as a communion. Zizioulas considers the articulation of christological and trinitarian understandings expressed by the early Councils to be expressions of the faith that informed the life of the Christian community and that was manifested most fully in the eucharistic celebration. Christians understood human beings as called to share in this communion and the Church as the realization of this new existence.

Zizioulas explains that the philosophical categories available prior to Nicaea for conceiving of the reality of God and the relationship between God and the world were not adequate for expressing the Christian experience. The Greek notion of "being" was impersonal and monistic and deterministic. Christians who relied heavily upon the various forms of Greek philosophy would end up in heresy. What was needed was an ontology that uncovered freedom and personhood and relationality in the core of being.

---

[7]John Zizioulas, *Being as Communion: Studies in Personhood and the Church* (Crestwood, NY: St. Vladimir's Press, 1985). A comprehensive approach to his work is Paul McPartlan, *The Eucharist Makes the Church: Henri de Lubac and John Zizioulas in Dialogue* (Edinburgh: T&T Clark, 1993).

[8]A brief introduction to Zizioulas' personalist ontology can be found in David A. Fisher, "Byzantine Theology: Reflections on the Thought of John Zizioulas," *Diakonia* 29 (1996) 57-63.

According to Zizioulas, this is what the Greek Fathers accomplished and what the early Councils confirmed. He focuses on two key historical developments: one that arises from Athanasius' debates against the Arians; a second that arises within the responses of the Cappadocian Fathers against Sabellianism.

Zizioulas claims that beyond meeting the challenges of the Arians, Athanasius introduced the category of relationality into Christian philosophy. Although Zizioulas points out also some serious limitations in Athanasius' approach, he finds there a key development in the discovery of how to articulate that at the core of being is communion. In other words, prior to Athanasius, a Christian relying upon Greek philosophy would end up thinking that being is prior to any relationality or communion; now the possibility is open to conceive of being as communion. Relationality is at the heart of existence.

It would take the Cappadocian Fathers, Gregory of Nazianzus, Gregory of Nyssa, and Basil of Caesarea, to develop further this line of thought. The Cappadocian Fathers introduce into the discussion clear distinctions between "being" and "nature" and "person." Without such distinctions, there is no adequate way to articulate parameters within which Christians can express what they believe about Jesus. One would end up with a Jesus who is either less than God or more than human, not one person who is fully divine and fully human. These insights informed the theology of the Council of Chalcedon. These categories do not pretend to express anything like a full understanding of the nature of Christ or of the triune God, but they give Christians a philosophical-theological framework that allows the conceptualization of the God encountered in the eucharistic celebration to escape being swallowed up in a deterministic monism.

By injecting the personal and the relational into the heart of being, Athanasius and the Cappadocian Fathers achieved a synthesis between Christian experience and Greek thought. Person is prior to and deeper than nature. Relationality is not something added on to already established substances, but is at the heart of being. Identity is not something that precedes relationship, but is something that is achieved within the context of relationship. The core of existence is not neutral but personal. Being is relational life and communion.

At the heart of God is not a neutral nature or substance or being-itself that precedes any distinction into personalities. God in God's deepest reality is three persons grounded in the person of the Father. God is personal, not simply a thing. God is radically free, not bound by any ontological necessity. God is ecstatic, self-expressive, not a dead, static reality. And the best way to appreciate God's relationality is as love. Relational love is the most basic reality of the universe.

Zizioulas believes this synthesis of Christian life and Greek thought was lost to the West through Augustine's reversion to identifying the being of God with "being" understood in a monistic manner. This basic move, charges Zizioulas, is recapitulated in every Western theological treatise that addresses the one God before the triune God.[9] God is implicitly identified with being as neutral substance rather than with being as communion. As Zizioulas sees it, the stage was set in the West for the Church as communion to dissolve into the Church as juridical institution, for the Church, too, came to be conceived of first as a neutral substance and only subsequently as a place for cultivating relationships.

For Zizioulas, to grasp the nature of the Church as communion is to appreciate it against the background of a free, relational, loving, communal God who wills to share with human beings the divine way of life through Christ. The main difficulty of human beings, caught in sin, is their experience of their existence as individualized, ego-centered entities. By being taken up into the personhood of Christ, individuals are transformed and affirmed in a new relational context. To be oneself is to be oneself in communion, in relation. This is God's way of being, and the Church is like a school in which Christians learn to *be* relationally in the way that God is. What the Church is is revealed most fully in the eucharistic celebration, in which a real foretaste of the divine life is shared. The Church is the corporate Christ, the communion of saints.

Like Tillard, Zizioulas highlights the link in the early Church between the Eucharist and the office of the bishop. The local community celebrates a Eucharist that includes all. The bishop represents both the oneness of the community and its interconnectedness with all other eucharistic communities. Zizioulas is so intent upon this link that he even suggests that what now exist as parishes might be headed by bishops, with the entire Church being restructured accordingly. This focus on the eucharistic community as local church gives Zizioulas' approach some overlap with the eucharistic ecclesiology of the Russian Nicholas Afanasiev.[10] Zizioulas remains radically distinct from Afanasiev, though, in that the latter so stresses the self-sufficiency of the local church as to minimize or even deny the necessity of larger connections. Communion is of course first of all for Zizioulas the existence of relationality, and this relationality finds its most important expression in the eucharistic assembly of a local church as presided over by the bishop. But this relationality also finds an important expression in the interlinking episcopal structures of the Church. Zizioulas is also open to discussion concerning the possibility of a Petrine ministry for the whole Church, so long as that is understood properly as serving rather than negating the Church's essential episcopal foundation.

---

[9]John Saward defends the West against this charge of Zizioulas in his review of *Being as Communion* in *New Blackfriars* 67 (January 1986) 45-8.

[10]Nicholas Afanasiev's major work is *L'Eglise du Saint-Esprit* (Paris: Cerf, 1975).

Volf's Free Church Version of Communion Ecclesiology

Miroslav Volf's recent work, *After Our Likeness: The Church as the Image of the Trinity*, articulates a version of communion ecclesiology from a Free Church perspective. Volf structures his book as a comparative dialogue with Joseph Ratzinger and John Zizioulas. Volf criticizes both of his dialogue partners for presenting concepts of Trinity and personhood that, despite their recognition of the complex interconnections between relationality and personhood, ultimately underemphasize the importance of the individual (*After* 181-9). Volf advocates an even stronger both/and on the subject of relationality and personhood that rescues individual personhood from its functionally subordinate status. Although Volf is careful to state his distance from many elements of contemporary consumerist culture, such a reading of Trinity and personhood supports both the traditional Free Church stress on personal confession as well as some contemporary values regarding freedom, equality, and democracy.

Where Volf's approach intersects most deeply with Tillard and Zizioulas is at the point where he finds in trinitarian communion the model of what Church should be. In sharp contrast with Schleiermacher, Volf holds that the doctrine of the Trinity does reveal to Christians something of what God is like in God's own self. Volf is careful to emphasize the analogical and therefore limited nature of knowing God in this way. Having made this qualification, he mines trinitarian theology for material to express the reality of Church. Like Ratzinger and Zizioulas, he finds that God is a communion, and that the Church, although eschatological and anticipatory, is also a communion. Much of the book is an extended reflection on the existence in complementarity of relationality and individual personhood, and on implications for individual Christians, for local churches, and for relations among local churches. Volf acknowledges problematic tendencies toward individualism within his own tradition as much as he criticizes what he perceives as the demise of the individual within the episcopal traditions.[11]

Some of Volf's positions stand directly in tension with Catholic and Orthodox versions of communion ecclesiology. Where Tillard and Zizioulas each in their own way attest to a shared Catholic vision in early Christian antiquity that links love, Eucharist, and bishop, Volf makes little reference to patristic authors; his vision of communion ecclesiology results from his reading of the New Testament. With the exception of Augustine, the patristic writer to whom Volf makes the

---

[11]This social vision is articulated in Miroslav Volf, "'The Trinity Is Our Social Program': The Doctrine of the Trinity and the Shape of Social Engagement," *Modern Theology* 14 (July 1998) 403-23.

most significant reference is Tertullian.[12] He finds in Tertullian's emphasis on Matthew 18:20 ("For where two or three are gathered in my name, I am there among them") a most basic understanding of what the Church is in relation both to scripture and to trinitarian theology. Where Ignatius held that the true Church is present wherever there is a bishop in apostolic succession who guides the handing on of the tradition, Tertullian came to emphasize what Volf interprets as a complementary point that Christ is present in any gathering of those who confess Christ. In contrast with John Smyth (1554-1612), however, the "first Baptist" who serves as a touchstone for Volf throughout the book, Volf affirms the ecclesiality of the episcopal traditions. Volf's position on apostolic succession is that it can be desirable but not necessary for catholicity (*After* 474-5). Ever consistent to the Free Church tradition, Volf finally grounds "catholicity" itself in the individual Christian in relation with other individual Christians who are "catholic" (*After* 278-82). That is, for Volf, each individual confessing Christian is "catholic" to the extent that he or she is open to relationship with other Christians who are also "catholic."

Volf tries to articulate a "both/and" position toward episcopal and Free Church traditions, though his preferences for the latter remain strong throughout. He holds that either type of tradition can be validly Christian as long as the final emphasis remains that ultimately Christ is sovereign, not earthly rulers. He concedes that an episcopal tradition might work best in a particular culture. Inculturation is for Volf a very important consideration, but hierarchical arrangements should not be considered to be essential structures of the Church (*After* 253-4).

For Volf, what Ignatius affirmed about the episcopacy represents one way of going about things that might have been desirable in a certain culture and might retain contemporary usefulness; what Tertullian affirmed, however, is even more fundamental. The Church in which Christ is to be found is present *par excellence* in local gatherings of confessing Christians. Volf holds that the Church universal is an eschatological reality that has yet to be achieved in this world. He is willing to follow Paul in calling the Church collectively the Body of Christ, but he does not consider the Body of Christ to exist in this world as a "subject" in its own right (*After* 144-5). Volf places exclusive emphasis on the local congregation as the locus where church can be found. He emphasizes his intersections with Zizioulas on this matter. Volf goes so far as

---

[12]Volf accepts the widely held view that Tertullian became a Montanist. My colleague, Maureen Tilley, an expert on Latin literature of late Christian Antiquity, informs me that recent scholarship has been challenging this notion. See Maureen A. Tilley, "Passion of Perpetua and Felicity (a commentary)," in *Searching the Scriptures: A Feminist-Ecumenical Commentary and Translation*, ed. Elisabeth Schüssler Fiorenza, 829-58 (New York: Crossroad, 1994).

to label Ratzinger's position that the papacy is essential to the ecclesiality of local churches as "ecumenically offensive" (*After* 59).

In contrast with Schleiermacher, Volf rejects an organic interpretation of the Body of Christ. Schleiermacher affirmed the organic development of the Church with its emergence of an episcopal structure. Schleiermacher affirmed further that it has been legitimate and necessary for various groups to break off from earlier groups; the original organic connection, though, remained crucial. Volf argues that the Body of Christ is a metaphor that does not refer to a physical, organic reality (*After* 142). The necessary connections among churches are simply that confessing Christians gather to bear witness to Christ and be open to other churches that do the same.

Volf, the Episcopacy, and the Papacy

Volf highlights his connections with Zizioulas regarding the focus on the local church. He does not, however, highlight as much the extent to which Zizioulas departs from him concerning the ecclesial necessity of episcopal connections among local churches. It is precisely on this point that Zizioulas takes pains to distinguish his own work from that of the Russian Afanasiev. Afanasiev's fault, in Zizioulas' eyes, was not that he focused on the fullness of the local church, but the manner in which he did so. Afanasiev stressed the self-sufficiency of the local church at the expense of the importance of larger connections with other churches. Even if Volf had made Afanasiev his dialogue partner instead of Zizioulas, however, a great difference between the Orthodox and Free Church position would remain in that the Orthodox focus on the ecclesial reality of the local church depends so integrally on the eucharistic assembly and the bishop.

Volf tries to affirm the ecclesiality of the episcopal traditions, but he does not give any substantial reasons concerning why an episcopal tradition might be desirable beyond the point that such an arrangement might work best in a particular culture. Although he stresses the importance of inculturation, he insists that hierarchical arrangements should not be considered essential structures of the Church. From the perspective of the episcopal traditions, Volf seems to give with one hand and take away with the other.

Traditional reasons for affirming the episcopacy are grounded in beliefs about organic development, sacramentality, the preservation of orthodoxy, and ultimately divine institution. As Zizioulas expresses it:

> If we understand the Church in this way, as an eschatological community existing in history, taking upon itself Christ's Cross, suffering in this world, celebrating its true identity in the Eucharist, then

all the institutions which result from this form part of its true identity and its Mystery. To my mind, institutions such as episcopacy or the structure of the eucharistic community to the distinction between laity, priests and bishops, or even conciliarity, stem from the Church as event and Mystery, precisely in the celebration of the Eucharist.[13]

If these grounds are removed, the Catholic and Orthodox rationales collapse. Catholic and Orthodox beliefs about episcopal office rest precisely upon the claim that these offices are more than simply "useful." Volf's attempt at a "both/and," here, while to be deeply appreciated, rests its case finally on one side of the divide.

Volf does not substantially address the matter of the papacy in *After Our Likeness*. In a recently published paper, however, Volf acknowledges the importance of a scripturally based ministry of unity.[14] He argues, though, mainly through a reading of John 17:22 ("that they may be one, as we are one") that this ministry should be based more directly on a trinitarian model than on a monarchical model. Such would result not simply in a triumverate, but in a "consistent practice of self-donation which is at the very heart of the Trinity's life."

Volf's attention to the papacy is to be appreciated in the light of recent Catholic discussions. Catholics maintain that the papacy is critical not simply within their own tradition but regarding ecumenical matters as well. As expressed by Avery Dulles, "No Catholic theologian will deny the desirability of all Christians coming to accept the Petrine office as exercised by the Bishop of Rome."[15]

The conversation in Catholic circles has focused of late on reforming the exercise of the primacy. John Paul II himself speaks of this in *Ut Unum Sit*, in which he asks forgiveness for past failings of the papacy (88) and speaks appreciatively of the fresh look being given to the office by other ecclesial communities (89). He asks Catholics and other Christians to consider together the forms that the Petrine ministry might take:

This is an immense task, which we cannot refuse and which I cannot carry out by myself. Could not the real but imperfect com-

---

[13]John Zizioulas, "The Mystery of the Church in Orthodox Tradition," *One in Christ* 24 (1988) 301.

[14]Miroslav Volf, "Trinity, Unity, Primacy: On the Trinitarian Nature of Ecclesial Unity and Its Implications for the Question of Primacy," in *Petrine Ministry and the Unity of the Church*, ed. James F. Puglisi (Collegeville, MN: Litugical Press, 1999) 171-84.

[15]Avery Dulles, "The Church as Communion," in *New Perspectives in Historical Theology: Essays in Memory of John Meyendorf*, ed. Bradley Nassif (Grand Rapids, MI: Eerdmans, 1996) 138. Dulles adds, though, that ecumenism cannot be reduced to this one objective.

munion existing between us persuade Church leaders and their theologians to engage with me in a patient and fraternal dialogue in which, leaving useless controversies behind, we could listen to one another, keeping before us only the will of Christ for his church? (96)

In an address that develops further points made in *Ut Unum Sint*, Archbishop John Quinn has said:

> In considering the papal office and the call to Christian unity, we have to confront the challenging truth that it is not permitted to defer unity until there is a pope who can fulfill everyone's expectations or agenda. We cannot hold unity hostage until there is a perfect pope in a perfect church. Christian unity will require sacrifice. But it cannot mean that all the sacrifices must be made by those who want full communion with the Catholic Church while the Catholic Church herself makes no significant sacrifices.[16]

Although ecumenical agreement on the papacy seems still a long way off, Volf's article on this issue, which he wrote specifically in response to John Paul II's request for suggestions in *Ut Unum Sint*, helps to move the discussion along.

Volf offers a powerful argument concerning why those from the episcopal traditions should accept the full ecclesiality of Free Churches. He writes:

> Today, such exclusivity is no longer credible. I am thinking less of the sociological fact that exclusive positions in modern societies are unpersuasive than of the observation that the dynamic life and the orthodox faith of the many, quickly proliferating Free Churches make it difficult to deny them full ecclesiality. Let me illustrate this difficulty by referring to a situation that, although doubtless atypical, must nonetheless be the touchstone of any ecclesiology precisely because it is a borderline case. Should, for example, a Catholic or Orthodox diocese whose members are inclined more to superstition than to faith and who identify with the church more for nationalistic reasons—should such a diocese be viewed as a church, while a Baptist congregation that has preserved its faith through the crucible of persecution *not* be considered such? Would not an

---

[16]Archbishop John Quinn, "The Exercise of the Primacy and the Costly Call to Unity," in *The Exercise of the Primacy: Continuing the Dialogue*, ed. Phyllis Zagano and Terrence W. Tilley (New York: Crossroad, 1998) 1-28, at 25. This Oxford Lecture of Quinn is also available in *Commonweal* 123 (12 July 1996) 11-20 and in *Origins* 26 (18 July 1996) 119-27.

understanding of ecclesiality that leads to such a conclusion take us to the brink of absurdity? Equally untenable is the early, though still widespread Free Church position that denies ecclesiality to episcopal churches. (*After* 133-4)

I hear this appeal to the witness of martyrs and those who suffer persecution as one that needs to be taken as seriously as the Catholic and Orthodox concerns about the status of the episcopacy. This is not just a matter of emotional persuasion but one of substance. True witness to the gospel can be argued to be as much an essential element of the Church as is any particular structure. Free Church proponents can garner a considerable amount of evidence that authoritative structures and true witness have not always gone hand in hand. Catholics acknowledge corruption, even deep corruption, but continue to hold, along with the Orthodox, to the essential importance of visible unity, based on apostolic succession linked with a particular, historical episcopacy.

I see no quick and easy way beyond this dilemma of, on the one hand, affirming episcopal structures as essential and, on the other hand, categorizing them as merely culturally desirable under certain circumstances. One must be cautious of trying to make a "both/and" out of what can only be a contradiction. Yet I do not think that the situation is entirely hopeless. Might there be a way both to affirm the essential necessity of the episcopacy and the universal links associated with it, and at the same time to affirm the essential necessity at key historical points of various independent groups forming to bear true witness to the gospel when the essential structures were wallowing in corruption? Can a repenting, reformed, and humble papacy serve again as a sign of unity for all Christians?

Such is a Catholic hope. From a Catholic perspective, such a "both/and" would need to avoid Schleiermacher's construal of the Catholic-Protestant relationship strictly as a dialectical polarity. Beyond the position of Volf, it would have to affirm not just the cultural desirability, but the sacramental, doctrinal, and ministerial rationales supporting the organic emergence of a particular, historical episcopacy in the early Christian centuries. But such a resolution seems a long way off on all sides.

A Shared Vision of the Shared Vision?

I have acknowledged in this chapter some not insignificant differences between Tillard and Zizioulas regarding their respective retrievals of the patristic witness of the Church as a communion. Zizioulas emphasizes more than Tillard how the Church reflects a philosophy of being in which God is understood as a community. Tillard emphasizes more than Zizioulas how the patristic vision of the Church has a deep texture accessible through the testimony of a wide range of the Church

Fathers. Although they agree on the essential nature of the episcopacy, Tillard emphasizes much more the organic development of world-wide episcopal connections, in contrast with Zizioulas' stronger emphasis on the role of the bishop in the local church. Of course they also differ in their views of the current status of the papacy. A very serious difference, one which I will not resolve here, has to do with their respective readings of Augustine and whether or not the vision of communion is something maintained in both East and West for the first millennium.

In my judgment, however, the similarities between the two figures go much deeper. In the end they articulate a shared vision of a Church of relatedness, a Church revealed by the triune God, a Church that sacramentally makes present in history the anticipated eschaton. This Church is one, holy, catholic, and apostolic. The communion of the Church exists visibly, through the office of the bishop and through the interconnectedness of bishops throughout the world. This is the vision of the early Church that is retrieved today as communion ecclesiology by Catholic and Orthodox thinkers.

Volf agrees with much of the language concerning Trinity and relatedness. He affirms strongly the role of the individual confessing Christian. He acknowledges the legitimacy of episcopal traditions. His ecclesial quibbles begin at certain interpretations of how the Church is the Body of Christ and grow into stronger and stronger disagreements as theologians begin to speak of episcopal structures as essential. For Volf, the passage on which Tertullian focused, "For where two or three are gathered in my name, I am there among them," runs deeper than any patristic-era developments concerning the reality of the Church. Yet Volf offers an approach to the Church understood in trinitarian terms as a communion, a challenging vision, one with a surprising number of significant intersections with Catholic and Orthodox understandings.

Tillard, Zizioulas, and Volf's use of communion ecclesiology stands in contrast with the tendency in internal Roman Catholic discussions to co-opt communion terms and concepts in support of particular theological agendas. These ecumenical theologians employ communion ecclesiology in a refreshingly honest way to clarify differences and to stretch toward agreement. There is much to be learned from their method and style.

ELEVEN

Touchstones for the Vision

Beyond Selective Readings of Vatican II

The Church is a multi-dimensional reality. To even begin to understand the Church, one needs to be attuned to its various dimensions.

In the comparative studies of the preceding chapters I have examined diverse figures who grapple with the complexities of conceiving of the Church as a communion. Each author studied has had something worthwhile to contribute to an overall vision. Yet in each study, certain tensions have arisen.

I have found in the early nineteenth-century works of Johann Adam Möhler a seminal voice of contemporary Catholic communion ecclesiology. Yet already in Möhler's own works there are tensions between a version that is historical-pneumatological-organic and another that is mystical-christological-aesthetic. Now, one can decide that the early Möhler was not quite mature and that the later Möhler got things right. Or, one can decide that the early Möhler got things right, but, like a groundhog frightened by the sight of his own shadow, retreated into his hole. With either of these readings, one can then move on to join the appropriate camp. I support, however, the reading of Michael Himes, who demonstrates, through a close study of the five editions of *Symbolik*, Möhler's continual quest toward a balance amid these tensions.[1]

A similar set of tensions surfaced in my comparative studies of Congar and Journet, Rahner and Balthasar, and the Brothers Himes and Ratzinger. Related tensions arose in the studies of Küng and Boff, as well as Johnson and Goizueta. Most of these figures work toward some type of balance in their own approaches. The tensions that have been explored are not intended to represent facile dichotomies; nor are

---

[1]Michael J. Himes, *Ongoing Incarnation: Johann Adam Möhler and the Beginnings of Modern Ecclesiology* (New York: Crossroad, 1997).

these tensions in every case the same. There are enough similarities, however, for a picture to emerge that is worth taking seriously.

Henri de Lubac has emerged in this study as one whose simultaneous commitment to the reality of the mystery of Christian revelation, to a radically inclusive meaning of catholicity, and to the social dimensions of the Church in its mission in the world, is, I believe, unparalleled among contemporary theologians. I do not by this mean to suggest that de Lubac's theology is without limitations, or that his positions on particular questions need to be adopted uncritically today. I believe, though, that de Lubac deserves imitation in regard to the generous inclusivity and multi-dimensionality of his vision. A communion ecclesiology inspired by his work will gracefully accept truth wherever it may be found. It will acknowledge that the world that is created and the world that is redeemed are accomplishments of the same God. Yet it will find a special beauty in Christian revelation, and foster an appreciation for the Church expressed in a wide range of images, the Mystical Body of Christ holding a special place among them.

In this final chapter, I consider what value communion ecclesiology might have within the cultural context of U.S. Catholicism. I then offer five "touchstones" that, taken together, can serve as a measure of the multi-dimensionality of any particular version of the vision.

The Cultural Context of U.S. Catholicism

A multi-dimensional and inclusive approach to catholicity becomes especially important in relation to the bishops' call at the Extraordinary Synod of 1985 to embrace a communion ecclesiology as a way beyond selective readings of the Council documents. These selective readings go hand in hand with the existence of left-right divisions in the Church today. What is the nature of these divisions? I focus here on the cultural context of U.S. Catholicism.

Prior to Vatican II, U.S. Catholicism formed a tightly knit subculture with its own institutions, customs, and worldview. Catholics drew strength from the certainty of their beliefs and from loyal devotion to the pope who guaranteed that certainty.[2] "The Church" included not just the hierarchy but everything associated with Catholicism, from its

---

[2]The history and importance of papal devotion in the U.S. is traced by Patricia Byrne in "American Ultramontanism," *Theological Studies* 56 (June 1995) 301-26. Byrne relies on Sandra Yocum Mize, *The Papacy in Mid-Nineteenth Century American Catholic Imagination* (Ph.D. dissertation, Marquette University, 1987) and on Patrick W. Carey, *Priests, People, and Prelates: Ecclesiastical Democracy and the Tensions of Trusteeism* (Notre Dame: University of Notre Dame Press, 1987) for much of this history.

beliefs and devotions, through its rituals and rules, to its saints and the Trinity itself. "The Church" was not understood as one theological element among others, but as the whole complex of all that made up the faith. Few U.S. Catholics could conceive in those days of leaving "the Church" and maintaining some kind of spirituality or connection with God. "The Church" and the entire life of faith tended to be part of a large undifferentiated mass. Criticism of "the Church" ran low, and a sense of the sacred through liturgy and devotion ran high. The life of the Catholic was filled with holy cards, statues, rosaries, medals, scapulars, meatless Fridays, grace before meals, May processions, priests and nuns in religious garb, and the sign of the cross before foul shots in basketball. After this life there was the promise of heaven, which was attained by every good Catholic who remained in a state of grace.

That subculture as a force of unity among all U.S. Catholics has disappeared. The few remnants testify to this disappearance by their scarcity and lack of vigor. Catholicism remains a large, strong, and influential force in the United States, but where once there was a deep sense of unity there is now a good deal of confusion.

The Second Vatican Council is less a cause of the loss of the Catholic subculture as it is a reflection of many deeper cultural causes. If the Council had not taken place, it is very likely that U.S. Catholicism would still have changed as radically and in similar ways. The virtually inevitable loss of that subculture for a variety of social and historical reasons is not in itself responsible for the cultural difficulties within U.S. Catholicism today; the challenge, rather, has more to do with what has or has not replaced that subculture. And for that the Council has tremendous potential for bringing about a renewal and providing the grounds for a new understanding of God, the Church, and spirituality.

Yet the interpretation and implementation of Vatican II has to date yielded no greatly shared common vision among U.S. Catholics. Like the papacy itself, what is intended to be a source of unity ironically functions at the same time as a source of division. Among U.S. Catholic intellectuals, the debate between the left and the right reaches a fever pitch. As William Shea laments, "Argument becomes perfunctory and a mode of attack or a solicitation of allies. One no longer argues with, one argues against. An argument is no longer an exchange meant to disclose truth but a way of upending the enemy."[3] Margaret O'Brien Steinfels depicts the right and the left as being in a symbiotic relationship in which each feeds off the dysfunctionalities of the other.[4] Both sides, she points out, share many more characteristics than they would

[3]William M. Shea, "Dual Loyalties in Catholic Theology," *Commonweal* 119 (31 January 1992) 11.

[4]Margaret O'Brien Steinfels, "The Unholy Alliance Between the Right and the Left in the Catholic Church," *America* 166 (2 May 1992) 376-82.

like to admit as they push their own partisan agendas to the detriment of the good of the Church.

Avery Dulles explains some of the complexity behind the left-right divisions by describing four major strategies in the United States for relating faith and culture: traditionalism, neo-conservatism, liberalism, and prophetic radicalism.[5] Dulles' approach aids in differentiating the contesting groups and explores in a beginning way some of the particularities and the history of each. Yet the more one understands the complex differences, the more a unifying vision seems a long way off.

Richard McBrien prefers more simply the categories right, center-right, center-left, and left.[6] McBrien expresses his strong reservations about various voices, including that of the Vatican, which claim that their own approach represents the "center" and which thereby misalign other groups along the spectrum. He is especially concerned that some Church officials consider the center-left to be marginal instead of mainstream, and consider the left to be off the map. In McBrien's opinion, the center-left is arguably more legitimately centrist than the center-right. Yet McBrien also recognizes that the categories of center, left, and right are of limited value from the start. After all, in order to call oneself a "center," all one has to do is to identify positions to either side and label them "extreme." And, as McBrien realizes, the centrist shell game is played by those at all points of the spectrum, not just those to the right.

The problem facing U.S. Catholicism today lies not so much in its diversity as in the lack of a unifying vision that mediates among the various stances and approaches to provide some sense of a shared Catholic identity. Even the sense of unity that existed in U.S. Catholicism prior to Vatican II worked amid a large variety of differences and debates.[7] Yet that sense of unity was strong, as was the subculture that supported it. Few desire or think it possible to return wholesale to the subculture of the days before the Council; what often worked well in those days is no longer viable for our times. But many Catholics, without at all being restorationist or rejecting the real advances of Vatican II, maintain a kind of selective nostalgia for the sense of unity, identity, loyalty, and connection with the sacred that the pre-Vatican II Church represented. As Raymond Brown has written:

---

[5]Avery Dulles, "Catholicism and American Culture: The Uneasy Dialogue," *America* 162 (27 January 1990) 54-9.

[6]Richard P. McBrien, "Conflict in the Church: Redefining the Center," *America* 167 (22 August 1992) 78-81.

[7]For an in-depth discussion of the significant diversity that existed in preconciliar U.S. Catholicism, see Philip Gleason, *Keeping the Faith: American Catholicism Past and Present* (Notre Dame: University of Notre Dame Press, 1987).

The generation that grew up in the 1970's, while being very aware of the new outlooks of Vatican II, were often painfully ignorant of much of their Catholic heritage. Those who taught the new were at times deaf to cries about loss of the old, equating all such cries with a traditionalist rejection of the Council. There were and are extremist Catholics opposed to Vatican II. . . . But others, and I would include myself among them, see no need for the concomitant losses, e.g., of inner-Catholic loyalty, obedience, and commitment to the church; of dignity in liturgy; of Gregorian chant; of a knowledge of the Latin tradition reaching from Augustine through Thomas to the Middle Ages. To try now to recoup some of those losses while still advancing the gains of Vatican II would make eminent good sense. Let us hope that the bitterness of the exchanges between extremists does not prevent that.[8]

Theological Diversity and Frameworks of Inclusion

Can communion ecclesiology provide a sense of unity to help Catholics address some of the divisions that plague us today? If communion ecclesiology is identified narrowly as one theological camp or school of thought, then the answer is no. But if communion ecclesiology is defined more inclusively to embrace a reasonable range of theological approaches, then it does have an important contribution to make in healing the pain of divisions and in achieving a sense of unity.

Communion ecclesiology, properly understood as multi-dimensional and inclusive, is like a playing field in which a range of diverse theological options can be played out with an awareness that all are contained within the same ballpark. There are boundaries to the playing field. Not everything is permissible. All who play on this field are called to strive for a multi-dimensional approach that includes the broad range of dimensions of the Church associated with the vision expressed in the documents of Vatican II.

There will remain, however, various strategies for achieving this multi-dimensionality and various configurations of the dimensions that constitute it. And there will remain serious disagreements about directions in which the Church should move concerning a host of controversial issues. Communion ecclesiology does not in and of itself directly resolve many important questions that face the Church today. Theologians can faithfully and deeply explore what it means for the Church to be a communion and still end up with significantly diverse views concerning these controversial matters. A multi-dimensional approach to communion

---

[8]Raymond Brown, *The Churches the Apostles Left Behind* (New York: Paulist Press, 1984) 118.

ecclesiology most often provides not immediate solutions to practical questions but rather offers frameworks of inclusion that can allow various partisans to see the practical questions in a new light. Communion ecclesiology can give indirect but highly significant aid in the resolution of the issues by creating an atmosphere and a turf that focus attention on a large host of important presuppositions that are mutually shared.

Communion ecclesiology's potential impact on the Church is like the story of a person who manifests many symptoms of illness. This person goes to see a physician. But the symptoms are so many and so varied and the problems so complex that the physician cannot come up with a simple diagnosis or cure. So the physician tells the person to take some time off, go away to a quiet place, eat well, exercise every day, drink a lot of water, read some classic books, and pray. The person does as the doctor suggests, and within a short time many of the symptoms disappear.

I will reiterate three frameworks of inclusion that have emerged within the historical and comparative studies in this book. First, an inclusive notion of catholicity operated in most of the authors studied, most notably in the works of Möhler, Congar, de Lubac, and Goizueta. These authors emphasized the need to be able to hold in tension positions that appear on the surface to be contradictory. Ideally speaking, as both Möhler and de Lubac stressed, the Church contains within itself all antitheses. Communion ecclesiology should not function as a weapon to drive people out of the Church. It can, however, function as an instrument for explaining to some people that through their own exclusivity or neglect of essential dimensions of the Church, they have excluded themselves from the larger communion. Even in these cases, though, those who make reference to communion ecclesiology should manifest a humble spirit of invitation, a generous striving to value what is legitimate in the person's position, and an inclusive drive to maintain communion if at all possible. Both Rahner and Balthasar in their later works stressed the need for a sense of complementarity in the often-competing schools of theological method.

My next door neighbor and I share a driveway that leads into our respective garages. Our deeds give each of us the right to exclude the other from using the driveway. This rule functions a bit in practice like this first framework of inclusion. Yes, either of us can exclude the other from using the driveway; we both know, however, that to exclude the other will ultimately lead to the exclusion of ourselves. The only way to secure our own inclusion is to act in an inclusive manner toward the other. Communion ecclesiology can function in a similar manner.

A second framework of inclusion that has emerged in the course of these studies is understanding the Church as a sacrament in a manner that draws upon Thomas Aquinas' distinction between two kinds of sacraments.[9] This distinction is discussed in chapter one as well as in the

---

[9]*Summa Theologiae*, part III, q. 84, a. 1.

comparative study of Ratzinger and the Himeses in chapter seven. There are those sacraments whose grace is incommensurable with what human beings can achieve on their own, and those sacraments whose grace is more in proportion with what human beings can achieve on their own. Is the Church more a sacrament that offers to the world that which it has not, or is the Church more a sacrament that makes explicit and gives aid to that grace which, through the presence of the Spirit, the world already has? Although the former deserves a certain priority, the question as posed presents a false dichotomy. The Church is a sacrament in both of these senses. Both senses are critical for understanding the Church in its relations with the modern world. Ratzinger may emphasize the former, and the Himeses the latter. But in the end each has not only to avoid denying the position of the other, but must also acknowledge it positively.

A third and most important framework of inclusion is provided by the multi-faceted nature of the documents of Vatican II. If communion ecclesiology is the key to interpreting Vatican II, the reverse is also true: Vatican II holds the key to a proper interpretation of communion ecclesiology. The communion ecclesiology expressed in the conciliar documents is not exhausted either by Rahner's emphasis on the self-actualization of the Church as a world Church or by John Paul II's manner of configuring the Council's achievements in preparation for the coming of the third millennium. Each of these figures offers a synthesis that includes a wide range of elements. The breadth of the Vatican II documents themselves does not permit a simplistic rejection of one in favor of the other. The Council documents are complex, and the roads to synthesis will be many. A communion ecclesiology that at this point in history simply chooses one school of thought over all others would betray the Council's variegated portrayal of the Church as both Body of Christ and as People of God, as Pilgrim on a journey and as the heavenly Church, and as a lay-centered, hierarchically structured institution and as the Communion of Saints. De Lubac compared the Church to Joseph's coat—it's one coat with many colors. So must the communion ecclesiology that tries to make as intelligible as humanly possible this mystery be multi-colored. Anything less represents a lack of fidelity to the multi-faceted teaching of Vatican II.

This is not a facile pluralism based on a liberal doctrine of tolerance for the sake of tolerance. It is based instead in the type of inclusive Catholic vision promoted by Henri de Lubac, whose theological method both before and after the Council combined an appreciation for the Church as a mystery with an appreciation for the Church as a social body in history. De Lubac's own Catholic spirit of inclusive generosity should serve as a model for our times.

Five Touchstones for the Vision

Practically speaking, communion ecclesiology in Catholic perspective is that vision of the Church that emerges from a generous, inclusive, and integrative reading and application of the documents of Vatican II.

Not every reading of Vatican II is a legitimate one. Not every legitimate reading of Vatican II is as good as every other legitimate reading. The call of the bishops at the Extraordinary Synod of 1985 for an end to readings that are overly selective means that Catholics on all points of the theological spectrum must strain to grasp what those on other points of that spectrum are trying to say. It also means, though, that one's own perspective deserves a respectful hearing.

I offer now not so much a single version of the vision as some touchstones intended to provide guidance for any articulation of communion ecclesiology that would claim the parentage of Vatican II. I use "touchstones" to refer to dimensions of the Church that ideally should be present in the various version of the vision of communion ecclesiology. These "touchstones" can serve as standards for assessing the degree of multi-dimensionality achieved. The chart that I introduced in chapter one to describe various dimensions of relationship that theologians describe as "communion" can serve as an entry point into various dimensions of the Church expressed in the Council documents. Vatican II proclaims a vision of the Church (1) as an invitation to share in the divine life and love of the three persons in one God; (2) as the Mystical Body of Christ and the Communion of Saints; (3) as sacramental communities of Christians who love each other, existing simultaneously as local churches and as embodiments of the Church universal; (4) as the pilgrim People of God on its journey through history; and (5) as leaven in the world. These dimensions of communion, which at times some theologies unfortunately tend to pit against each other in actual theological discussion, need to be read as complementary.

Divine

A communion ecclesiology based in the documents of Vatican II must maintain an openness to understanding the Church as an invitation to share in the divine life and love of the three persons in one God. Communion has necessarily a vertical dimension. Personhood and community go hand in hand and are not to be dichotomized. This divine dimension of the reality of the Church has ecumenical implications. Communion is first of all with God. Disruptions of communion on the horizontal plane, while they do not help in relating with God, are not to be understood necessarily as shutting off the vertical relationship with God for parties on either side of the split.

Mystical

A communion ecclesiology based in the documents of Vatican II must also maintain an openness to understanding the Church as the Mystical Body of Christ and as the Communion of Saints. This mystical dimension of the Church also finds expression in typological readings of scripture as exemplified by Balthasar, who finds representatives of what the Church is in Mary, John, Peter, Paul, and other figures. The Church is not simply a mundane reality, but it includes dimensions that transcend this place and this time. We are all members of one Body. We who are still in this life are connected with those who have gone before us in death through the grace of God. This dimension of the Church has ecumenical implications because of its attention to scripture and because of its use of images that can include Christians of various denominations.

Sacramental

A communion ecclesiology based in the documents of Vatican II must maintain an openness to understanding the Church as a sacrament. The Church consists in sacramental communities of Christians who love each other, existing simultaneously as local churches and as embodiments of the Church universal. The Eucharist and the episcopacy both function as essential structures that bring unity to the local church and forge connections with all of the other local churches. The Eucharist is the celebration *par excellence* through which the reality of the Church finds its fullest expression. The bishop, in his connection with the Eucharist, symbolizes the unity of love that exists among the people of a local church (diocese). The Church universal exists in and is formed out of these local church communities; conversely, the local churches exist in and are formed out of the Church universal. The Church universal, which exists as a reality in its own right, and not simply as the sum of local churches or as a federation, is realized as, in Tillard's phrase, a "Church of churches, . . . a communion of communions."[10] The college of bishops with the pope as their head, in a way that is prior to and deeper than any juridical understanding, symbolizes the love that connects all Catholics throughout the world in their bondedness in Christ. This sacramental dimension of the Church has ecumenical implications insofar as the Church is recognized as having both visible and invisible elements, and insofar as various denominations can be recognized to at least be in partial communion with each other.

---

[10]Jean-Marie Tillard, *Church of Churches: The Ecclesiology of Communion*, trans. R.C. DePeaux (Collegeville, MN: Liturgical Press, 1992 [French orig. 1987]) 29.

Historical

A communion ecclesiology based in the documents of Vatican II must also maintain an openness to understanding the Church as the pilgrim People of God on its journey through history. The ecclesiology of Vatican II envisions the Church as having emerged organically and continually as communities that have grown from the love that exists among Jesus and his disciples. It continues to exist as an actual historical relatedness between human beings and the three-personed God. It is thus that the Church represents the visible breaking in of the kingdom of God about which Jesus preached, and is the seed of that kingdom, present among us, not yet having attained its fullness. As de Lubac pointed out, the Church that can be typified in scripture as the Bride of Christ can also be typified as a harlot. It is the Church as fallible human beings who are called to embrace the cross of Christ. It is the Church as a society in which all members share a fundamental equality and common dignity in Christ, and within which some are called to roles of leadership. This dimension of communion has ecumenical implications in that it can recognize the real ecclesial existence of Christian churches outside the visible confines of Roman Catholicism. It is a Church that acknowledges that in the history of Christianity, there have been many rights and wrongs on all sides. It is a Church that accepts that the future of Christian interrelationships depends not only on the openness of other ecclesial communities but also on the continuing reform and renewal of the Catholic Church itself.

Social

A communion ecclesiology based in the documents of Vatican II, finally, must maintain an openness to understanding the Church as a social body with a commitment to justice and to global relationality. Christian solidarity is complemented by human solidarity. The Church is called to be as a leaven in the world.

Numerically it is noteworthy that well over 99 percent of Catholics are lay people and that the sacrament of matrimony is received many times more often than is holy orders. Practically speaking, a huge percentage of the Church's mission as it is actually carried out consists in lay activity in the world. In *Christifideles laici* (1989), John Paul II spells out the proper mission of the laity in the spheres of family, work, and society. The transformation of Christians and the transformation of the world go hand in hand. The Church as a communion is not simply an ideal vision, but also a historical phenomenon. This dimension of the Church has ecumenical implications in that its concrete manifestation lies in lay people living out their lives in interconnectedness not only with other Christians but also with a wide variety of people. Catholic ecclesiologist Catherine Nerney speaks of the Church on this concrete, global level as a "corporate personality."[11] Historicity and global human solidarity are not additional, optional considerations for communion ecclesiology, but themselves constitute part of the core of what the mystery of the Church is.

The Church is such a multi-dimensional and many-layered reality that it must be understood analogically. It is possible and often necessary to focus on one or two dimensions or levels at a time; one should do so, however, without losing sight of the Church as a multi-faceted mystery. Like a parable, the mystery of the Church brings forth many meanings. The quality of mystery belongs not simply to what I have identified as the divine, mystical, and sacramental dimensions, but also to the historical and the social.

Such is my attempt at expressing five touchstones for Catholic versions of the vision of communion ecclesiology. Inevitably, every particular expression of the vision becomes a version. Some versions, however, are more broadly inclusive of a wider range of Catholic ecclesial concerns than others.

Communion Ecclesiology and Church Renewal

Worthwhile reform in the Catholic Church will take place only if it goes hand in hand with a renewed appreciation of the mystery of the Church as the Body of Christ and as the Communion of Saints. Catholics of today cannot afford to choose between the mystical and the practical. Too often these days those in Catholic reform movements operate with a bitterness and a narrowness that does not allow them to see beyond human failings and limitations, even when encountered as structural sin, in order to apprehend the beauteous splendor of the Church, which continues the sacramental presence of Christ on this earth. This wondrous beauty is present not only when the Eucharist and the other sacraments are celebrated, but also when the sacramental nature of the Church is lived out in the ordinary lives of Christians in the world. On the other hand, though, too many of those who do battle against the internal Catholic reform movements fail to appreciate adequately the importance of the issues being raised and the genuine frustrations of those who participate.

On its own, communion ecclesiology will not cause renewal or reform in the Catholic Church. The human dimension of the causes of such happenings are complex and varied, and it does not seem to be the usual *modus operandi* of the Holy Spirit to bring about renewal simply

---

[11]Catherine Nerney, S.S.J., "Response," in *Small Christian Communities: Imagining Future Church*, ed. Robert Pelton, C.S.C. (Notre Dame: University of Notre Dame Press, 1997) 64-5.

through theology. One of the main tasks of theology is to remove intellectual obstacles and to open up intellectual possibilities that can aid movements of renewal and reform whose motivations are moral and religious, practical and contextual, and aesthetic and devotional.

Communion ecclesiology can contribute to Church renewal first of all by re-awakening the Catholic people to the mystery of the Church as the Mystical Body of Christ in a way that transcends but includes its institutional structures. God has come to us in the saving work of Jesus Christ, whose sacramental presence continues in the Church through the person of the Holy Spirit. The Church is fundamentally the Communion of Saints, the sharing in love between those who have gone before us in death and those who are on their earthly journey. The Church is the Bride of Christ, the spotless Spouse of the spotless Lamb, whose faithfulness will be of lasting merit in the end times. The Church is our Mother, who brings us to birth into the new life of grace. Communion ecclesiology can give support to Catholics who are true believers, who believe in Jesus, in his presence in the Eucharist, and in the efficacy of the sacraments, and in the need to transform the world through Christ.

I do not think that even images as age-old and as associated with the sacred as the above should be immune from gender or other forms of culturally based critique. Such images can and have functioned in unhealthy ways. And I think further that a creative plurality of images that goes far beyond the above sampling is desirable. But approaches that completely cut Catholics off from these aesthetic avenues of appreciating the mystery of the Church are far too narrow.

Communion ecclesiology is further a tool for Church renewal in that it provides a theological framework within which structural reform, through bold implementations of the concepts of collegiality and inculturation, can take place in a way that can be seen as supporting rather than threatening some of the deepest held beliefs of the Catholic tradition. Most people rarely change through aggressive interventions and attacks; more often they grow gradually through a complex interaction of affirmation and criticism. The same principle applies to organizations. Too many in the American reform movements today are without conceptual means of affirming the legitimate claims of the Church universal as they work for change. For Catholics, these claims are based not simply on organizational strategy but on revelation as expressed in scripture and in the historical developments of tradition.

Communion ecclesiology can provide a framework for theological discourse within which Catholics on all parts of the spectrum can feel that there are at least a few crucial things that are mutually understood. It values a variety of approaches, not polemics. It offers tools, not weapons. Communion ecclesiology expresses and brings together a range of elements of Catholicism, both mystical and practical, both old and new, that span some of the great divides that plague the Church today. The label "communion ecclesiology" will at times be misused by those who automatically co-opt any approach to serve their own narrow views; the true reality of communion ecclesiology, however, will always work to subvert and overturn such narrowness. The communion ecclesiology that has its roots in theologians such as Möhler, Journet, Congar, and de Lubac will serve as a tool for promoting the broad and inclusive Catholic vision expressed in the documents of Vatican II.

Bibliography

Abbott, Walter M., ed. *The Documents of Vatican II*. New York: Guild Press, 1966.

Afanasiev, Nicholas. *L'Eglise du Saint-Esprit*. Paris: Cerf, 1975.

Alberigo, Giuseppe, Jean-Pierre Jossua, and Joseph A. Komonchak, eds. *The Reception of Vatican II*. Translated by Matthew J. O'Connell. Washington, DC: The Catholic University of America Press, 1987 [French orig. 1985].

Alberigo, Giuseppe, and Joseph A. Komonchak, eds. *History of Vatican II*. 3 vols (of projected five). Maryknoll, NY: Orbis Books; Leuven: Peeters, 1995, 1997, 2000.

Anderson, Floyd, ed. *Council Daybook, Vatican II, Sessions 1-4*. Washington, DC: National Catholic Welfare Conference, 1965-66.

Ashley, Benedict. *Justice in the Church: Gender and Participation*. Washington, DC: Catholic University of America Press, 1996.

Bacik, James. *Apologetics and the Eclipse of Mystery: Mystagogy according to Karl Rahner*. Notre Dame: University of Notre Dame Press, 1980.

Balthasar, Hans Urs von. *The Christian State of Life*. Translated by Sister Mary Frances McCarthy. San Francisco: Ignatius Press, 1983 [German orig. 1977].

——— *Church and World*. New York: Herder and Herder, 1967 [German orig. *Sponsa Verbi, 1960]*.

——— "Conversion in the New Testament." *Communio* 1 (Spring 1974) 47-59.

——— "Current Trends in Catholic Theology and the Responsibility of the Christian." *Communio* 5 (Spring 1978) 77-85.

——— *The Glory of the Lord*. 7 Vols. Edited by Joseph Fessio et al. San Francisco: Ignatius Press, 1982-89 {German orig. 3 vols. 1961-69].

——— *Love Alone*. Translated by Alexander Dru. New York: Herder and Herder, 1969 [German orig. 1963].

——— *New Elucidations*. Translated by Sister Mary Theresilde Skerr. San Francisco: Ignatius Press, 1996 [German orig. 1979].

——— *The Office of Peter and the Structure of the Church*. Translated by Andree Emery. San Francisco: Ignatius Press, 1986 [German orig. 1974].

——— *Our Task: A Report and a Plan*. Translated by John Saward. San Francisco: Ignatius Press, 1994 [German orig. 1984].

——— *The Theology of Henri de Lubac: An Overview*. Translated by Joseph Fessio, S.J., and Michael M. Waldstein. San Francisco: Ignatius Press, 1983 [German orig. 1976].

——— *The Theology of Karl Barth*. Translated by John Drury. New York: Holt, Rinehart and Winston, 1971 [German orig. 1951].

——— *The Von Balthasar Reader*. Edited by Medard Kehl and Martin Löser. New York: Crossroad, 1982.

Baum, Gregory. *Religion and Alienation: A Theological Reading of Sociology*. New York: Paulist Press, 1975.

Baxter, Michael J. "The Non-Catholic Character of the 'Public Church.'" *Modern Theology* 11 (2 April 1995) 243-58.

Beauchesne, Richard. "Heeding the Early Congar Today, and Two Recent Roman Catholic Issues: Seeking Hope on the Road Back." *Journal of Ecumenical Studies* 27 (1990) 535-60.

Bertoldi, Francesco. "The Religious Sense in Henri de Lubac." *Communio* 16 (Spring 1989) 6-31.

Blondel, Maurice. *Action (1893): Essay on a Critique of Life and a Science of Practice*. Translated by Olivia Blanchett. Notre Dame: University of Notre Dame Press, 1984.

Boff, Leonardo. *Church: Charism and Power*. Translated by John W. Diercksmeier. New York: Crossroad, 1985 [Portuguese orig. 1981].

———— *Ecclesiogenesis: The Base Communities Reinvent the Church*. Translated by Robert Barr. Maryknoll, NY: Orbis Books, 1986 [Portuguese orig. 1977].

———— *The Maternal Face of God: The Feminine and Its Religious Expressions*. Translated by Robert R. Barr and John W. Diercksmeier. San Francisco: Harper and Row, 1987 [Portuguese orig. 1979].

———— *The Path to Hope: Fragments from a Theologian's Journey*. Translated by Phillip Berryman. Maryknoll, NY: Orbis Books, 1993.

———— *Trinity and Society*. Translated by Paul Burns. Maryknoll, NY: Orbis Books, 1988 [Portuguese orig. 1986].

Brown, Raymond. *The Churches the Apostles Left Behind*. New York: Paulist Press, 1984.

Byrne, Patricia. "American Ultramontanism." *Theological Studies* 56 (June 1995) 301-26.

Carey, Patrick W. *Priests, People, and Prelates: Ecclesiastical Democracy and the Tensions of Trusteeism*. Notre Dame: University of Notre Dame Press, 1987.

Carter, David. "Review of Jean-Marie Tillard, *L'Eglise locale*." *One in Christ* 32 (1996) 378-85.

Chapp, Larry S. *The God Who Speaks: Hans Urs von Balthasar's Theology of Revelation*. San Francisco: International Scholars Publications, 1996.

———— "Who Is the Church? The Personalistic Categories of Balthasar's Ecclesiology." *Communio* 23 (Summer 1996) 322-38.

Coffele, Gianfranco. "De Lubac and the Theological Foundations of the Missions." *Communio* 23 (Winter 1996) 757-75.

Congar, Yves. *After Nine Hundred Years*. Translated by faculty and staff at Fordham University. New York: Fordham University, 1959 [French orig. 1954].

———— "Bulletin D'Ecclésiologie (I)." *Revue des Sciences Philosophiques et Théologiques* 53 (October 1969) 693-706.

———— *Challenge to the Church: The Case of Archbishop Lefebvre*. Translated by Paul Inwood. Huntingdon, IN: Our Sunday Visitor, 1976 [French orig. 1976].

———— *Dialogue Between Christians*. Translated by Philip Loretz. Westminster, MD: Newman Press, 1966 [French orig. 1964].

———— *Divided Christendom: A Catholic Study of the Problem of Reunion*. Translated by M.A. Bousefield. London: G. Bles, 1939 [French orig. 1937].

———— *Diversity and Communion*. Translated by John Bowden. Mystic, CT: Twenty-Third Publications, 1985 [French orig. 1982].

———— *Fifty Years of Catholic Theology: Conversations with Yves Congar*. Edited by Bernard Lauret. Philadelphia: Fortress Press, 1988.
———— *I Believe in the Holy Spirit*. 3 vols. Translated by David Smith. New York: Seabury; London: Geoffrey Chapman, 1983 [French orig. 1979, 1980].
———— *Lay People in the Church*. Translated by Donald Attwater. Westminster, MD: Newman, 1957 [French orig. 1953].
———— *L'Eglise de Saint Augustin à l'epogue moderne*. Paris: Cerf, 1970.
———— "My Path-Findings in the Theology of Laity and Ministries." *The Jurist* 32 (1972): 169-88.
———— *The Mystery of the Church*. Translated by A.V. Littledale. Baltimore: Helicon, 1969 [French orig., two separate books, 1956].
———— *Power and Poverty in the Church*. Translated by Jennifer Nicholson. Baltimore: Helicon, 1964 [French orig. 1953].
———— *Sainte église: études et approches ecclésiologique*. Paris: Cerf, 1964.
———— *Tradition and the Traditions*. Translated by Michael Naseby and Thomas Rainborough. New York: Macmillan, 1966. [French orig. 1960, 1963].
———— *Vraie et fausse reforme dans l'eglise*. Paris: Cerf, 1950. Rev. ed. 1968.
Cooke, Bernard. *Sacraments and Sacramentality*. Mystic, CT: Twenty-Third Publications, 1983.
Cox, Harvey. *The Silencing of Leonardo Boff: The Vatican and the Future of World Christianity*. Oak Park, IL: Meyer-Stone Books, 1988.
D'Ambrosio, M. "*Ressourcement* Theology, *Aggiornamento*, and the Hermeneutics of Tradition." *Communio* 18 (Winter 1991) 530-55.
Delisi, Mark. *Ecclesiological Divergence and Convergence: A Study of How the Congregation for the Doctrine of the Faith and Leonardo Boff Understand the Hierarchy*. Dayton: University of Dayton Master's Thesis, 1993.
De Lubac, Henri. *Aspects of Buddhism*. Translated by George Lamb. New York: Sheed and Ward, 1954 [French orig. 1951].
———— *Catholicism*. Translated by Lancelot C. Sheppard. London: Burns and Oates, 1950; Universe Books Edition, 1961 [French orig. 1938].
———— *Christian Resistance to Anti-Semitism: Memories from 1940-1944*. Translated by Sister Elizabeth Englund, O.C.D. San Francisco: Ignatius Press, 1990 [French orig. 1988].
———— *The Church: Paradox and Mystery*. Translated by James R. Dunne. New York: Alba House, 1969 [French orig. 1967].
———— *Corpus Mysticum: L'Eucharistie et l'église au moyen âge: Etude historique*. Paris: Aubier, 1944.
———— *The Drama of Atheistic Humanism*. Translated by Edith M. Riley. New York: Sheed and Ward, 1950 [French orig. 1944].
———— "Le Mystèry du surnatural." *Recherches de science religieuse* 36 (1949) 80-121. English translation in *Theology in History*, trans. Anne Englund Nash (San Francisco: Ignatius Press, 1996) 281-316.
———— *The Mystery of the Supernatural*. Translated by Rosemary Sheed. New York: Herder and Herder, 1967 [French orig. 1965].
———— *Paradoxes of Faith*. Translated by Paule Simon, Sadie Kreilkamp, and Ernest Beaumont. San Francisco: Ignatius Press, 1987 [French originals 1948, 1955, 1958].
———— *The Splendour of the Church*. Translated by Michael Mason. New York: Sheed and Ward, 1956 [French orig. 1953].

———— *Surnaturel*. Paris: Aubier, 1946; new edition Paris: Desclee de Brouwer, 1985.

———— *Theological Fragments*. San Francisco: Ignatius Press, 1989.

———— *Theology in History*. Translated by Anne Englund Nash. San Francisco: Ignatius Press, 1996.

———— "A Witness to Christ and the Church: Hans Urs von Balthasar." *Communio* 2 (Fall 1975) 228-49.

Dietrich, Donald J. and Michael J. Himes, eds. *The Legacy of the Tübingen School: The Relevance of Nineteenth-Century Theology for the Twenty-First Century*. New York: Crossroad, 1997.

Doyle, Dennis M. *The Church Emerging from Vatican II*. Mystic, CT: Twenty-Third Publications, 1992.

———— "Communion Ecclesiology and the Silencing of Boff." *America* (12 September 1992) 139-43.

———— "Henri de Lubac and the Roots of Communion Ecclesiology." *Theological Studies* 60 (June 1999) 209-27.

———— "Journet, Congar, and the Roots of Communion Ecclesiology." *Theolgical Studies* 58 (September 1997) 461-79.

———— "Möhler, Schleiermacher, and the Roots of Communion Ecclesiology." *Theological Studies* 57 (September 1996) 467-80.

———— "Utopia and Utopianism." *New Catholic Encyclopedia*. Vol. 18. Washington, DC: The Catholic University of America Press, 1989.

Dulles, Avery. "Catholicism and American Culture: The Uneasy Dialogue." *America* 162 (27 January 1990) 54-9.

———— "The Church as Communion." In *New Perspectives in Historical Theology: Essays in Memory of John Meyendorf*. Edited by Bradley Nassif, 125-39. Grand Rapids, MI: Eerdmans, 1996.

———— "Henri de Lubac: In Appreciation." *America* 165 (28 September 1991) 180-2.

———— *Models of the Church*. Garden City, NY: Image Books, 1974, expanded edition 1987.

Emonet, Pierre-Marie. *Le Cardinal Journet: Portrait Intérieur*. Chambray-les-Tours: C.L.D., 1983.

Extraordinary Synod of 1985. "The Final Report." *Origins* 15 (19 December 1985) 444-50.

Fenton, Joseph Clifford. "Father Journet's Concept of the Church." *American Ecclesiastical Review* 127 (November 1952) 370-80.

Fesquet, Henri. *The Drama of Vatican II*. Translated by Bernard Murchland. New York: Random House, 1967 [French orig. 1966].

Fields, Stephen, S.J., "Balthasar and Rahner on the Spiritual Senses." *Theological Studies* 57 (1996) 224-41.

Fisher, David A. "Byzantine Theology: Reflections on the Thought of John Zizioulas." *Diakonia* 29 (1996) 57-63.

Ford, John. "*Koinonia* and Roman Catholic Theology." *Ecumenical Trends* 26 (March 1997) 42-4.

Galvin, John P. "The Church as Communion: Comments on a Letter of the Congregation for the Doctrine of the Faith." *One in Christ* 29 (1993) 310-7.

García-Rivera, Alejandro. *The Community of the Beautiful: A Theological Aesthetics*. Collegeville, MN: Michael Glazier, 1999.

Gleason, Philip. *Keeping the Faith: American Catholicism Past and Present*. Notre Dame: University of Notre Dame Press, 1987.

Goizueta, Roberto S. *Caminemos con Jesús: Toward a Hispanic/Latino Theology of Accompaniment*. Maryknoll, NY: Orbis Books, 1995.

—— "U.S. Hispanic Popular Catholicism as Theopoetics." In *Hispanic/Latino Theology: Challenge and Promise*. Edited by Ada María Isasi-Díaz and Fernando F. Segovia, 261-88. Minneapolis: Fortress, 1996.

Gustafson, James M. *Treasure in Earthen Vessels: The Church as a Human Community*. New York: Harper, 1961.

Gutiérrez, Gustavo. *A Theology of Liberation: History, Politics, and Salvation*. Translated by Sister Caridad Inda and John Eagleson. Maryknoll, NY: Orbis Books, 1973, revised 1988 [Spanish orig. 1971].

Häring, Hermann and Karl-Josef Kuschel, eds. *Hans Küng: His Work and His Way*. Translated by Robert Nowell. Garden City, NY: Image/Doubleday, 1980.

Healy, Nicholas. "Communion Ecclesiology: A Cautionary Note." *Pro Ecclesia* 4 (Fall 1995) 442-53.

Himes, Michael J. "'A Great Theologian of Our Time': Möhler on Schleiermacher." *Heythrop Journal* 37 (January 1996) 24-46.

—— *Ongoing Incarnation: Johann Adam Möhler and the Beginnings of Modern Ecclesiology*. New York: Crossroad, 1997.

Himes, Michael J. and Kenneth Himes. *Fullness of Faith: The Public Significance of Theology*. New York: Paulist Press, 1993.

Hinze, Bradford E. *Narrating History, Developing Doctrine*. Atlanta: Scholar's Press, 1993.

Hitchcock, James. "Why Communio?" *Communio* 1 (Spring 1974) 112.

Hollenbach, David. "The Common Good Revisited." *Theological Studies* 50 (March 1989) 70-94.

Hollenbach, David, ed. "Theology and Philosophy in Public: A Symposium on John Courtney Murray's Unfinished Agenda." *Theological Studies* 40 (December 1979) 700-715.

Imbelli, Robert. "The Unknown Beyond the Word: The Pneumatological Foundations of Dialogue." *Communio* 24 (Summer 1997) 326-35.

Jenson, Robert W. "Some Contentious Aspects of Communion." *Pro Ecclesia* (1993) 133-7.

John Paul II, Pope. "Address to the Roman Curia." *Acta Apostolicae Sedis* 83 (1991) 745-7.

—— *Tertio Millennio Adveniente* (As the Third Millennium Draws Near) *Origins* 24 (24 November 1994) 401-16.

Johnson, Elizabeth A. "Does God Play Dice? Divine Providence and Chance." *Theological Studies* 57 (1996) 3-18.

—— *Friends of God and Prophets: A Feminist Theological Reading of the Communion of Saints*. New York: Continuum, 1998.

—— *She Who Is: The Mystery of God in Feminist Theological Discourse*. New York: Crossroad, 1996.

Jossua, Jean-Pierre. *Yves Congar: Theology in the Service of God's People*. Chicago: Priory Press, 1968 [French orig. 1967].

Journet, Charles. "Cordula ou l'épreuve décisive." *Nova et vetera* 43 (1968) 147-54.

——— "De le théologie a l'anthropologie: un périple aujourd'hui centenaire." *Nova et vetera* 41 (1966) 229-34.

——— "Intercommunion?" *Nova et vetera* 45 (1970) 1-9.

——— *L'Eglise du Verbe incarné.* 3 vols. Paris-Bruges: Desclée De Brouwer, 1941, 1951, 1969. Only the first volume appears in English as *Church of the Word Incarnate.* Vol. 1. Translated by A. H. C. Downs. New York: Sheed and Ward, 1955.

——— "La synthèse du P. Teilhard de Chardin: Est-elle dissociable?" *Nova et vetera* 41 (1966) 144-51.

——— *The Meaning of Evil.* Translated by Michael Barry (New York: P.J. Kenedy, 1963 [French orig. 1961]).

——— "Note sur un accord entre theologians Anglicans et Catholiques touchant la doctrine eucharistique." *Nova et vetera* 46 (1971) 250-1.

——— *The Primacy of Peter: from the Protestant and from the Catholic Point of View.* Translated by John Chapin. Westminster, MD: Newman Press, 1954 [French orig. 1953].

——— "Secularisation, hermeneutique, orthopraxis selon E. Schillebeeckx et P. Schoonenberg." *Nova et vetera* 44 (1969) 300-12.

Komonchak, Joseph A. "The Church Universal as the Communion of Local Churches." In *Where Does the Church Stand? Concilium,* vol. 146, 30-5. Edinburgh: T&T Clark, 1981.

——— "Conceptions of Communion, Past and Present." *Cristianesimo nella storia* 16 (1995) 321-40.

——— "The Cultural and Ecclesial Roles of Theology." *Proceedings of the Catholic Theological Society of America* 40 (1985) 15-32.

——— "Ecclesiology and Social Theory: A Methodological Essay." *The Thomist* 45 (April 1981) 262-83.

——— "The Enlightenment and the Construction of Roman Catholicism." *Annual of the Catholic Commission on Intellectual and Cultural Affairs* (1985) 31-59.

——— "The Local Church," *Chicago Studies* 28 (1989) 320-35.

——— "Missing Person," *Commonweal* 124 (12 September 1997) 34-5.

——— "The Return of Yves Congar." *Commonweal* 110 (15 July 1983) 402.

——— "Theology and Culture at Mid-Century: The Example of Henri de Lubac." *Theological Studies* 51 (1990) 579-602.

Kress, Robert. "Journet, Charles." *New Catholic Encyclopedia.* Vol. 17. Washington, DC: Catholic University of America Press, 1979.

Küng, Hans. *Christianity: Essence, History, Future.* Translated by John Bowden. New York: Continuum, 1995 [German orig. 1994].

——— *The Church.* Garden City, NY: Doubleday, 1967 [German orig. 1967].

Küng, Hans, ed. *Yes to a Global Ethic.* Non-English articles translated by John Bowden. New York: Continuum, 1996 [German orig. 1995].

Küng, Hans, ed., with Leonard Swidler. *The Church in Anguish: Has the Vatican Betrayed Vatican II?* San Francisco: Harper and Row, 1987 [German orig. 1986].

LaCugna, Catherine Mowry. *The Theological Methodology of Hans Küng.* Chico, CA: Scholars Press, 1982.

Latourelle, René, ed. *Vatican II: Assessment and Perspectives, Twenty-Five Years After.* 3 vols. New York: Paulist Press, 1988, 1989.

Lawler, Michael G. and Thomas J. Shanahan. *Church: A Spirited Communion.* Collegeville, Minn.: Liturgical Press, 1995.

Lennan, Richard. *The Ecclesiology of Karl Rahner.* Oxford: Clarendon Press, 1995.

Mannheim, Karl. *Ideology and Utopia.* Translated by L. Wirth and E. Shils. London, 1936 [German orig. 1929].

McBrien, Richard P. "Church and Ministry: The Achievement of Yves Congar." *Theology Digest* 32 (1985) 203.

——— "Conflict in the Church: Redefining the Center." *America* 167 (22 August 1992) 78-81.

McPartlan, Paul. *The Eucharist Makes the Church: Henri de Lubac and John Zizioulas in Dialogue.* Edinburgh: T&T Clark, 1993.

Milbank, John. *Theology and Social Theory: Beyond Secular Reason.* Oxford: Basil Blackwell, 1990.

Möhler, Johann Adam. *Athanasius der Grosse und die Kirche seiner Zeit.* Mainz: Florian Kupferberg, 1827.

——— *Unity in the Church, or the Principle of Catholicism Presented in the Spirit of the Church Fathers of the First Three Centuries.* Translated with an Introduction by Peter C. Erb. Washington, DC: The Catholic University of America Press, 1996 [German orig. 1825].

——— *Symbolism: Exposition of the Doctrinal Differences between Catholics and Protestants as Evidenced by Their Symbolical Writings.* Translated by James Burton Robinson. New York: Crossroad Herder, 1997 [German orig. 4 editions between 1832 and 1835].

Molnar, Paul. "Can We Know God Directly: Rahner's Solution from Experience." *Theological Studies* 46 (June 1985) 228-261.

——— "The Function of the Immanent Trinity in the Theology of Karl Barth." *Scottish Journal of Theology* 42 (1989) 367-99.

National Catholic Welfare Conference. *Council Daybook.* Vatican II, Session 4. Edited by Floyd Anderson. Washington, DC: National Catholic Welfare Conference, 1996.

National Pastoral Life Center, in conjunction with Cardinal Bernardin. "Called to Be Catholic: Church in a Time of Peril." *Origins* 26 (29 August 1996) 165-70.

Nerney, Catherine, S.S.J. "Response." In *Small Christian Communities: Imagining Future Church.* Edited by Robert Pelton, C.S.C., 58-68. Notre Dame: University of Notre Dame Press, 1997.

Novak, Michael. *Freedom with Justice: Catholic Social Thought and Liberal Institutions.* San Francisco: Harper and Row, 1984.

Oakes, Edward T. *Pattern of Redemption: The Theology of Hans Urs von Balthasar.* New York: Continuum, 1994.

O'Meara, Thomas F. "The Teaching Office of Bishops in the Ecclesiology of Charles Journet." *The Jurist* 49 (1989) 23-47.

Quinn, John Archbishop. "The Exercise of the Primacy and the Costly Call to Unity." *Commonweal* 123 (12 July 1996) 11-20. Also in *Origins* 26 (18 July 1996) 119-27.

Rahner, Karl. *The Church and the Sacraments.* Translated by W.J. O'Hara. Freiburg: Herder, 1963.

——— *Faith in a Wintry Season: Conversations and Interviews with Karl Rahner in the Last Years of His Life.* Edited by Paul Imhof and Hubert Biallowans.

English translation edited by Harvey D. Egan. New York: Crossroad, 1990 [German orig. 1986].

―――― *Foundations of the Christian Faith: An Introduction to the Idea of Christianity*, Translated by William V. Dych. New York: Crossroad, 1982 [German orig. 1976].

―――― "Membership of the Church according to the Teaching of Pius XII's Encyclical, 'Mystici Corpus Christi.'" *Theological Investigations*. Translated by Karl-H. Kruger. Vol. 2, 1-88. Baltimore: Helicon Press, 1963.

―――― *The Shape of the Church to Come*. Translated by Edward Quinn. New York: Seabury, 1974 [German original 1972].

―――― *Spiritual Exercises*. Translated by Kenneth Baker. New York: Herder and Herder, 1965 [German original 1965].

―――― "Theology of the Symbol." In *Theological Investigations*. Translated by Kevin Smyth, vol. 4, 221-52. Baltimore: Helicon Press, 1966.

―――― "Towards a Fundamental Theological Interpretation of Vatican II." Translated by Leo J. O'Donovan. *Theological Studies* 40 (December 1979) 716-27.

―――― "Utopia and Reality." *Theology Digest* 32 (Summer 1985) 139-44.

Ratzinger, Joseph Cardinal. *Called to Communion: Understanding the Church Today*. Translated by Adrian Walker. San Francisco: Ignatius Press, 1996 [German orig. 1991].

―――― *Church, Ecumenism, and Politics*. Translated by Robert Nowell. New York: Crossroad, 1988 [German orig. 1987].

―――― *Introduction to Christianity*. Translated by J.R. Foster. New York: Herder and Herder, 1970 [German orig. 1968].

―――― *The Meaning of Christian Brotherhood*. Translated by W.A. Glen-Doeple. San Francisco: Ignatius Press, 1993 [German original, 1960].

―――― *The Ratzinger Report*. With Vittorio Messori. Translated by Salvator Attanasio and Graham Harrison. San Francisco: Ignatius Press, 1985.

―――― *Turning Point for Europe?* Translated by Brian McNeil, C.R.V. San Francisco: Ignatius Press, 1994 [German orig. 1991].

Rausch, Thomas P. "The CDF Letter on Communion: Reactions and Reflections." *Ecumenical Trends* (April 1993) 51-52.

Roberts, Louis. "The Collision of Rahner and Balthasar." *Continuum* 5 (1968) 753-57.

Sacred Congregation for the Doctrine of the Faith. "Doctrinal Congregation Criticizes Brazilian Theologian's Book." *Origins* 14 (4 April 1985) 683-87.

―――― "Instruction on Christian Freedom and Liberation." *Origins* 15 (17 April 1986) 713-28.

―――― "Some Aspects of the Church Understood as a Communion." *Origins* 22 (25 June 1992) 108-12.

Savon, Hervé. *Johann Adam Möhler: The Father of Modern Theology*. Mahwah, NJ: Paulist Press, 1966.

Saward, John. *The Mysteries of March: Hans Urs von Balthasar on the Incarnation and Easter*. Washington, DC: Catholic University of America Press, 1990.

―――― "Review of John Zizioulas, *Being as Communion*." *New Blackfriars* 67 (January 1986) 45-8.

Schillebeeckx, Edward. *Christ the Sacrament of Encounter with God*. Translated by Paul Barrett. English text revised by Mark Schoof and Laurence Bright. New York: Sheed and Ward, 1963 [Dutch orig. 1960].

Schindler, David L. *Heart of the World, Center of the Church: Communio Ecclesiology, Liberalism, and Liberation*. Grand Rapids, MI: Eerdman's/Edinburgh: T&T Clark, 1996.

——— "On the Catholic Common Ground Project: The Christological Foundations of Dialogue." *Communio* 23 (Winter 1996) 823-51.

Schleiermacher, Friedrich. *The Christian Faith*. 2 vols. Edited by H.R. Mackintosh and J.S. Stewart. New York: Harper and Row, 1963 [German orig. 1821-22; revised in 1830].

——— *On Religion: Addresses in Response to Its Cultured Critics*. Translated with an introduction and notes by Terrence N. Tice. Richmond: John Knox Press, 1969 [German orig. 1821. Earlier editions appeared in 1799 and 1806. A fourth edition in 1831 had only minor corrections].

——— "On the Discrepancy between the Sabellian and Athanasian Method of Representing the Doctrine of the Trinity in the Godhead." Translated by M. Stuart. In *Schleiermacher and Stuart on the Doctrine of the Trinity*. Reprinted in book form [no publication data] from the *Biblical Repository and Quarterly Observer* (April and July 1835).

Seckler, Max. "'*Potentia obedientialis*' bei Karl Rahner (1904-1984) und Henri de Lubac (1896-1991)." *Gregorianum* 74 (1997) 699-718.

Shea, William M. "Dual Loyalties in Catholic Theology." *Commonweal* 119 (31 January 1992) 9-14.

Staudt, Brian. "The Lay-Cleric Distinction: Tragedy or Comedy?" *Church* 12 (Fall 1996) 47-50.

Steinfels, Margaret O'Brien. "Dissent and Communion." *Commonweal* 121 (18 November 1994) 9-15.

——— "The Unholy Alliance Between the Right and the Left in the Catholic Church." *America* 166 (2 May 1992) 376-82.

Swidler, Leonard, ed. *Küng in Conflict*. Garden City, NY: Image/Doubleday, 1981.

Tanner, Norman P. *Decrees of the Ecumenical Councils*. 2 vols. Washington, DC: Georgetown University Press, 1990.

Tillard, Jean-Marie. *The Bishop of Rome*. Wilmington, DE: Michael Glazier, 1983 [French orig. 1982].

——— *Church of Churches: An Ecclesiology of Communion*. Translated by R.C. De Peaux. Collegeville, MN: Liturgical Press, 1992 [French orig. 1987].

——— *L'Eglise locale: Ecclésiologie de communion et catholicité*. Paris: Cerf, 1995.

——— "The Ministry of Unity." *One in Christ* 33 (1997) 97-111.

Tilley, Maureen A. "Passion of Perpetua and Felicity (a commentary)." In *Searching the Scriptures: A Feminist-Ecumenical Commentary and Translation*. Edited by Elisabeth Schüssler Fiorenza, 829-58. New York: Crossroad, 1994.

Tracy, David. *The Analogical Imagination: Christian Theology and the Culture of Pluralism*. New York: Crossroad, 1981.

Triulzi, Daniel A., S.M. "The Tract, *De Ecclesia Christi*, in the Seminary Manuals Predating the Second Vatican Council." Unpublished paper, 1986.

United States Catholic Conference. *The Küng Dialogue: Facts and Documents*. Washington, DC: United States Catholic Conference, 1980.

Volf, Miroslav. *After Our Likeness: The Church as the Image of the Trinity*. Grand Rapids, MI: William B. Eerdmans, 1998.

——— "'The Trinity Is Our Social Program': The Doctrine of the Trinity and the Shape of Social Engagement." *Modern Theology* 14 (July 1998) 403-23.

——— "Trinity, Unity, Primacy: On the Trinitarian Nature of Ecclesial Unity and Its Implications for the Question of Primacy." In *Petrine Ministry and the Unity of the Church*. Edited by James F. Puglisi. Collegeville, MN: Liturgical Press, 1999.

Vorgrimler, Herbert, ed. *Commentary on the Documents of Vatican II*. 5 vols. Translated by William Glen-Doepel et al. New York: Herder and Herder, 1968 [German orig. 1967].

Weber, Max. *The Protestant Ethic and the Spirit of Capitalism*. Translated by Talcott Parsons. New York: Scribner, 1958 [German orig. 1904].

Williams, Rowan. "Balthasar and Rahner." In *The Analogy of Beauty: The Theology of Hans Urs von Balthasar*, ed. John Riches, 11-34. Edinburgh: T&T Clark, 1986.

Wood, Susan K. *Spiritual Exegesis and the Church in the Theology of Henri de Lubac*. Grand Rapids, MI: Eerdman's/Edinburgh: T&T Clark, 1998.

World Council of Churches. *On the Way to Fuller Koinonia: Official Report of the Fifth World Conference on Faith and Order*. Faith and Order Paper no. 166. Edited by Thomas F. Best and Günther Gassmann. Geneva: World Council of Churches, 1994.

Yocum Mize, Sandra. *The Papacy in Mid-Nineteenth Century American Catholic Imagination*. Ph.D. dissertation, Marquette University, 1987.

Zagano, Phyllis and Terrence W. Tilley, eds. *The Exercise of the Primacy: Continuing the Dialogue*. New York: Crossroad, 1998.

Zizioulas, John. *Being as Communion: Studies in Personhood and the Church*. Crestwood, NY: St. Vladimir's Press, 1985.

——— "The Mystery of the Church in Orthodox Tradition." *One in Christ* 24 (1988) 294-303.

Index